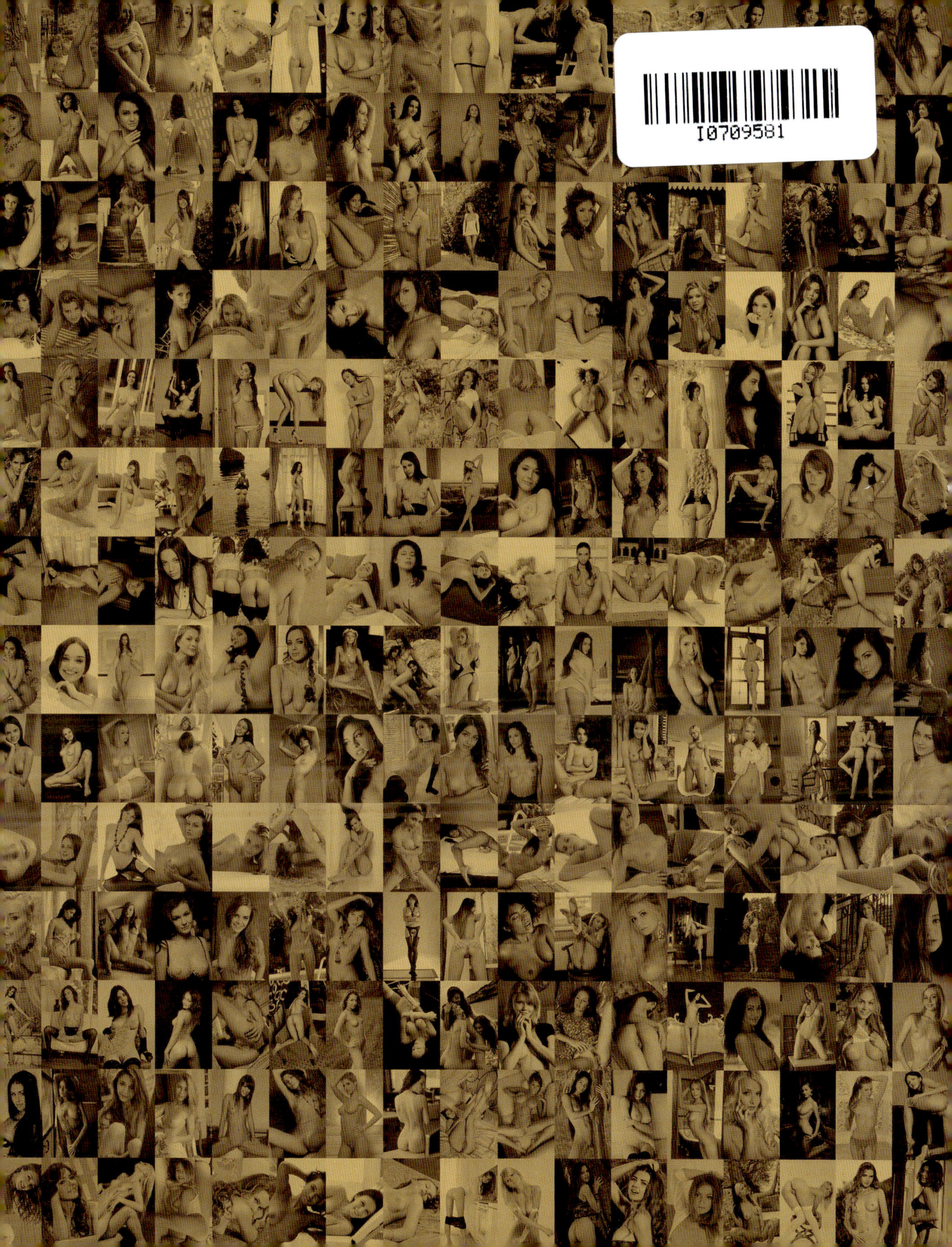
I0709581

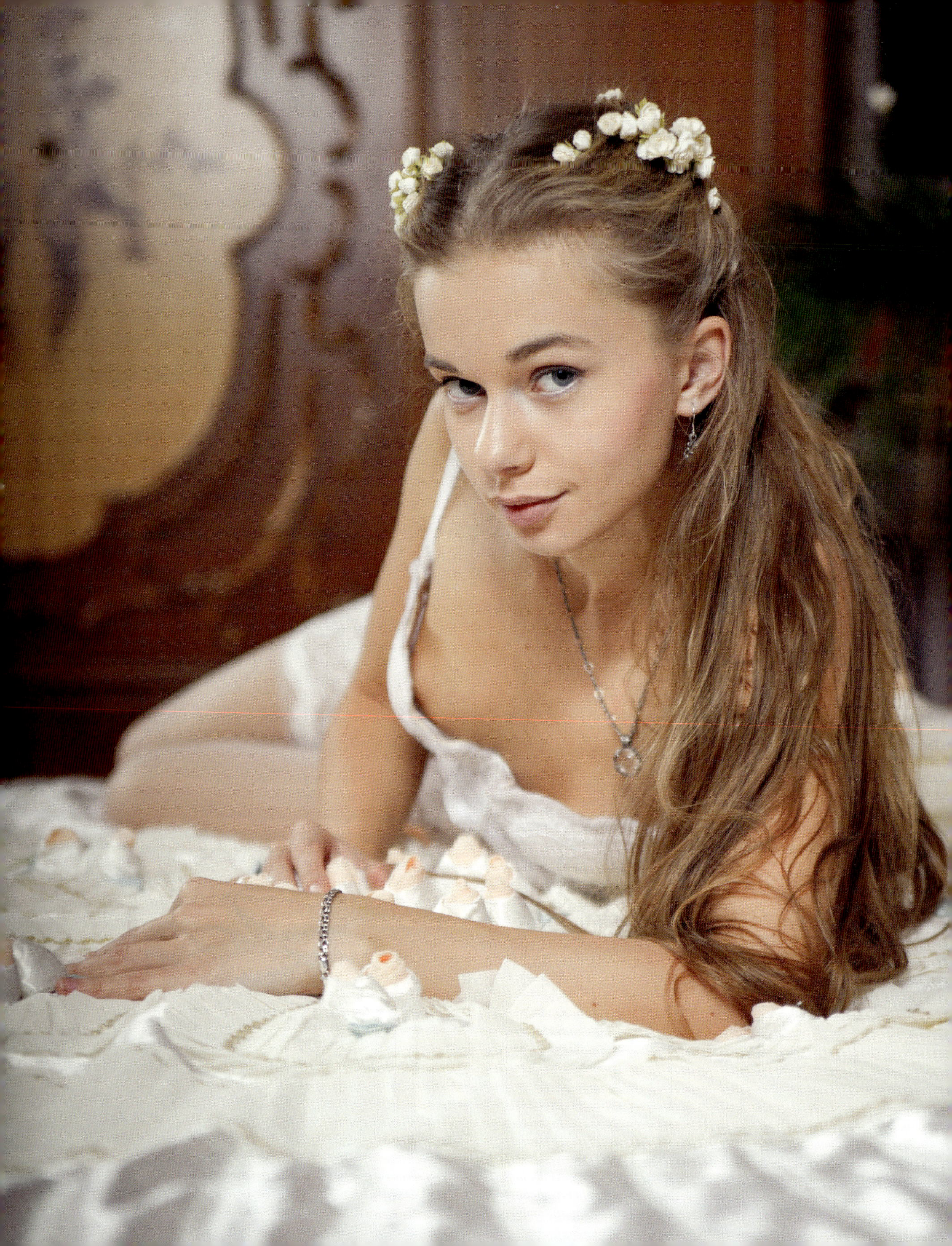

TOP MODELS OF
MetArt.com
WHERE FLAWLESS BEAUTY MEETS ART

MILENA D

COLLECTED AND EDITED BY ISABELLA CATALINA

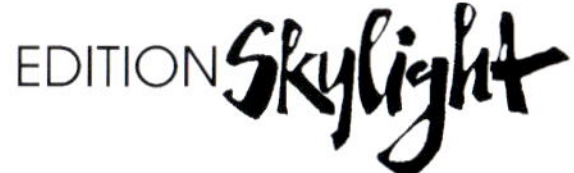
EDITION Skylight

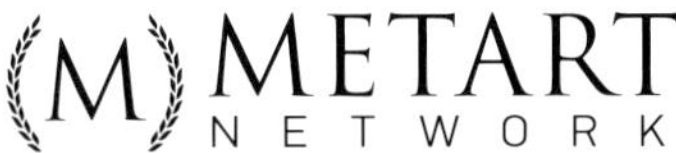

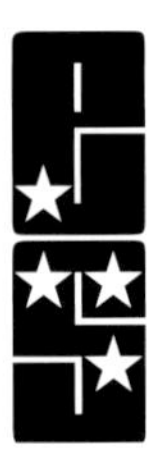

First edition 2024
Copyright © 2024 by Edition Skylight

EDITION SKYLIGHT
Rosengartenstrasse 13B
CH-8608 Bubikon / Zürich
Switzerland
info@edition-skylight.com
www.edition-skylight.com

ISBN 978-3-03766-696-8

Bibliographic information published by Die Deutsche Bibliothek
Die Deutsche Bibliothek lists this publication in the
Deutsche Nationalbibliografie; detailed bibliographic data
are available in the Internet at http://dnb.ddb.de.

Printed in Czech Republik

LOOKING AT MILENA IS LIKE SEEING AN ANGEL!

We can never get tired of Ukrainian models. This one, Milena D from Metart, is extremely sexy! Milena is 22 years old and her measurements are 89/58/89. This is what our friends of Metart say about her: "Looking at Milena is like seeing an angel. Her perfectly smooth skin and impeccable body make it hard not to fall in love with immediately. In person Milena is very approachable and kind. In fact, she can be very shy when it comes to anyone complimenting on her looks."
A model for four years, avid blogger, and photographer, she has fascinated a large and devoted fanbase. We're certainly thrilled to be part of her admirers. With her flowing and very long blonde hair and endearing personality, Milena is a delight to collaborate with and the ideal companion for an evening. Milena is a finance student and show-ballet dancer. She loves dancing, which serves as a delightful way to maintain her fitness and keep her body in top shape. Milena possesses a dynamic character, being charming and outgoing with her friends, but can exhibit a tough and opposing side if something doesn't sit well with her. Milena ventured into nude modeling, and desiring to capture some stunning images of herself. This stunning Ukrainian leaves a sprinkle of enchantment everywhere she goes. And those captivating blue eyes? This hair? Absolutely spellbinding!

Wir können uns nie an ukrainischen Models sattsehen. Dieses hier, Milena D von Metart, ist extrem sexy! Milena ist 22 Jahre alt und ihre Maße sind 89/58/89. Das sagen unsere Freunde von Metart über sie: «Wenn man Milena ansieht, ist es, als würde man einen Engel sehen. Ihre perfekte glatte Haut und ihr makelloser Körper machen es schwer, sich nicht sofort in sie zu verlieben. Persönlich ist Milena sehr zugänglich und freundlich. Aber sie kann sehr schüchtern reagieren, wenn es darum geht, ihr Komplimente für ihr Aussehen zu geben.» Seit vier Jahren ist sie Model, eifrige Bloggerin und Fotografin und fasziniert eine große und treue Fangemeinde. Wir sind definitiv begeistert, Teil ihrer Bewunderer zu sein. Mit ihrem fließenden und sehr langen blonden Haar und ihrer liebenswerten Persönlichkeit ist Milena eine sonnige Freude, mit der man zusammenarbeitet und sicher die ideale Begleiterin für einen Abend. Milena ist Finanzstudentin und Show-Balletttänzerin. Sie liebt das Tanzen, was eine herrliche Möglichkeit bietet, ihre Fitness zu erhalten und ihren Körper in Topform zu halten. Milena besitzt einen dynamischen Charakter, ist charmant und kontaktfreudig mit ihren Freunden, kann aber eine harte und gegensätzliche Seite zeigen, wenn ihr etwas nicht passt. Milena wagte sich in die Aktfotografie und wollte einige atemberaubende Bilder von sich selbst einfangen. Diese atemberaubende Ukrainerin hinterlässt überall, wo sie hingeht, einen Hauch von Verzauberung. Und diese fesselnden blauen Augen? Dieses Haar? Absolut fesselnd!

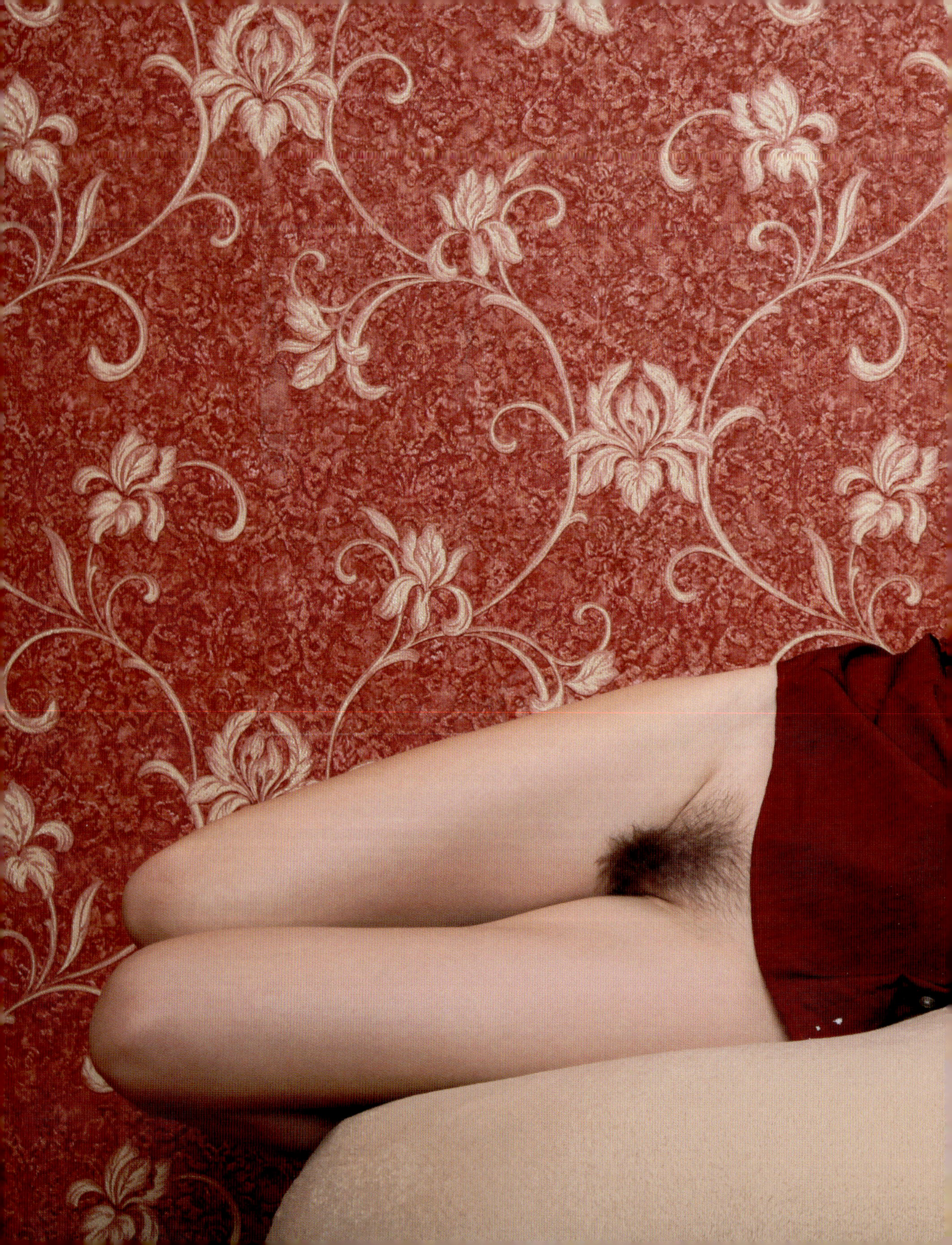

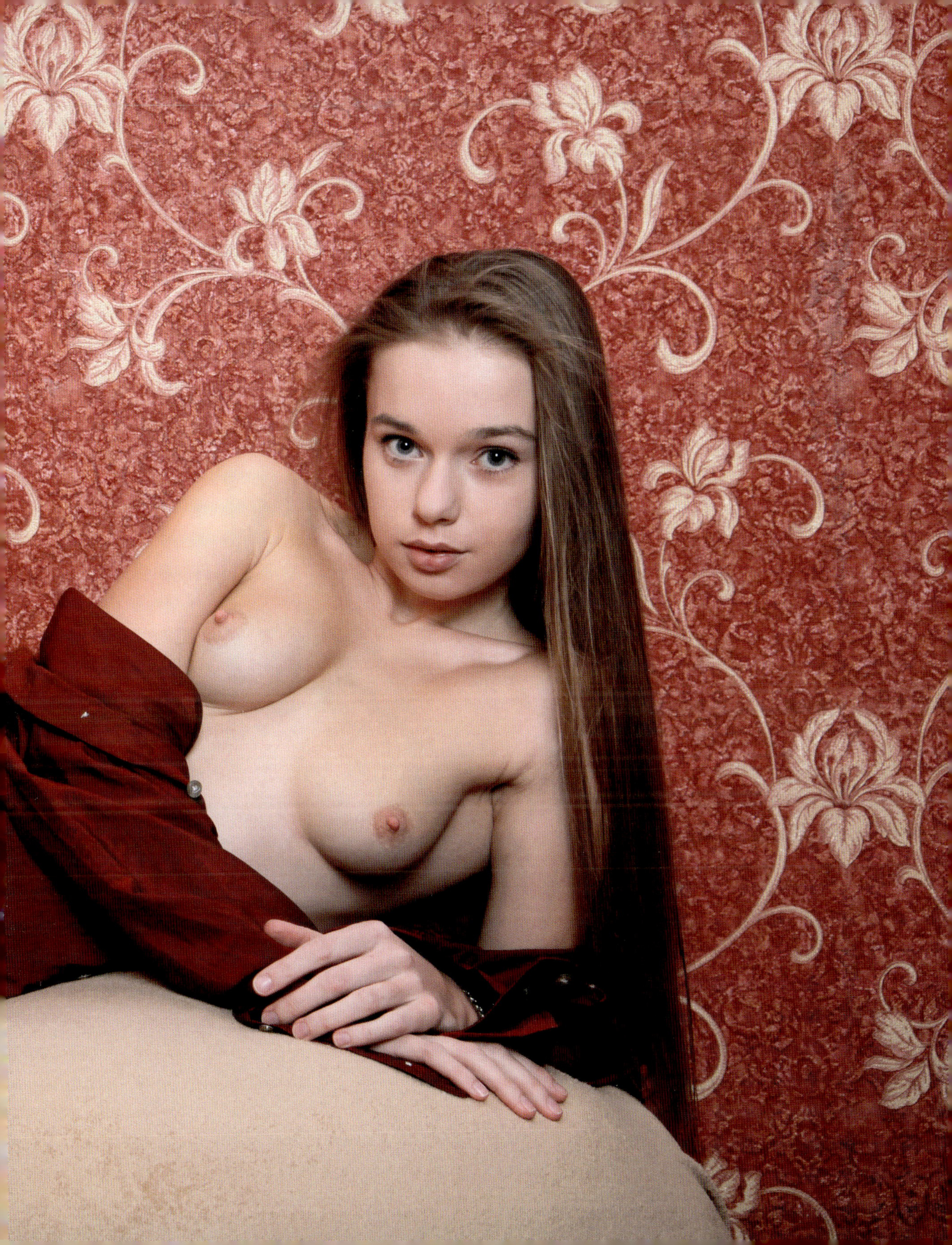

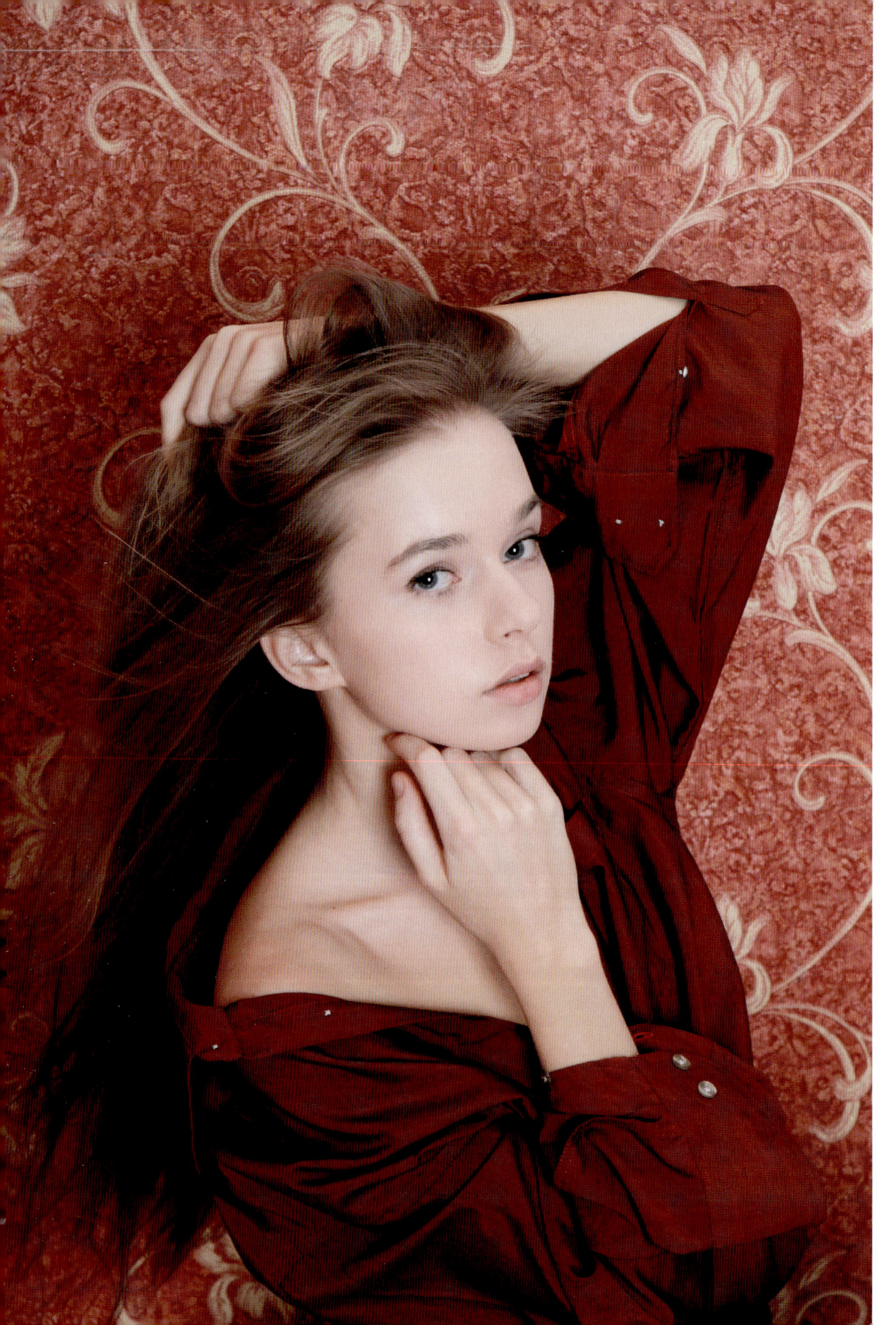

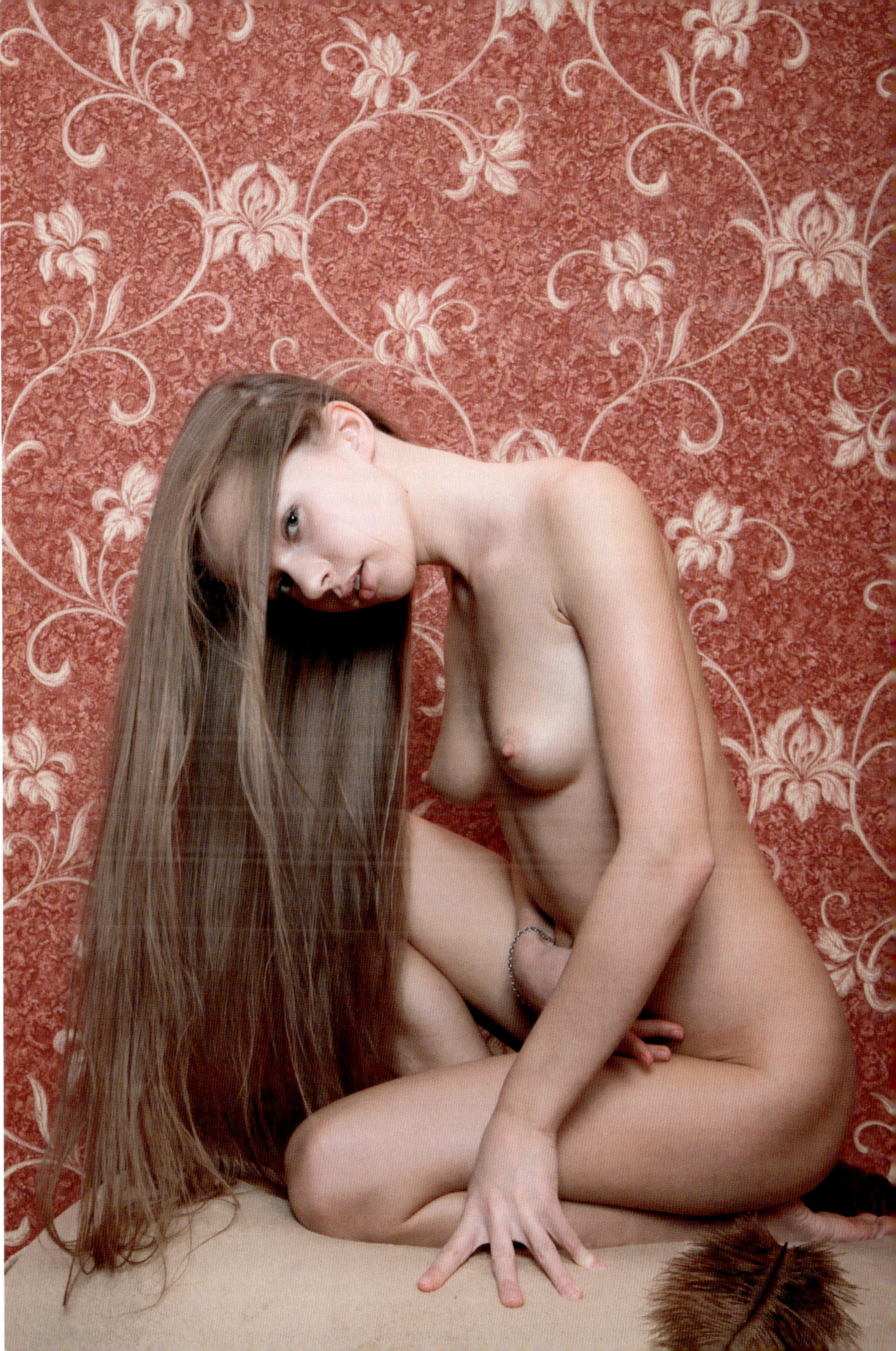

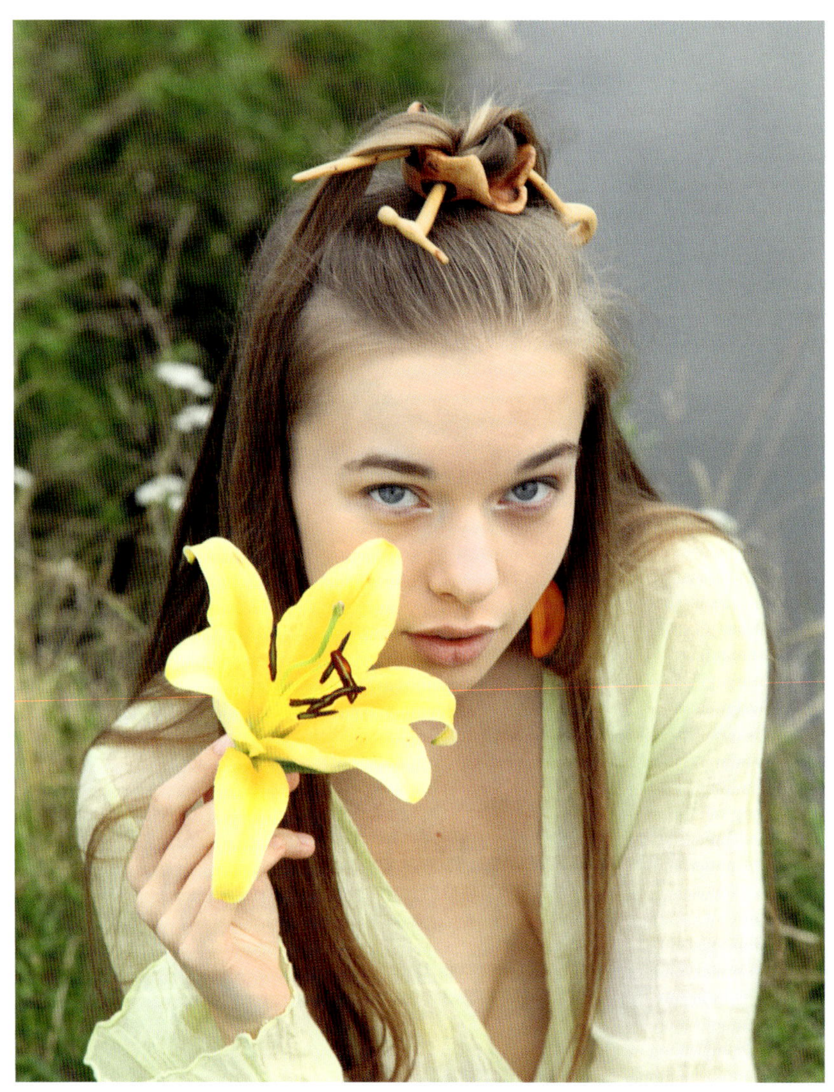

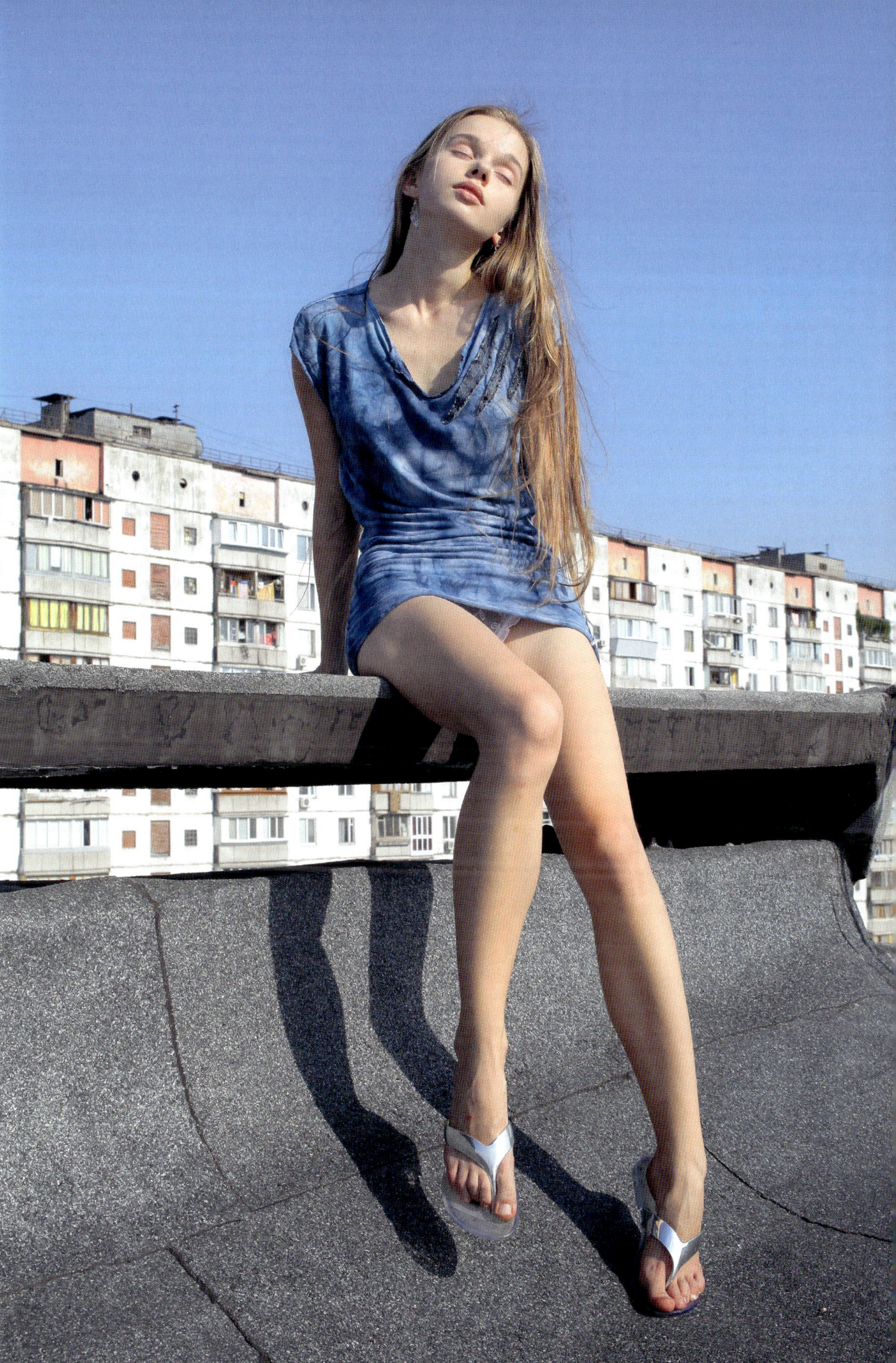

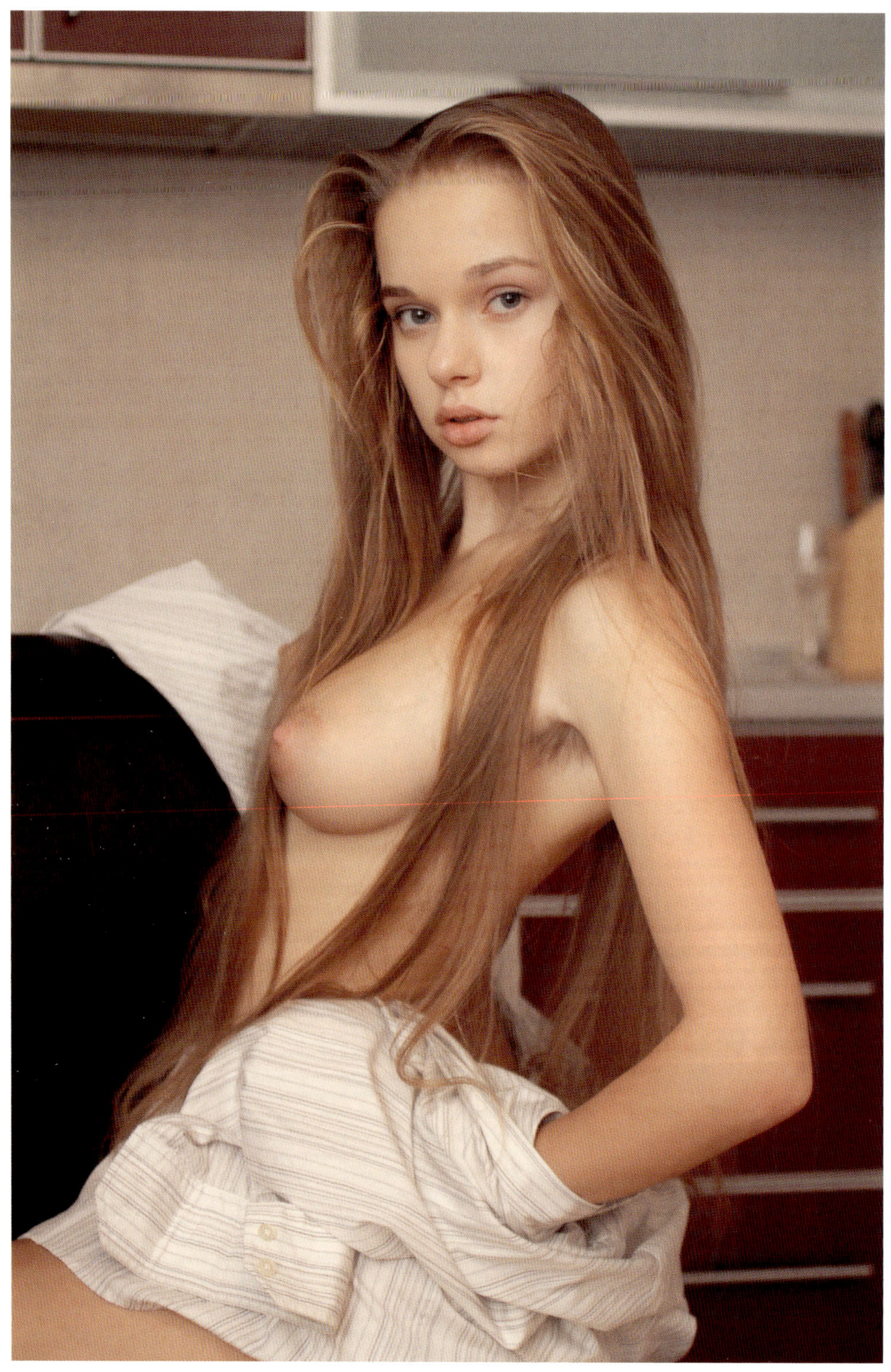

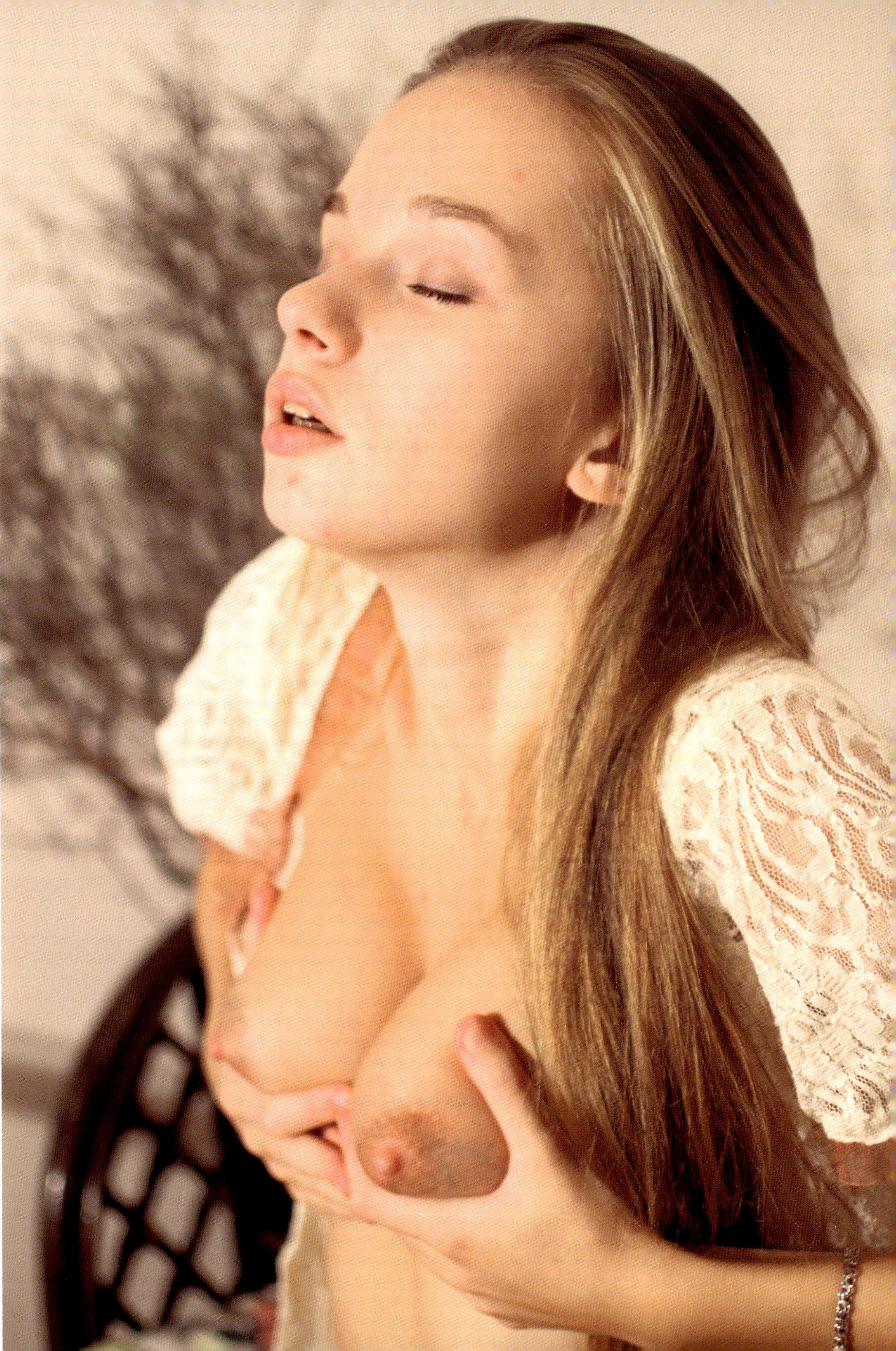

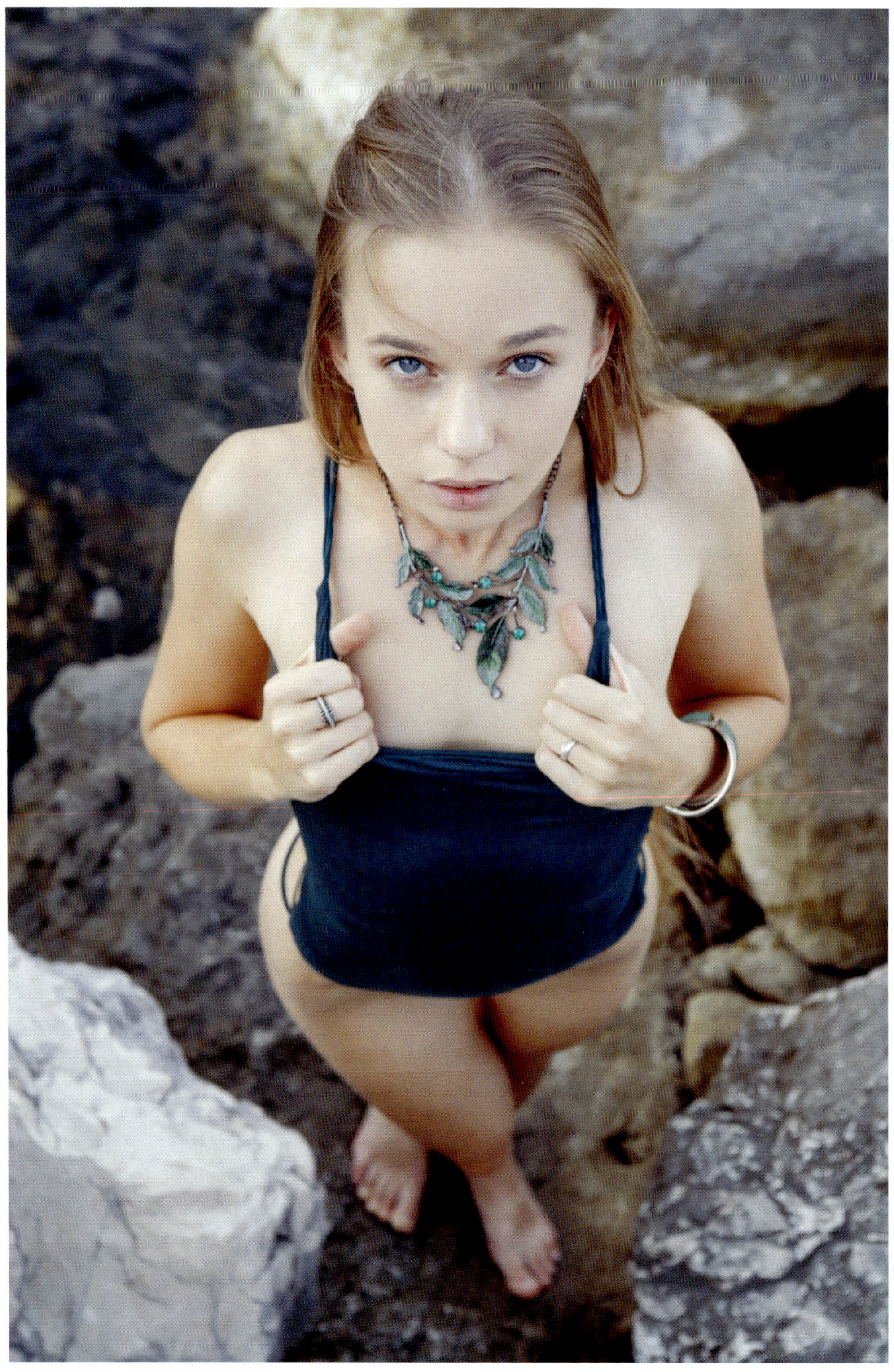

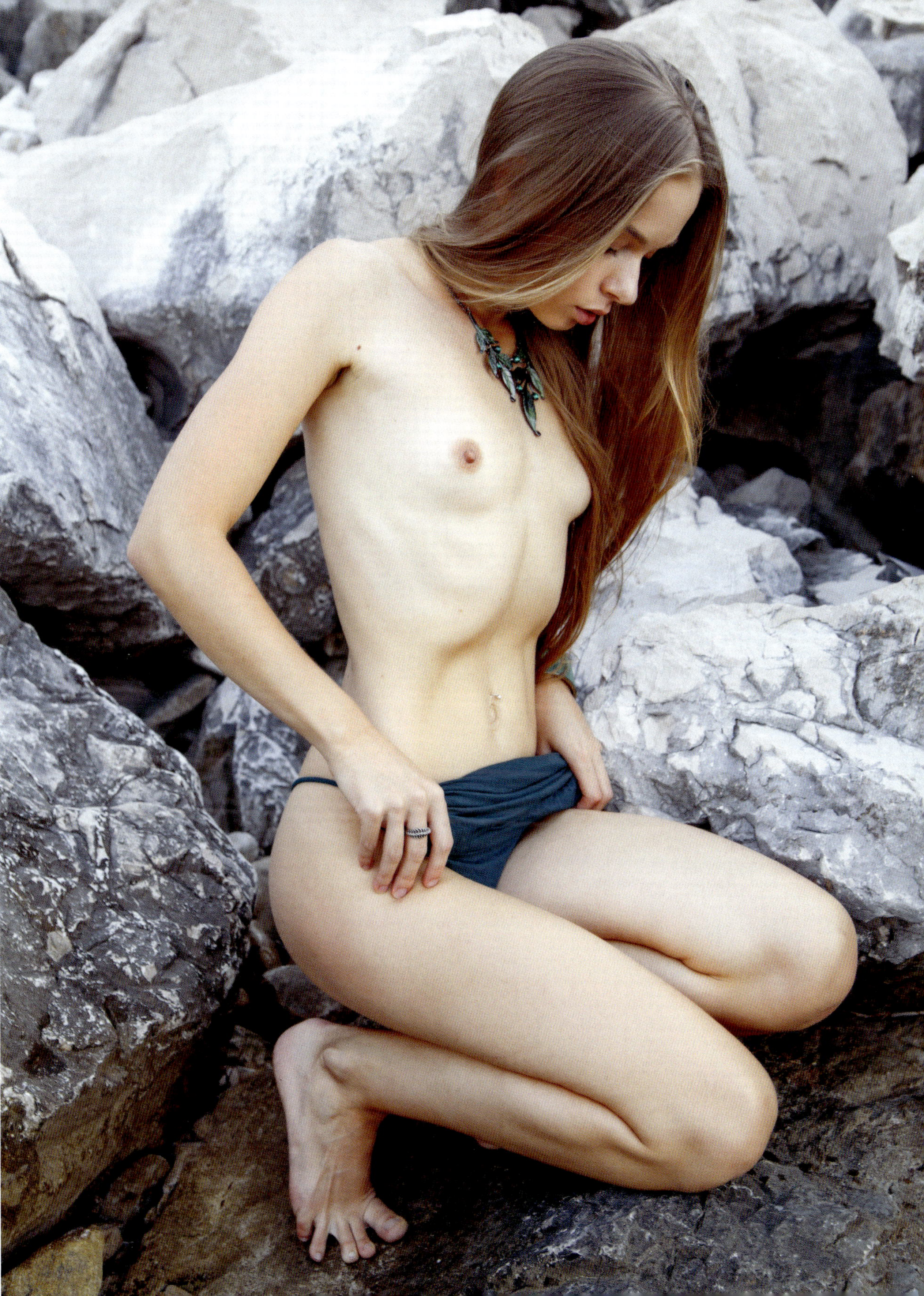

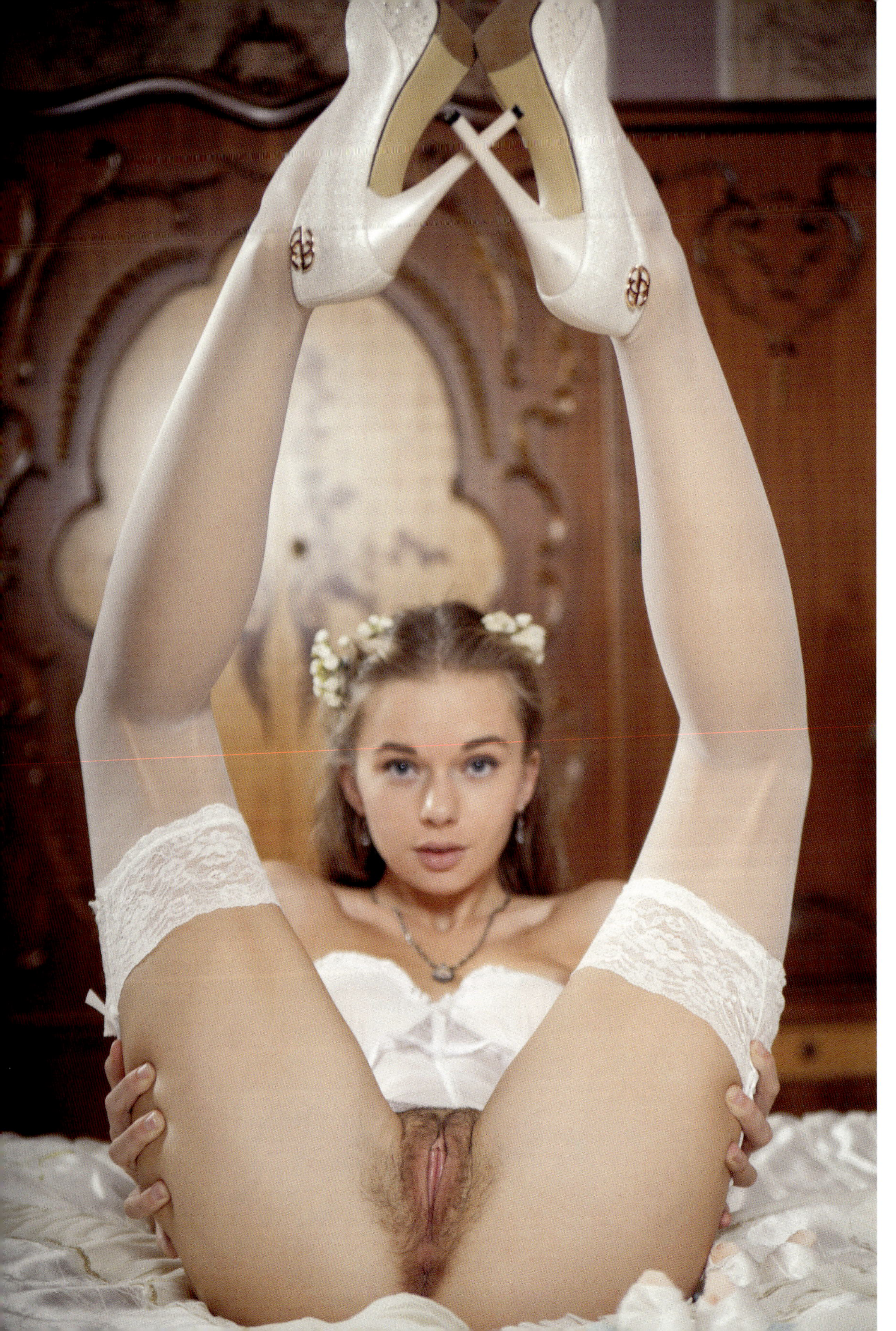

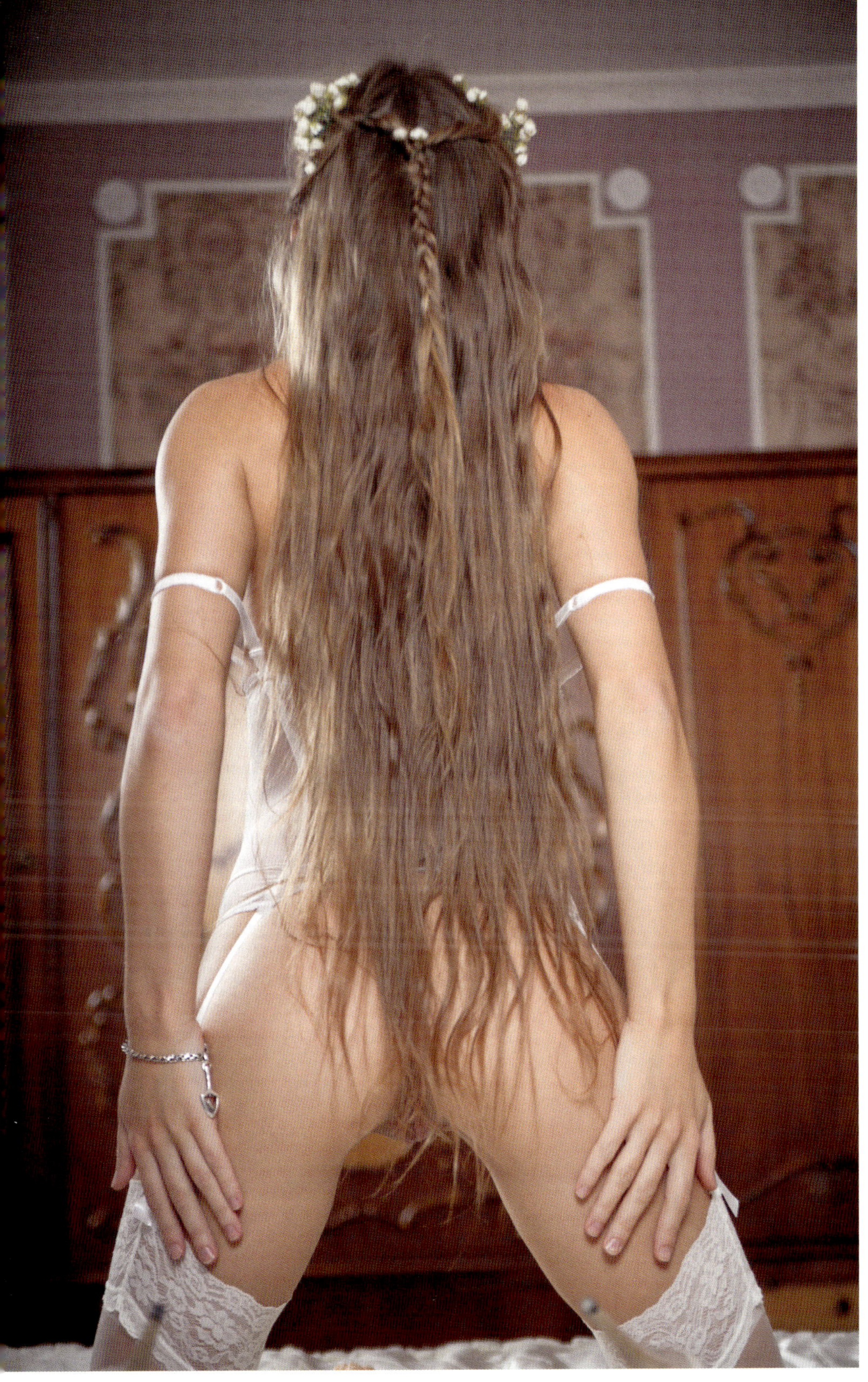

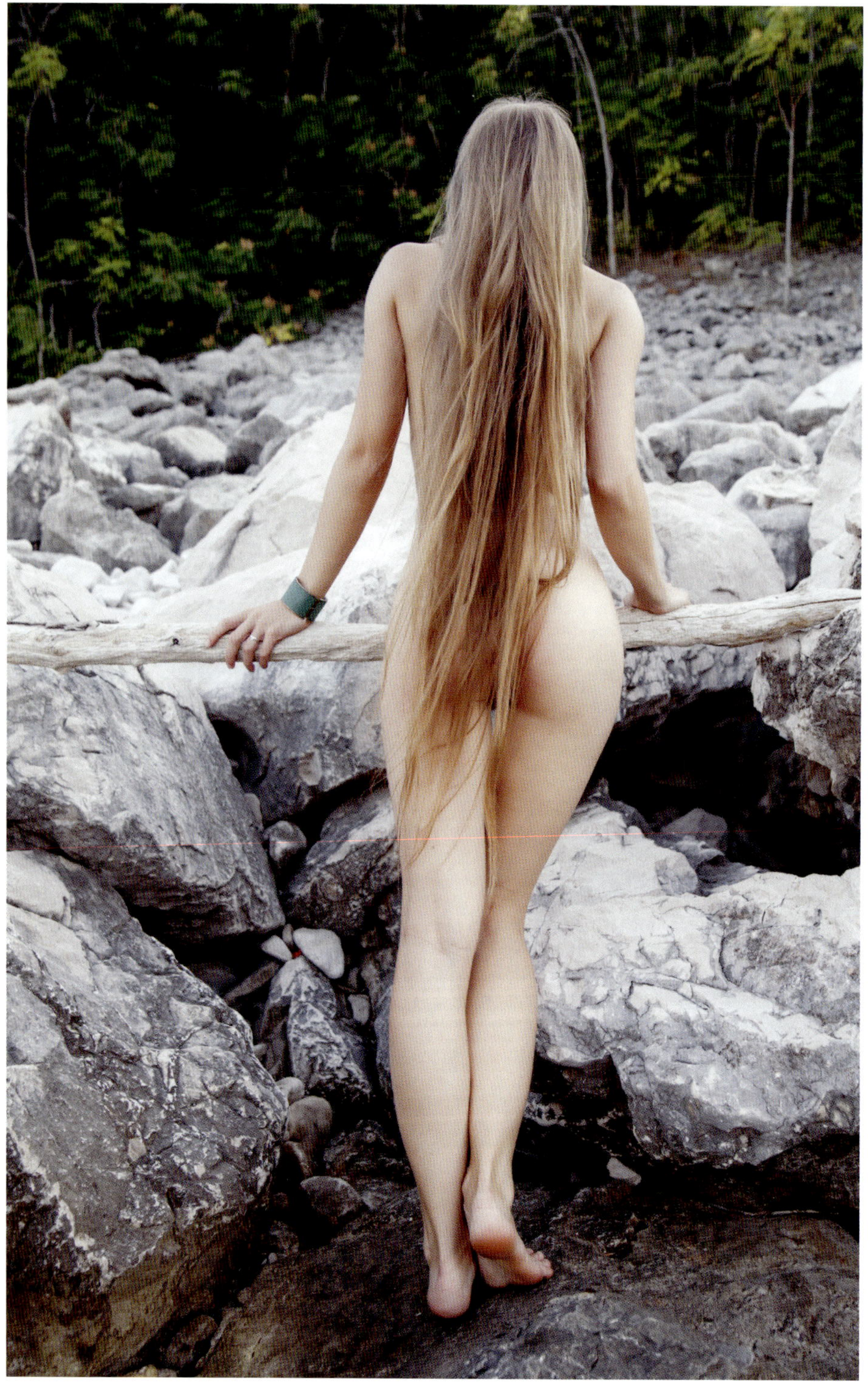

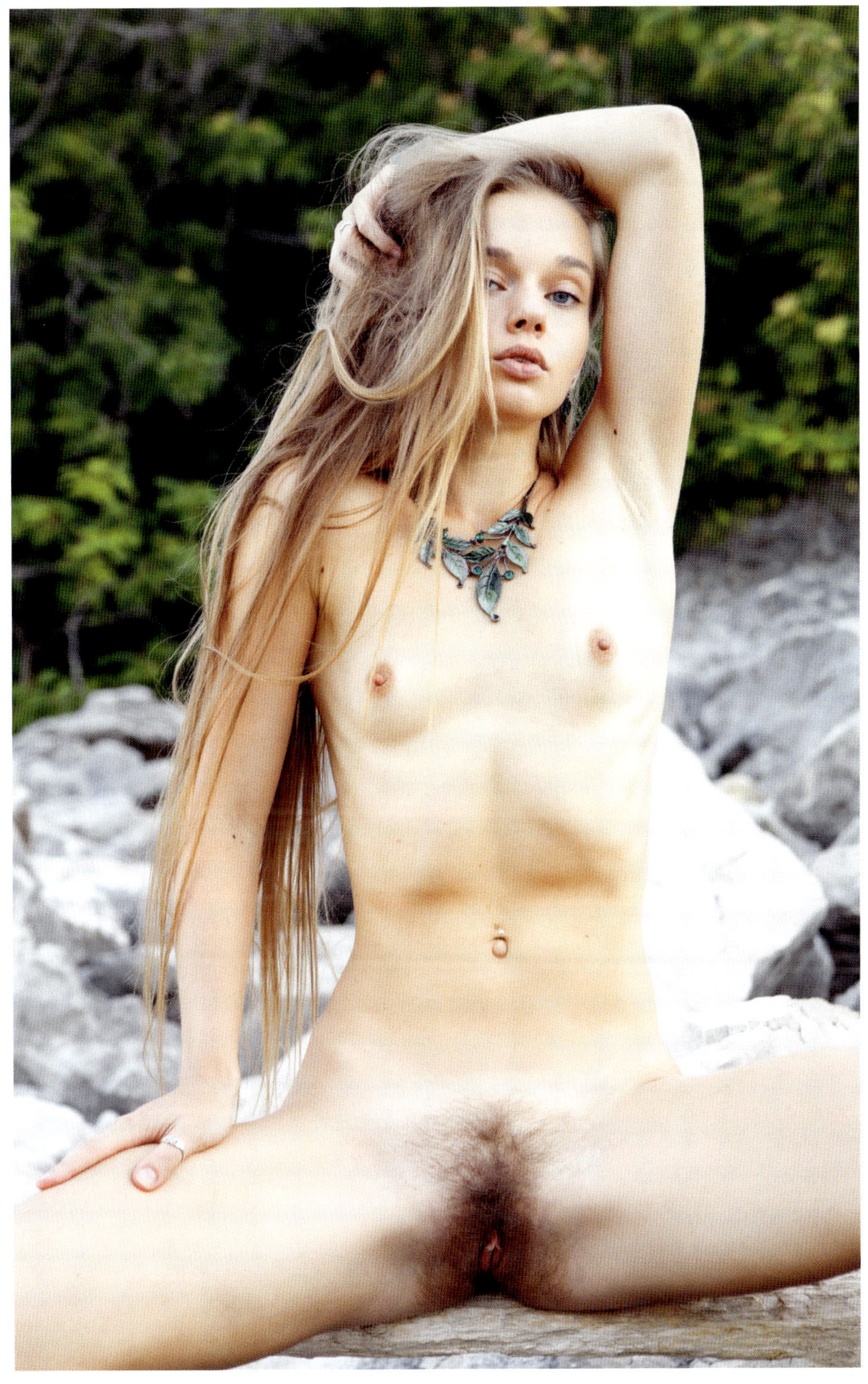

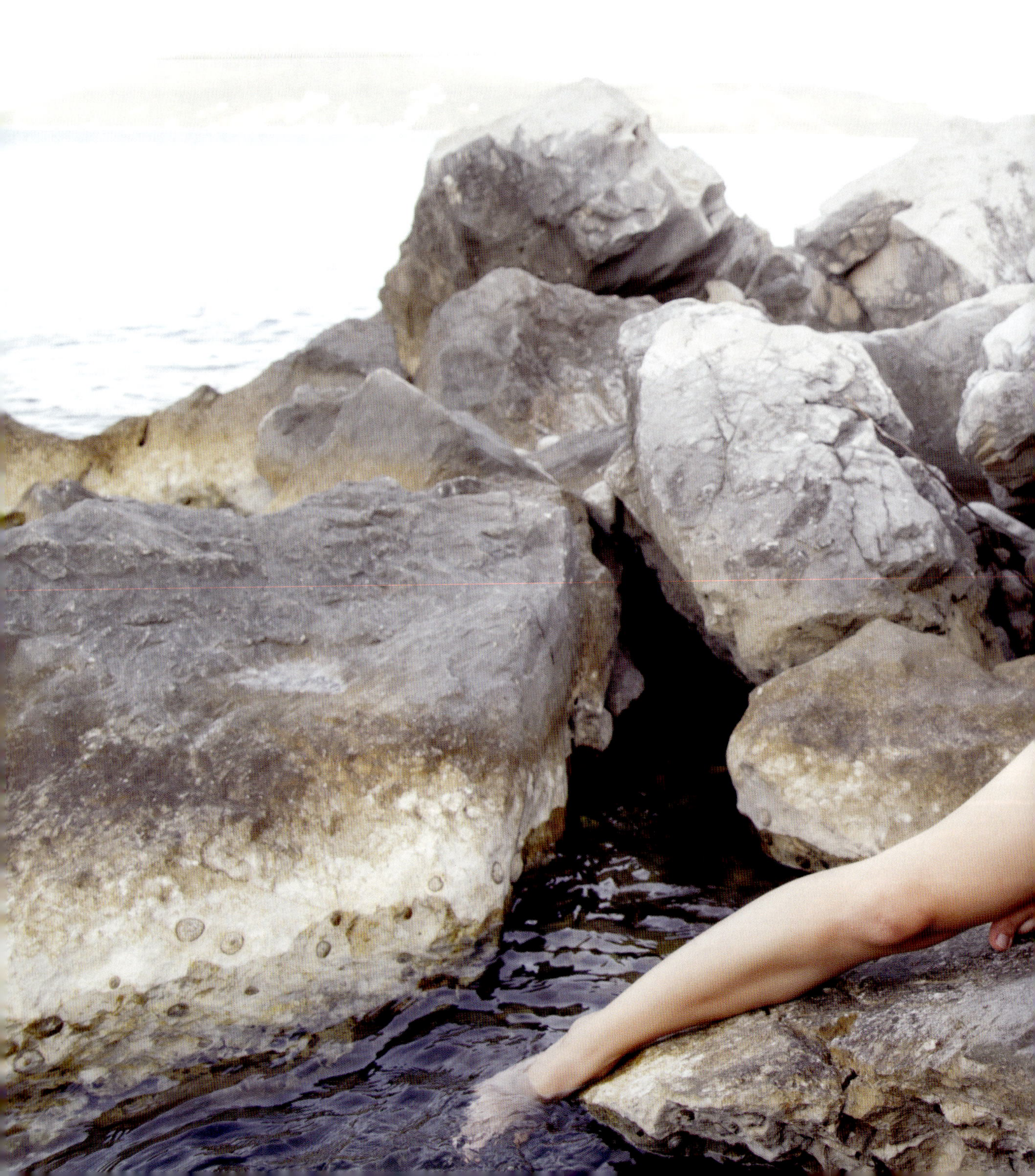

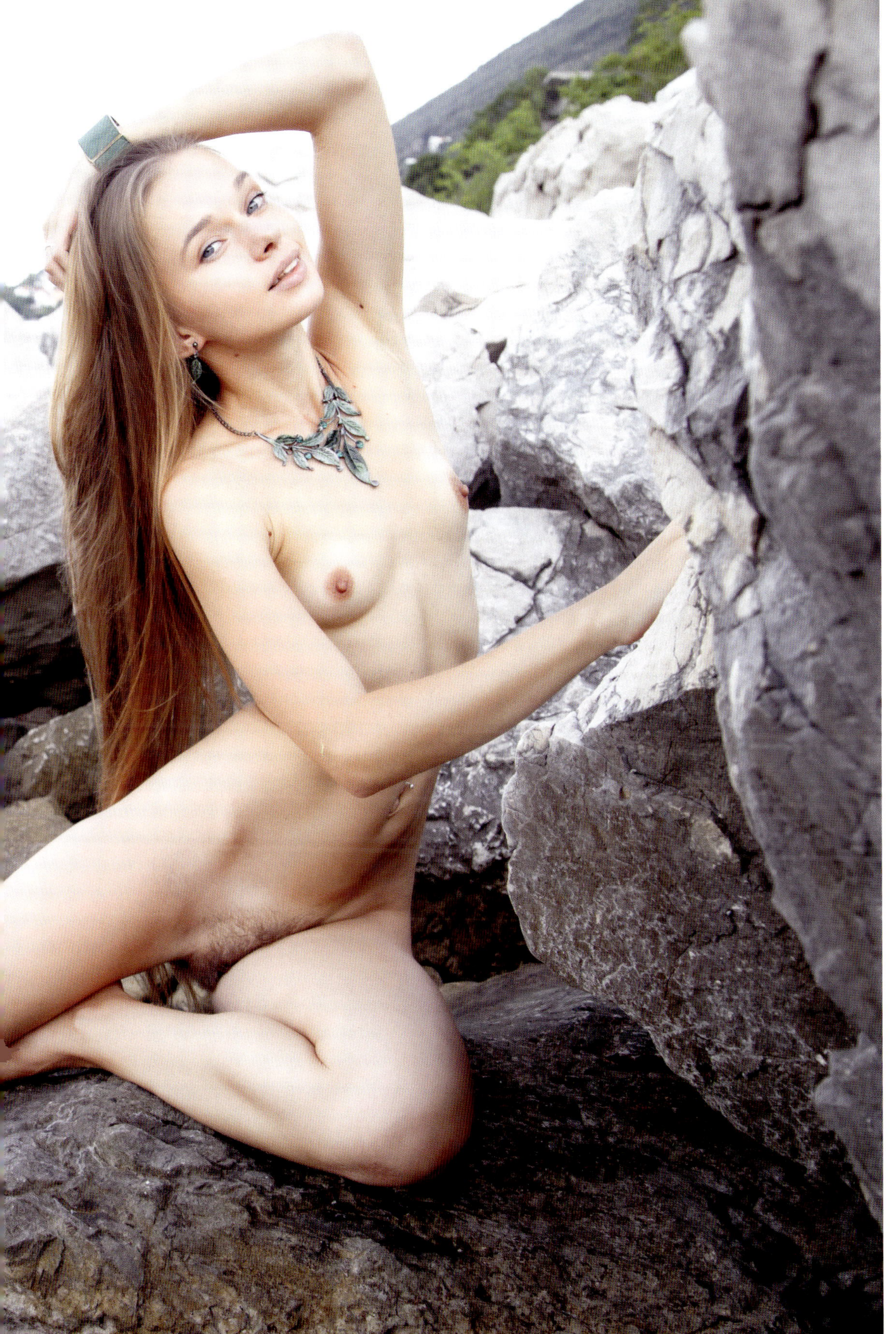

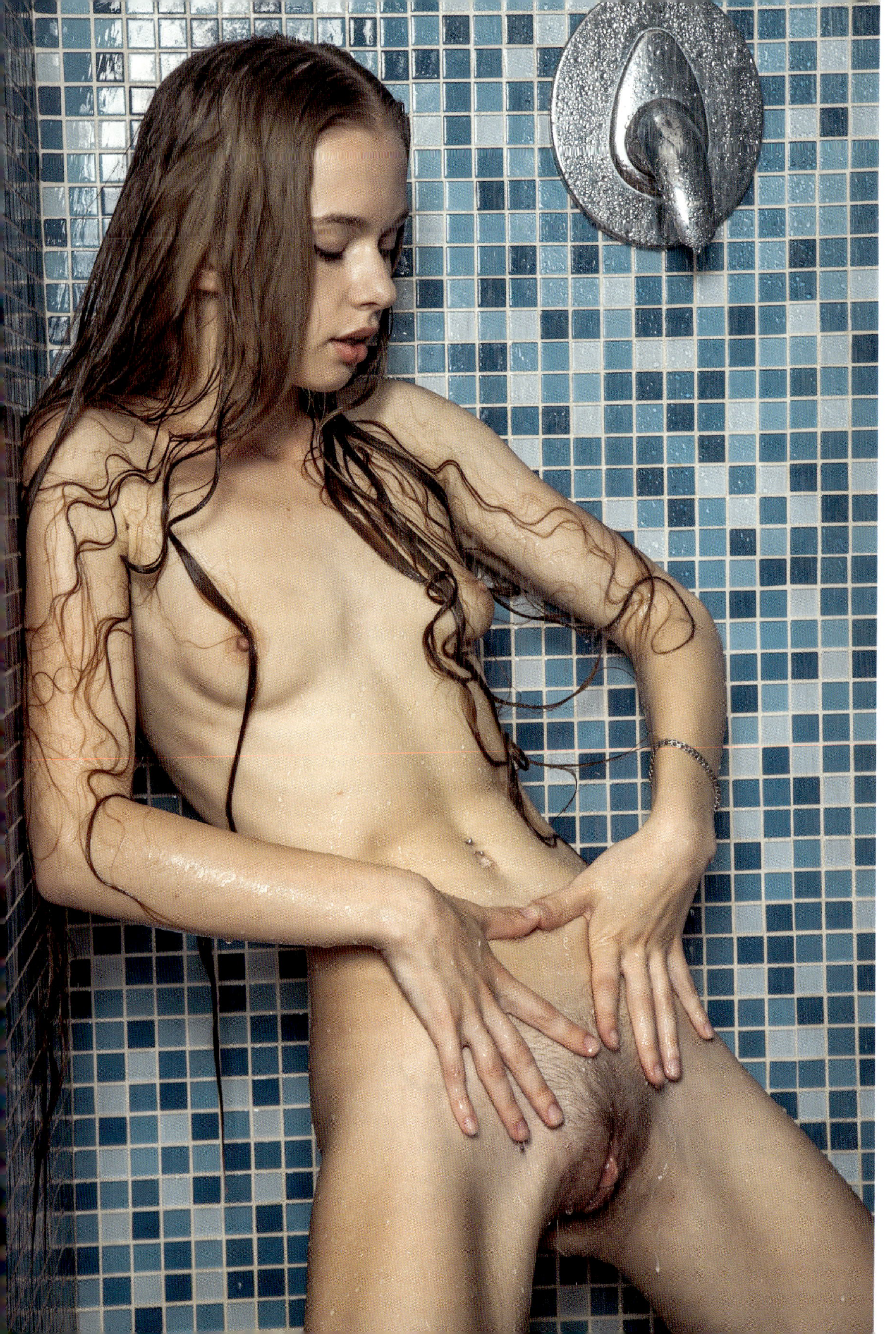

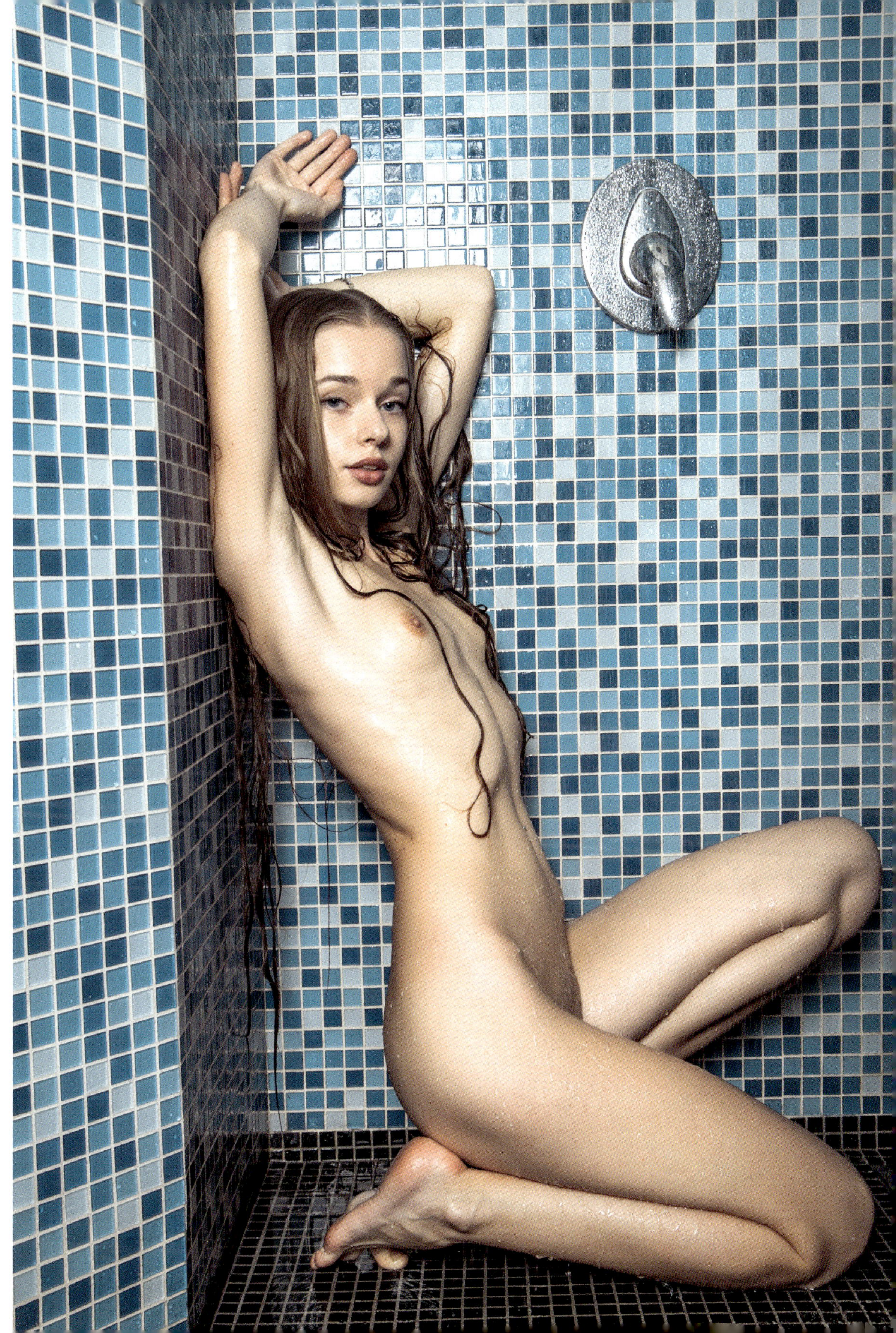

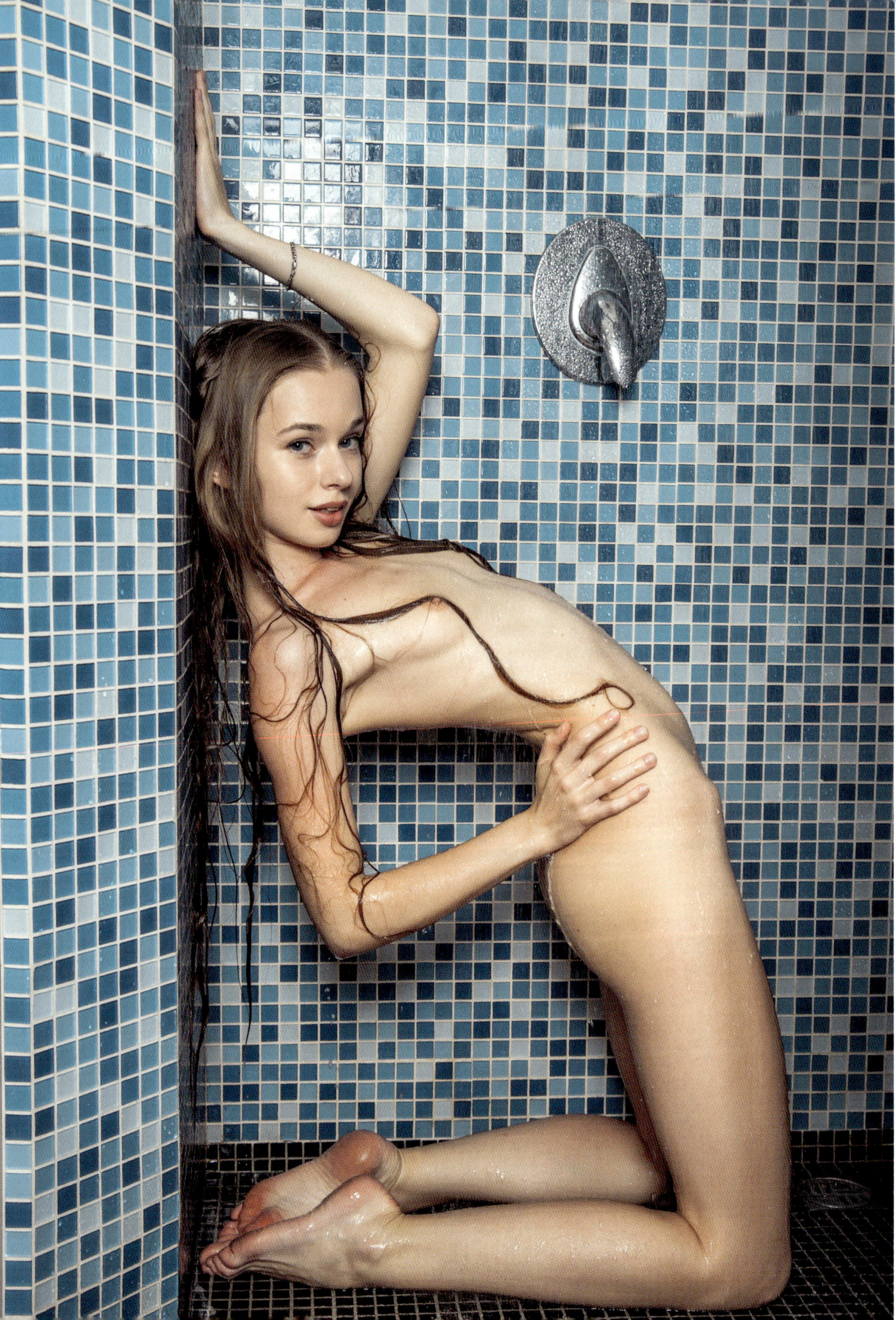

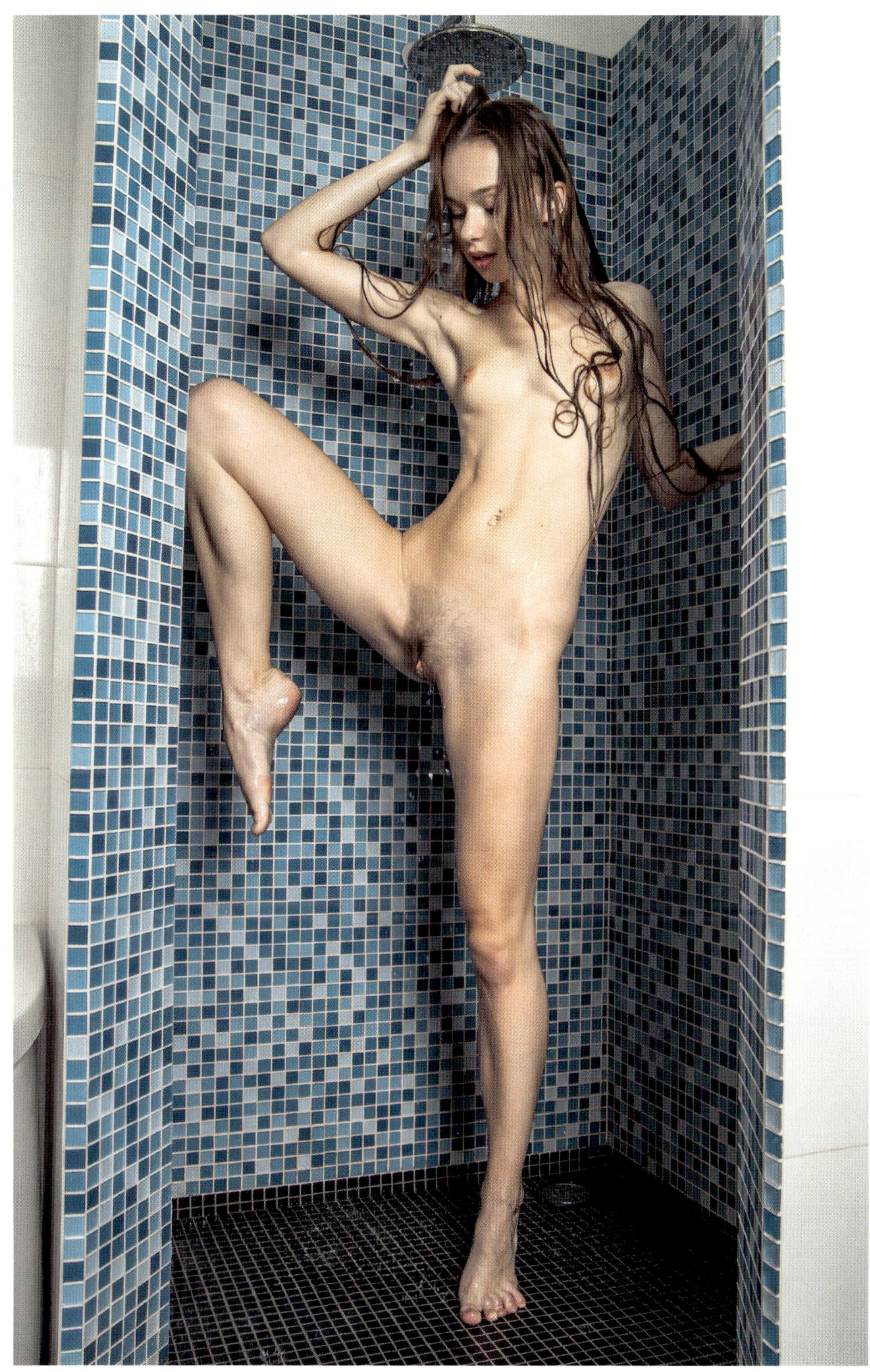

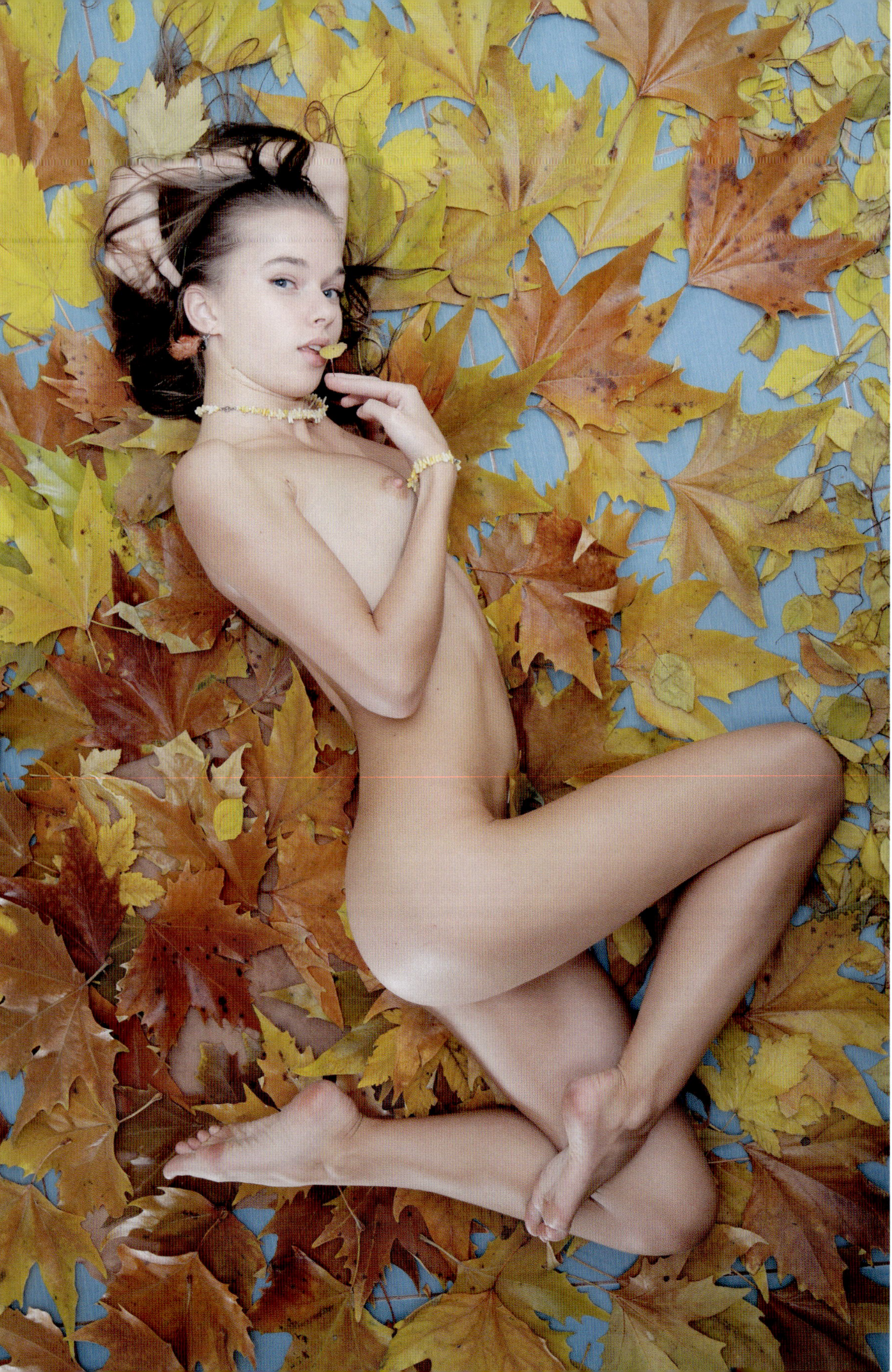

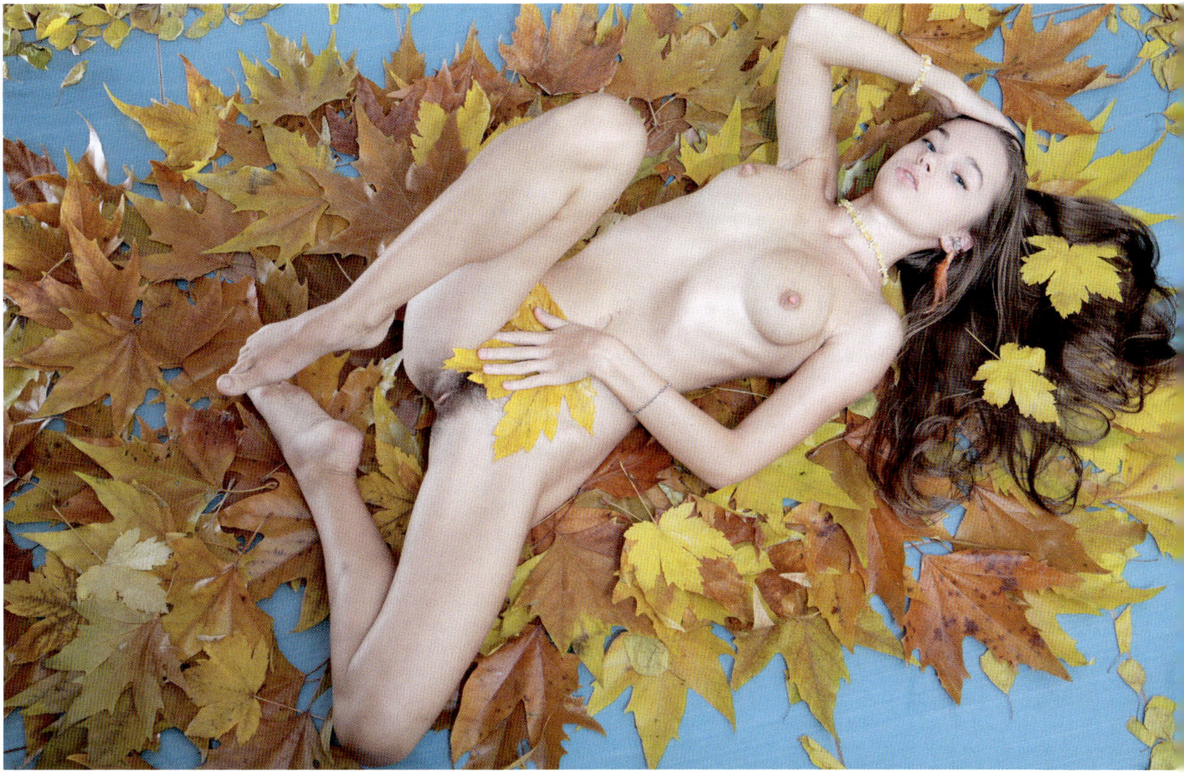

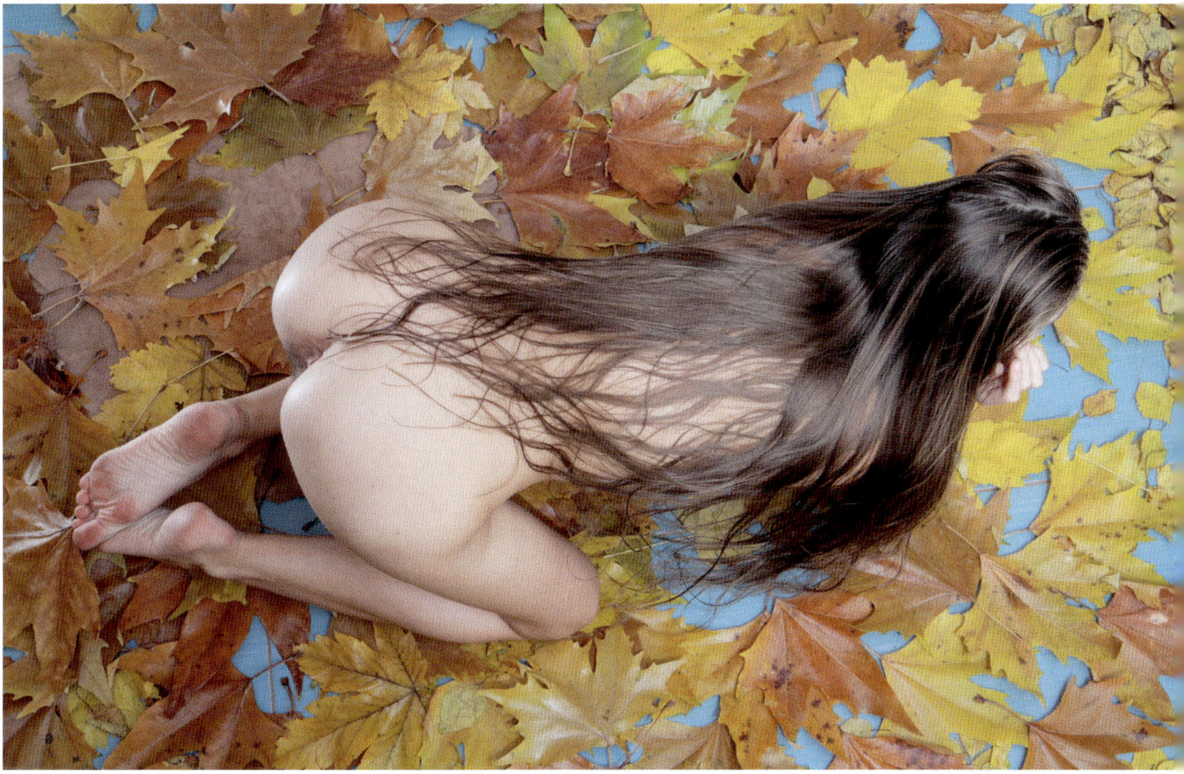

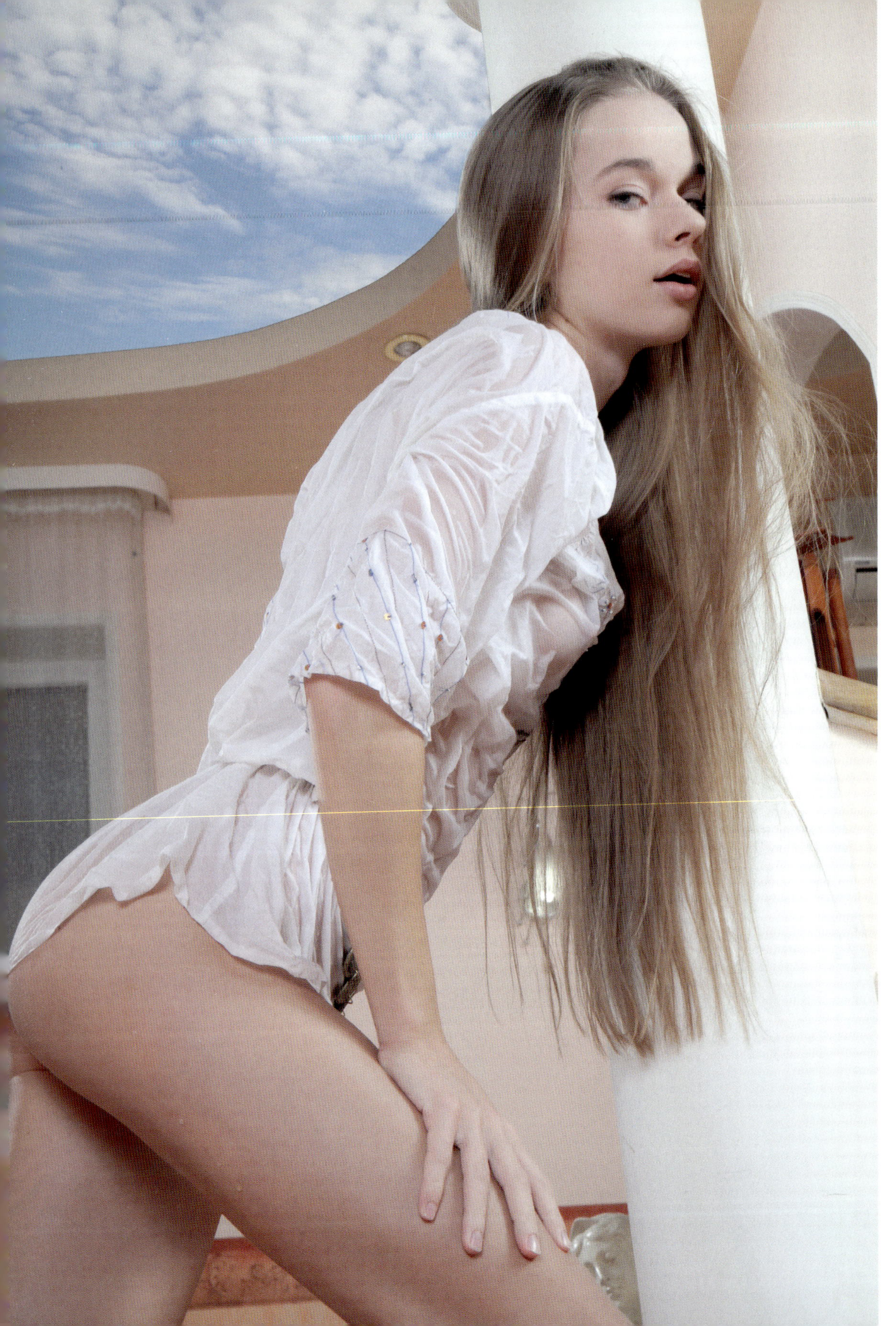

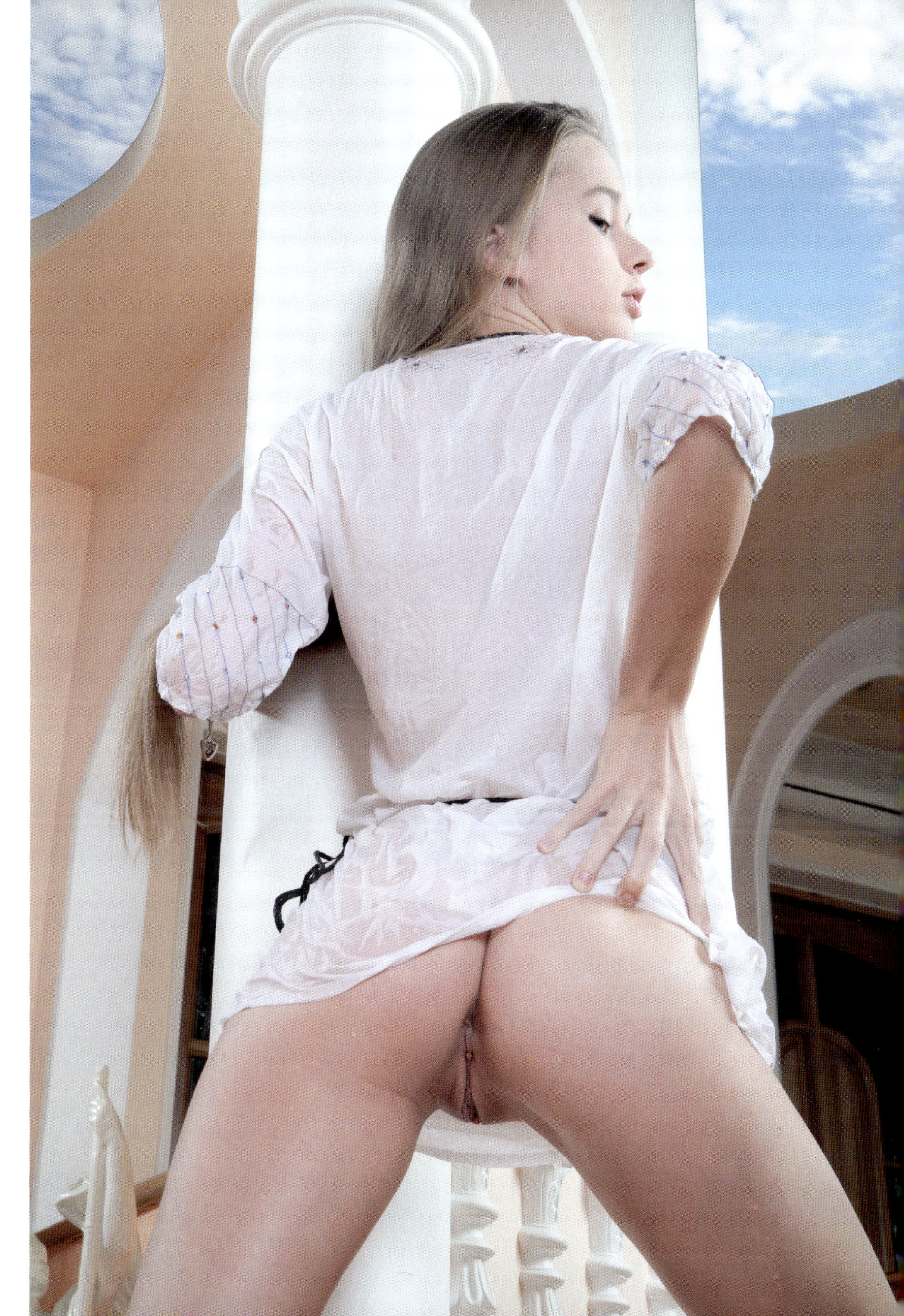

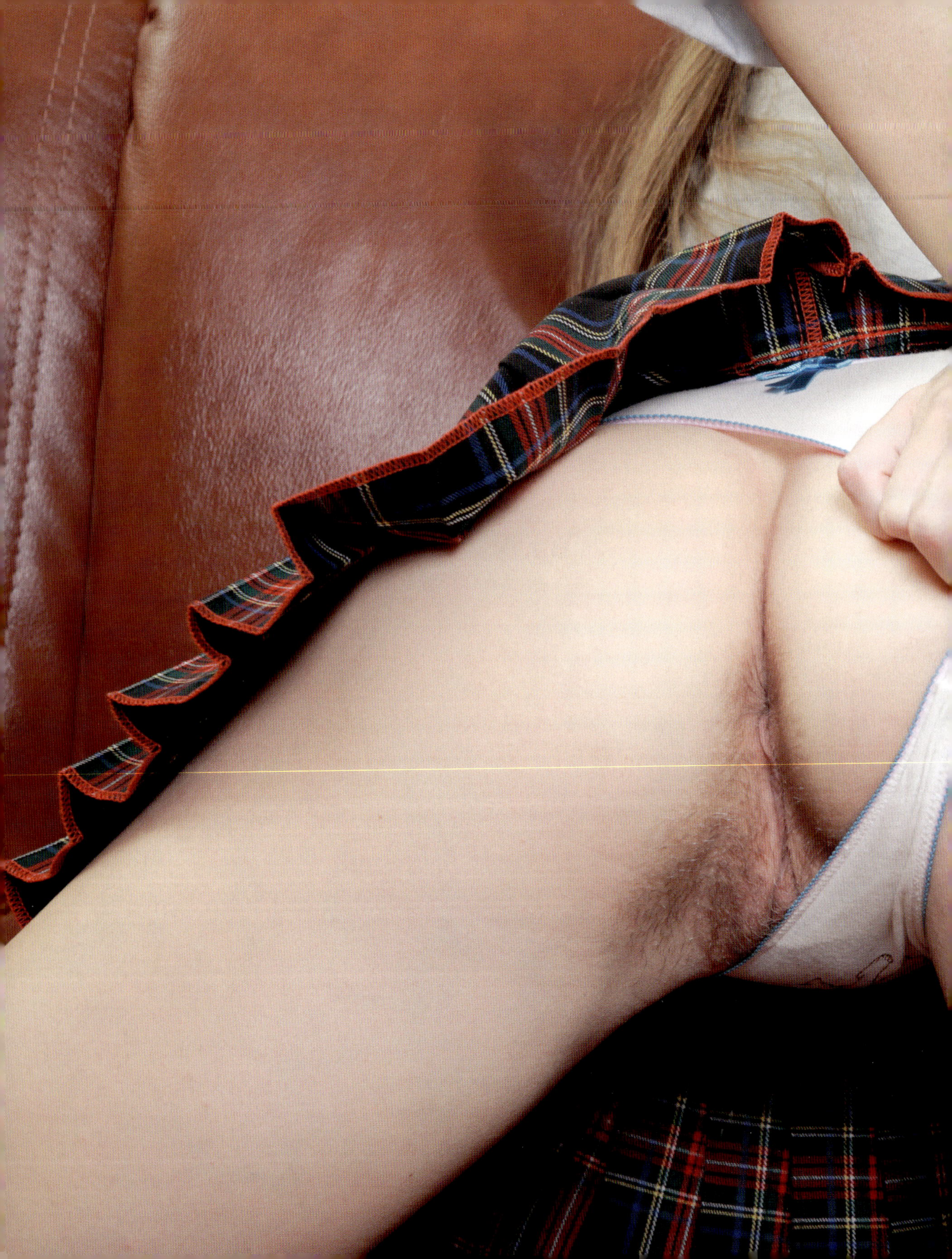

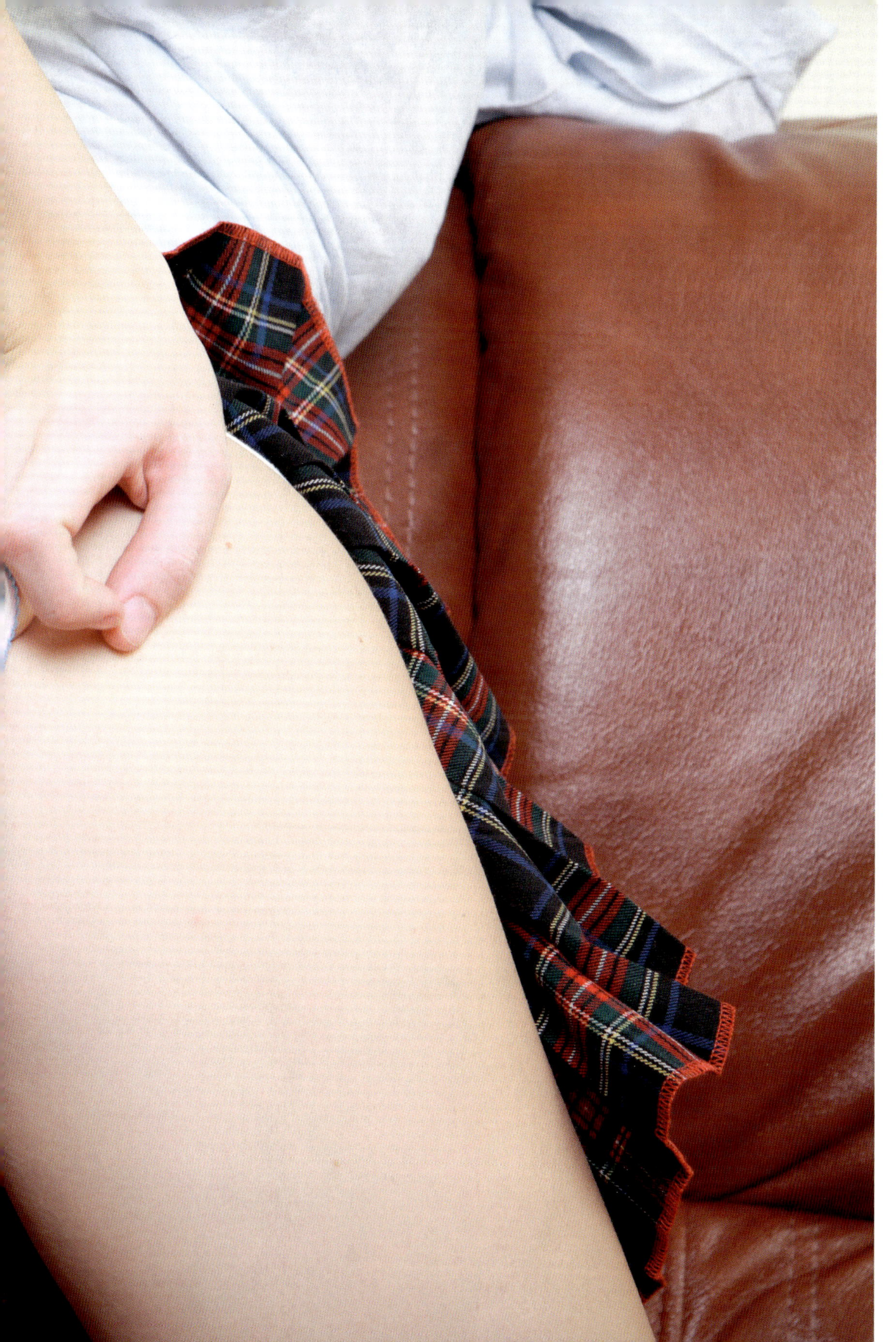

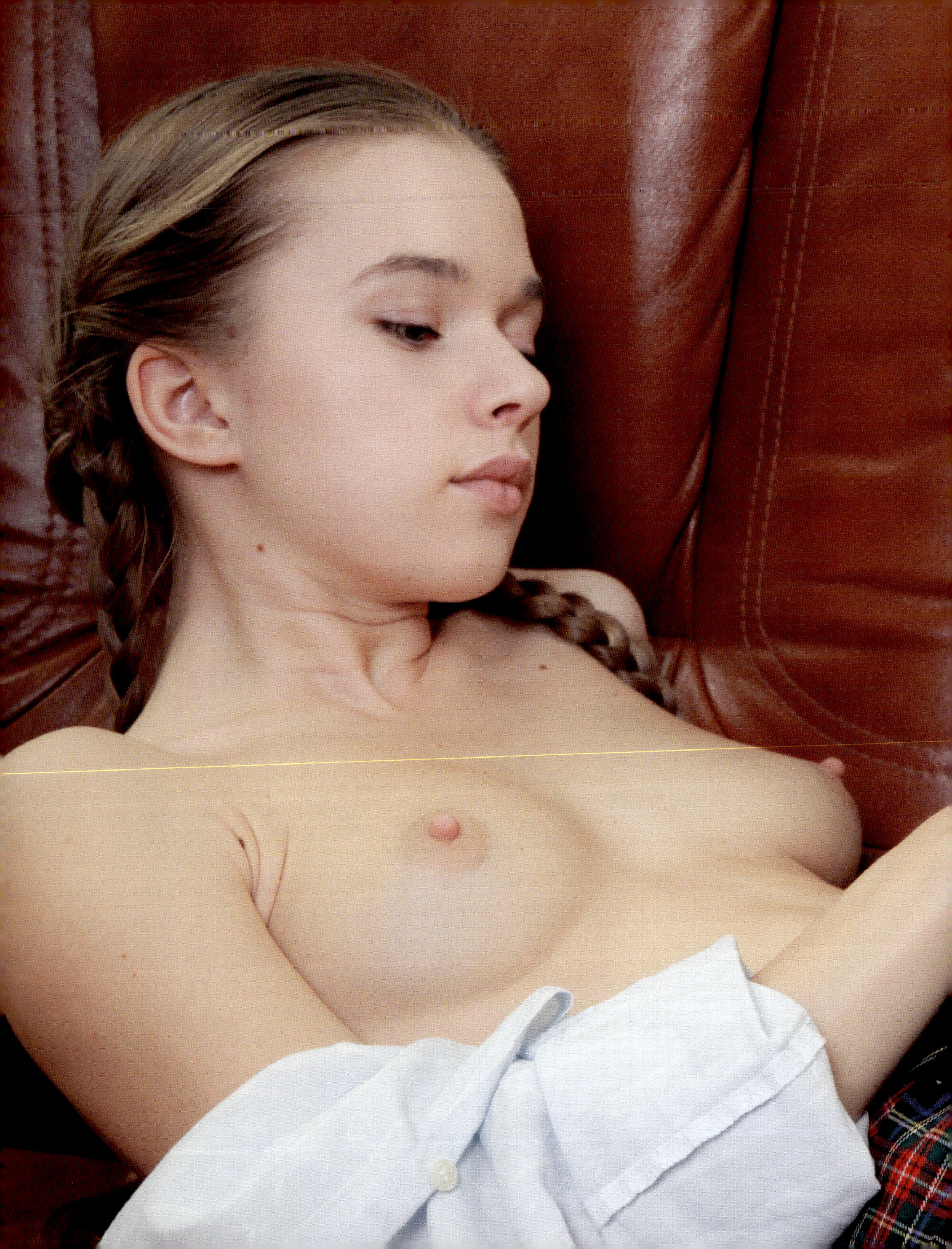

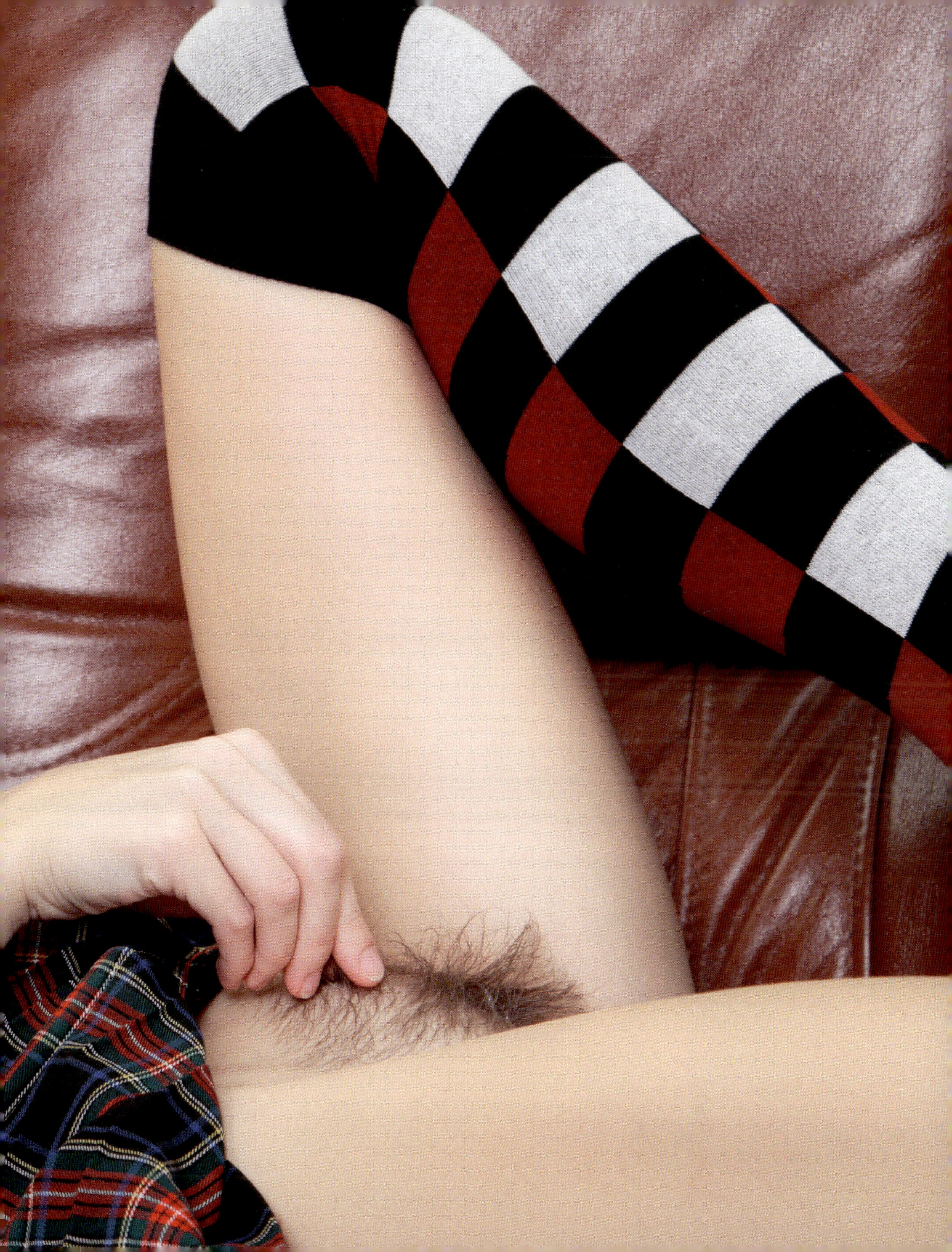

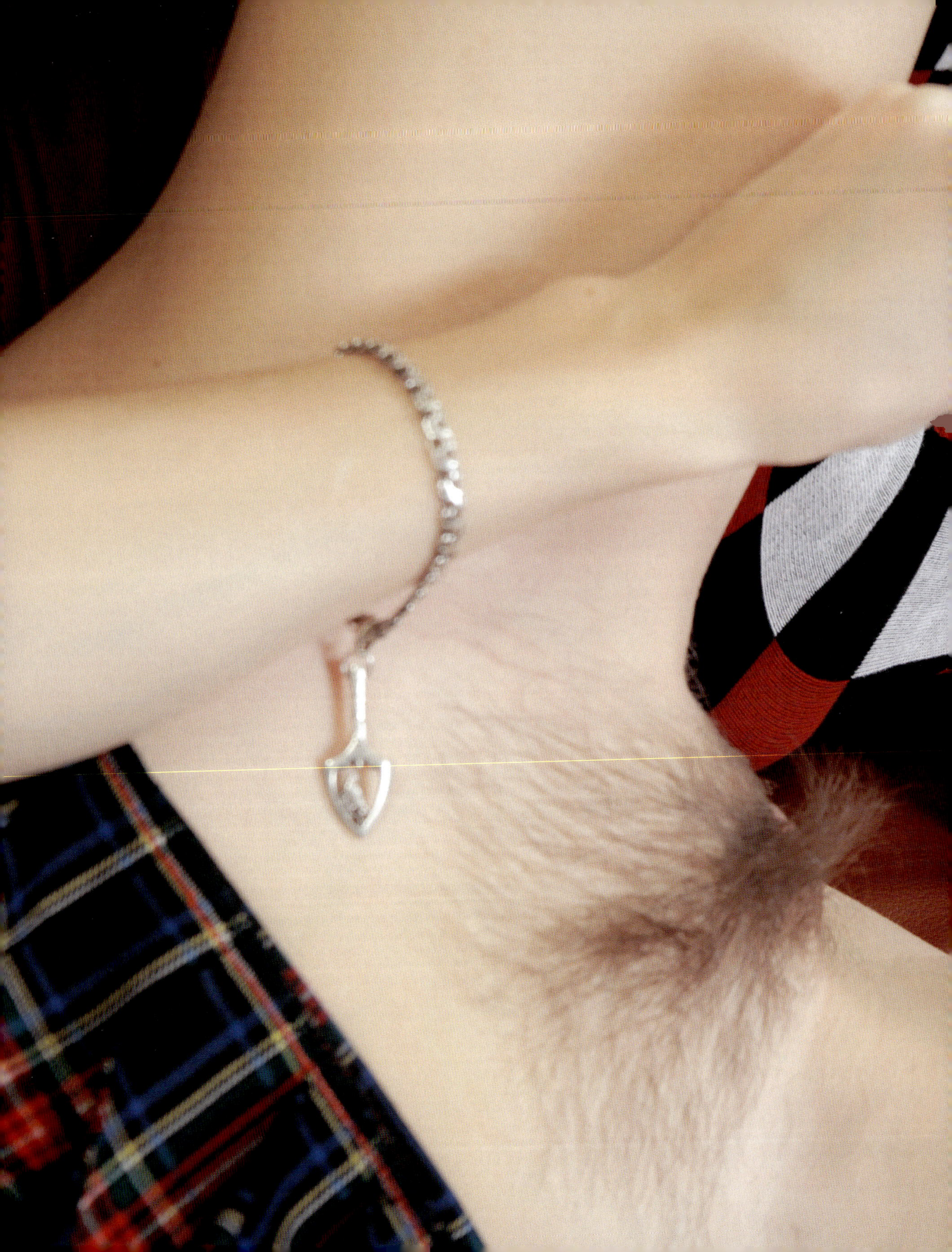

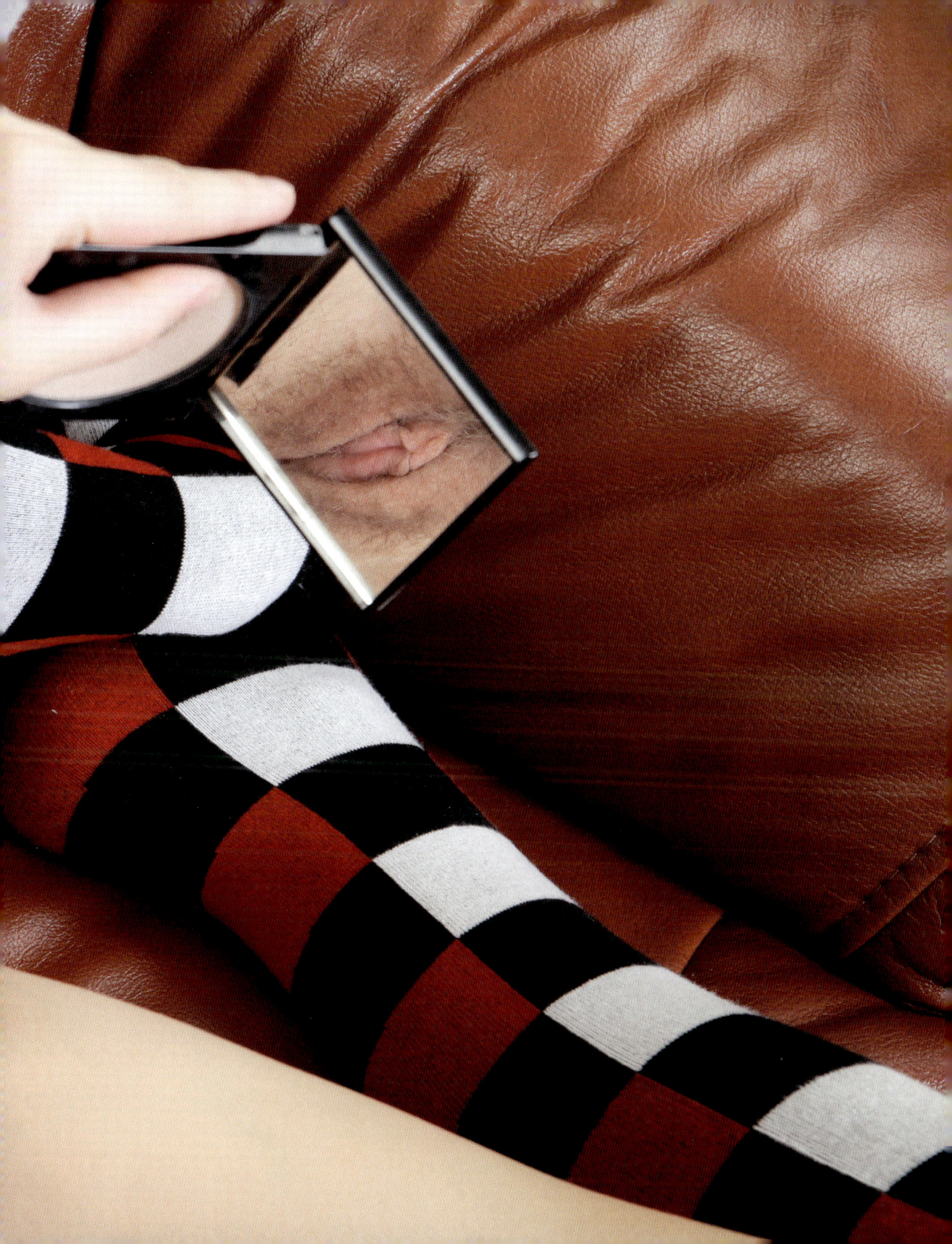

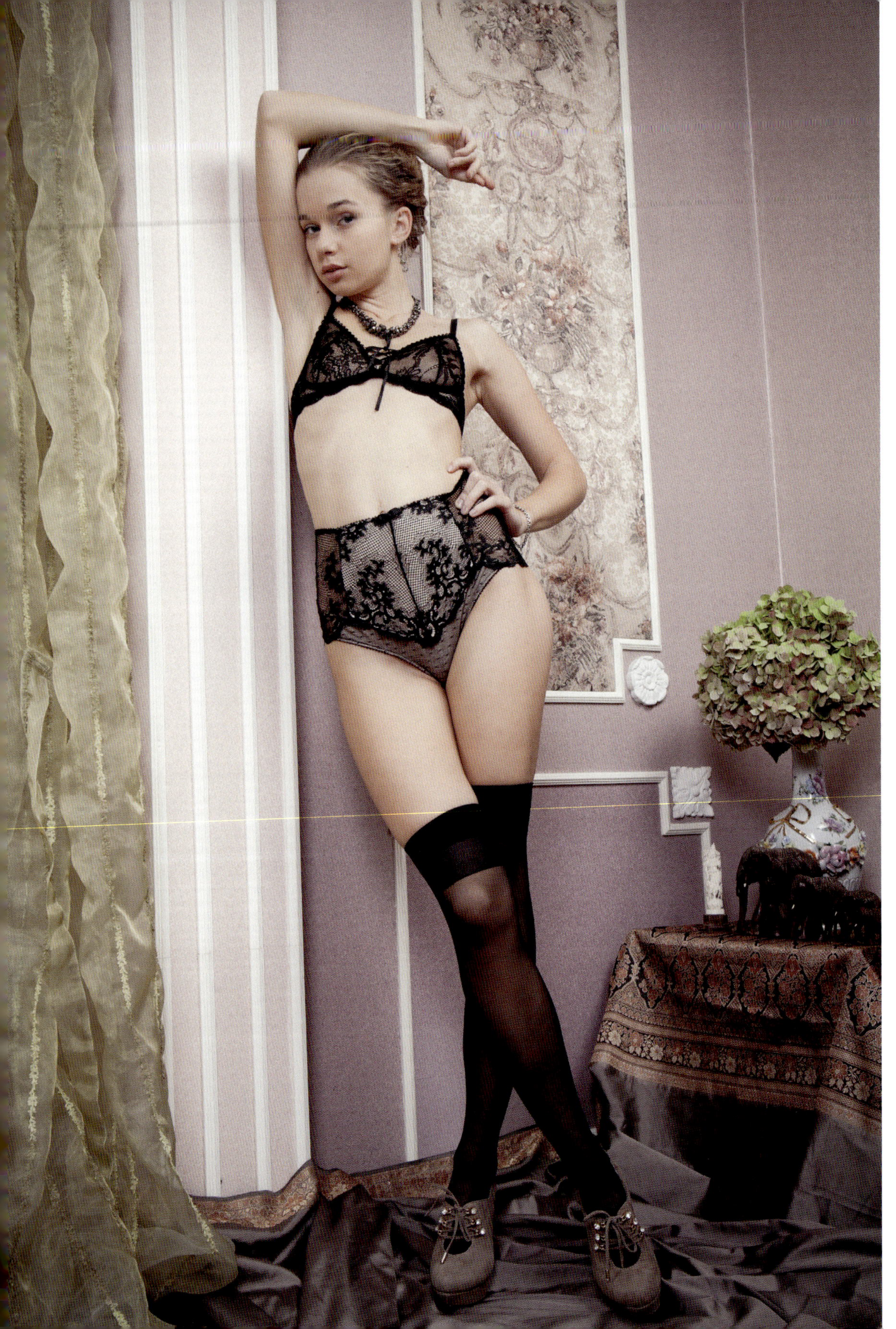

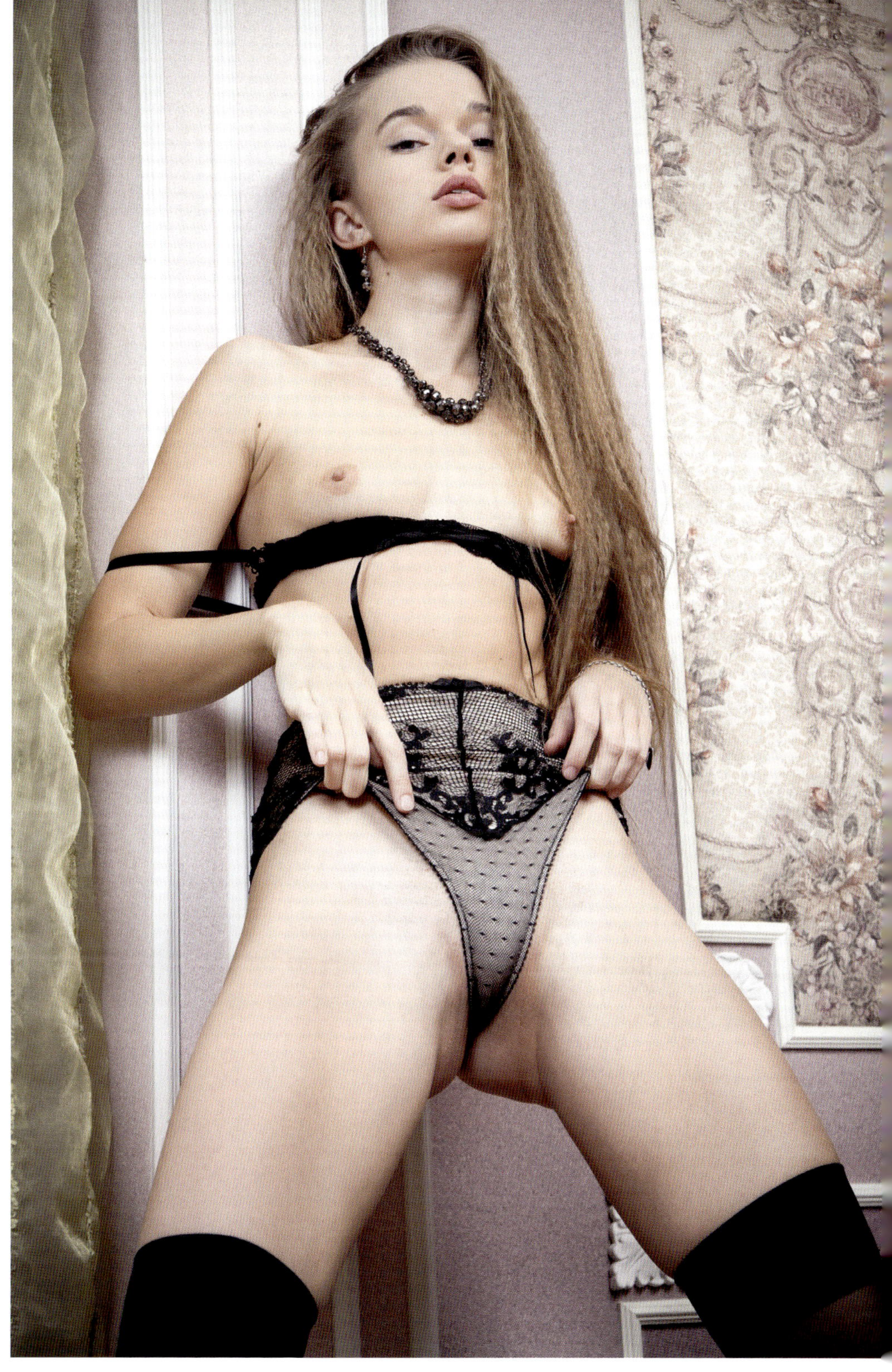

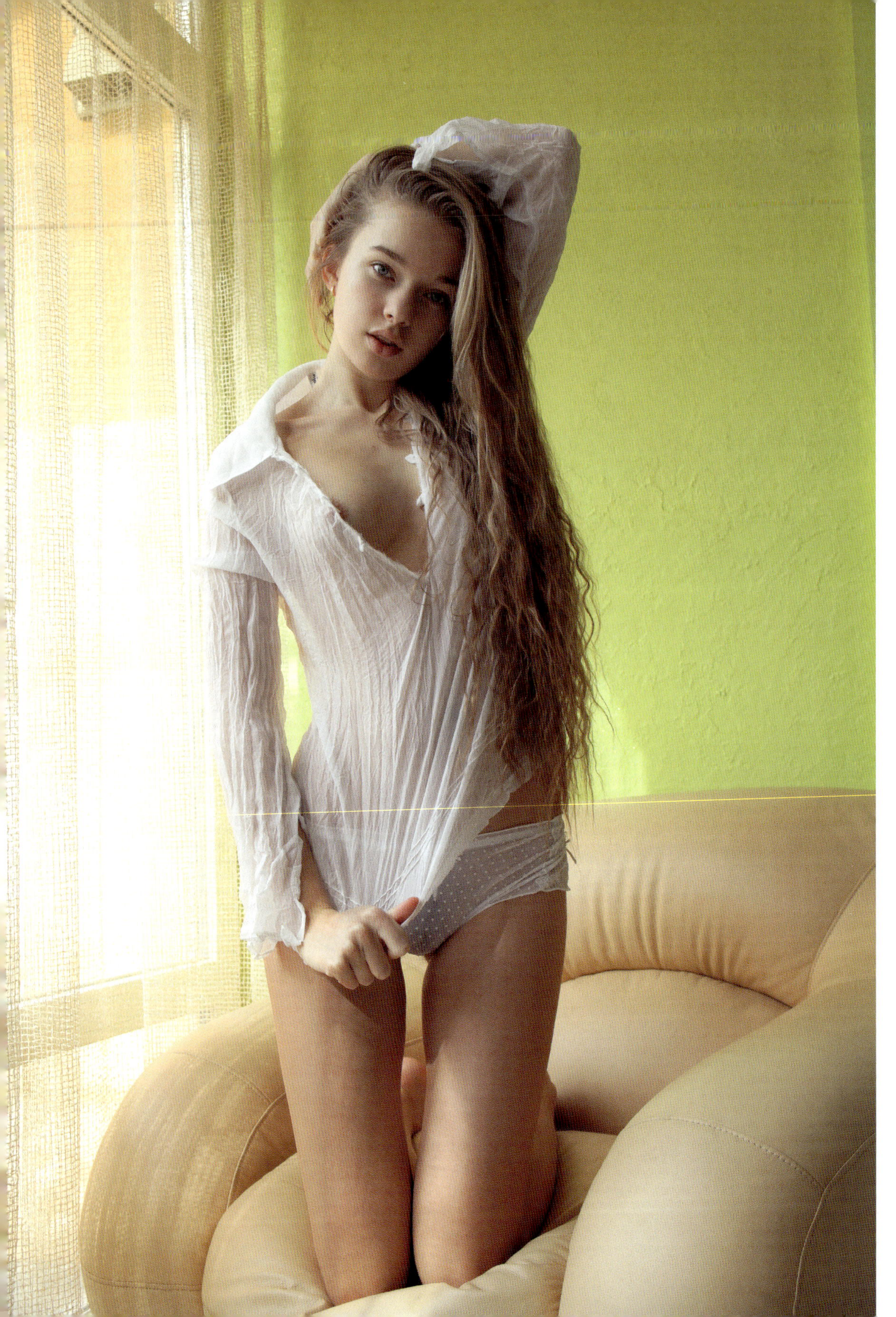

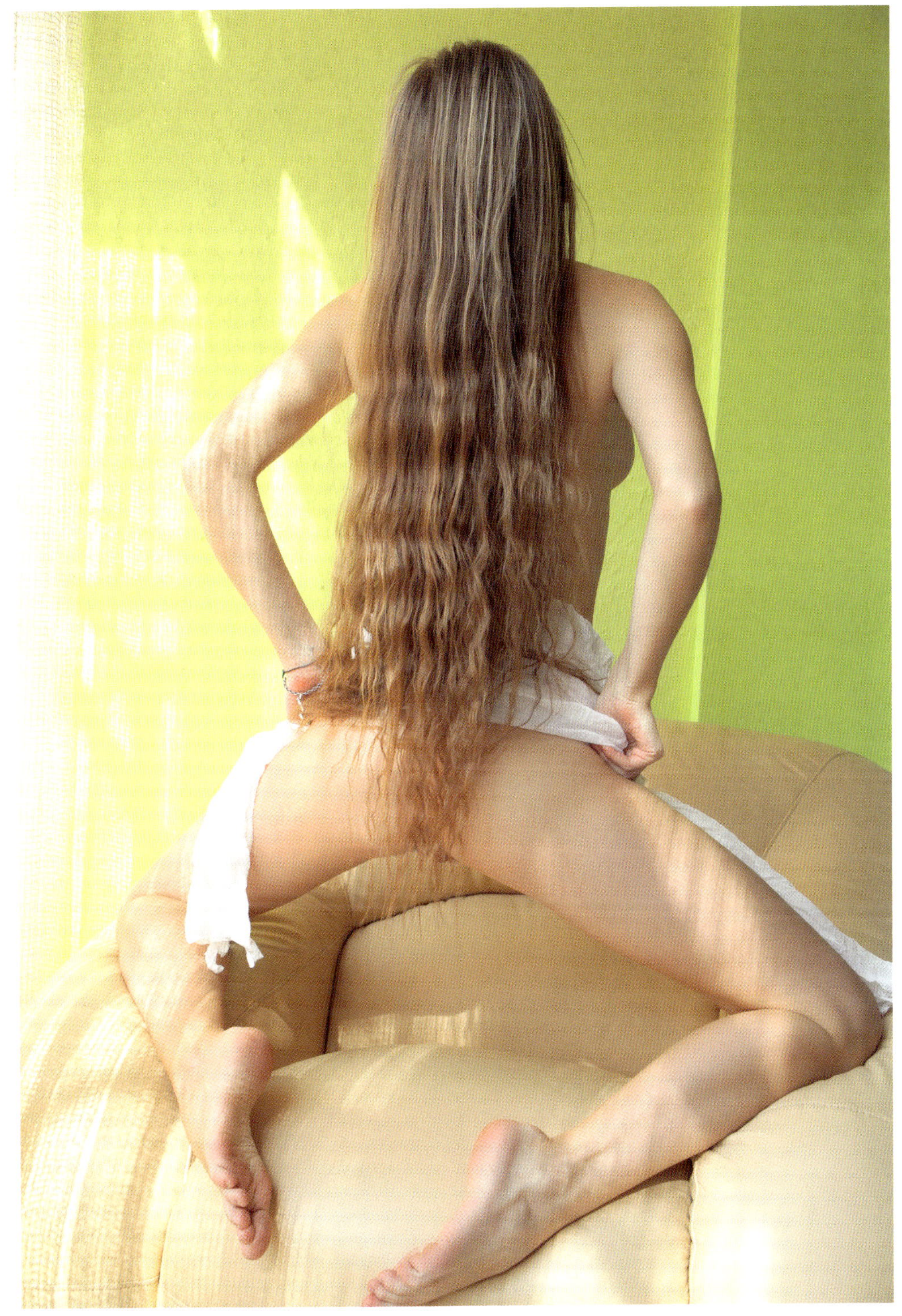

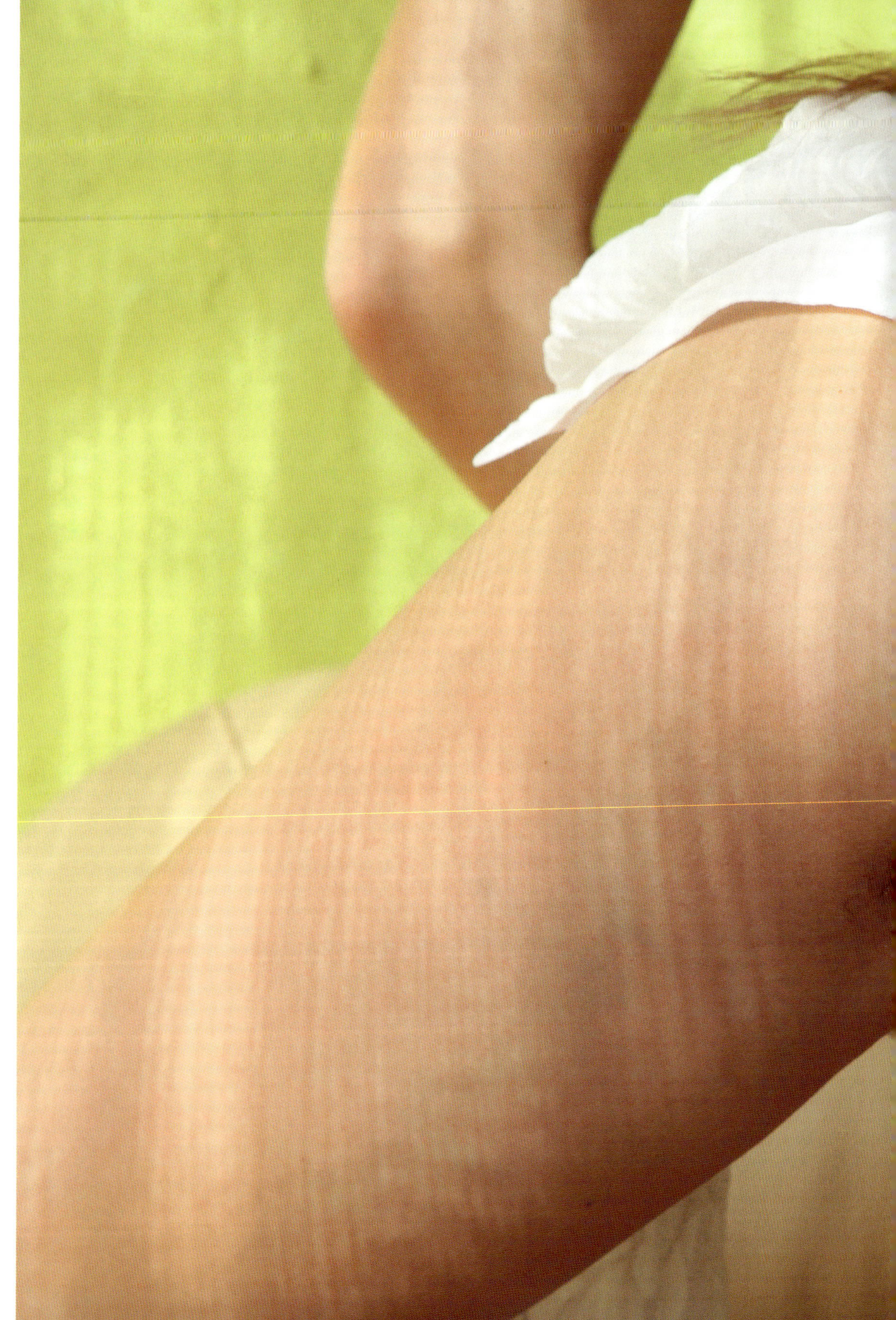

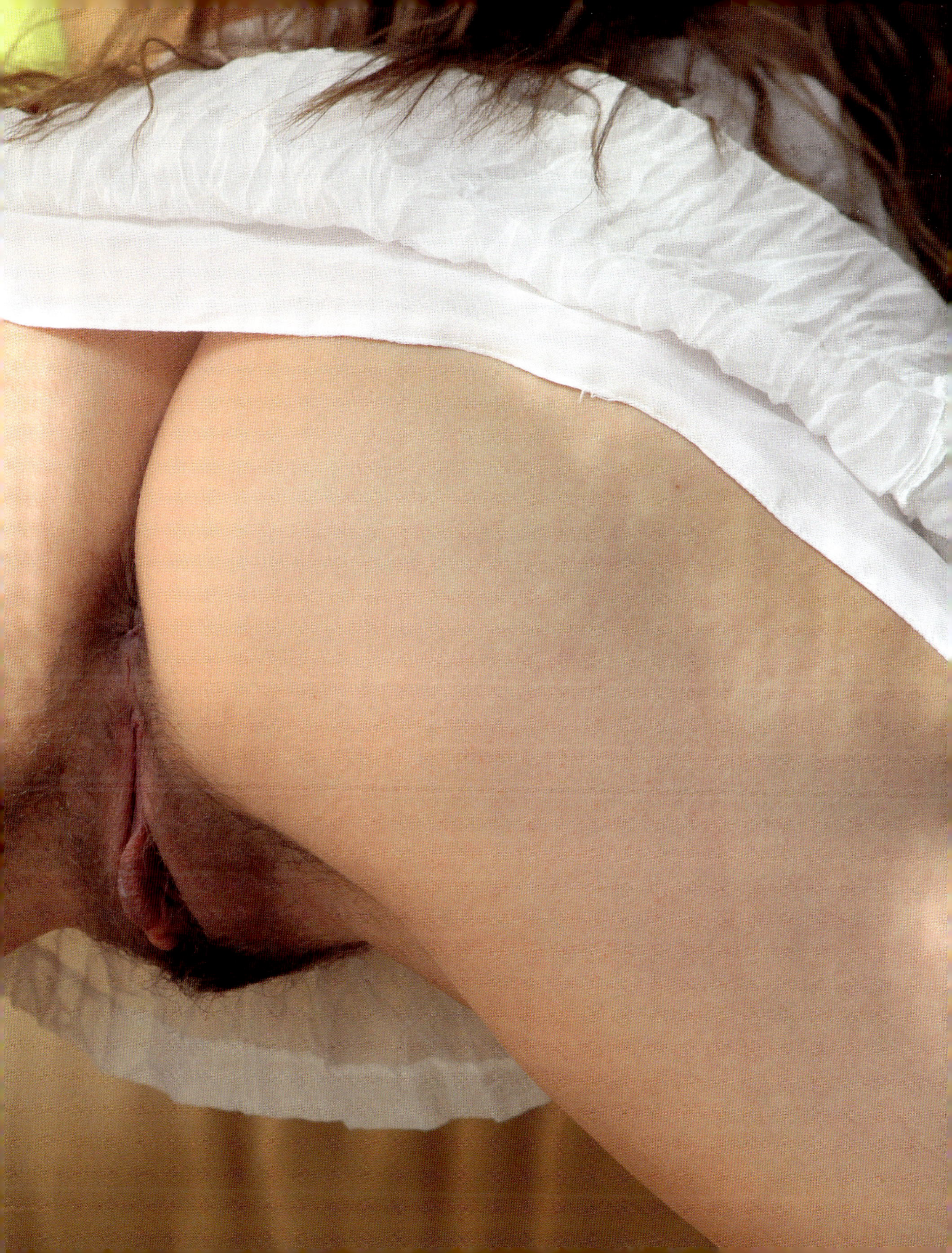

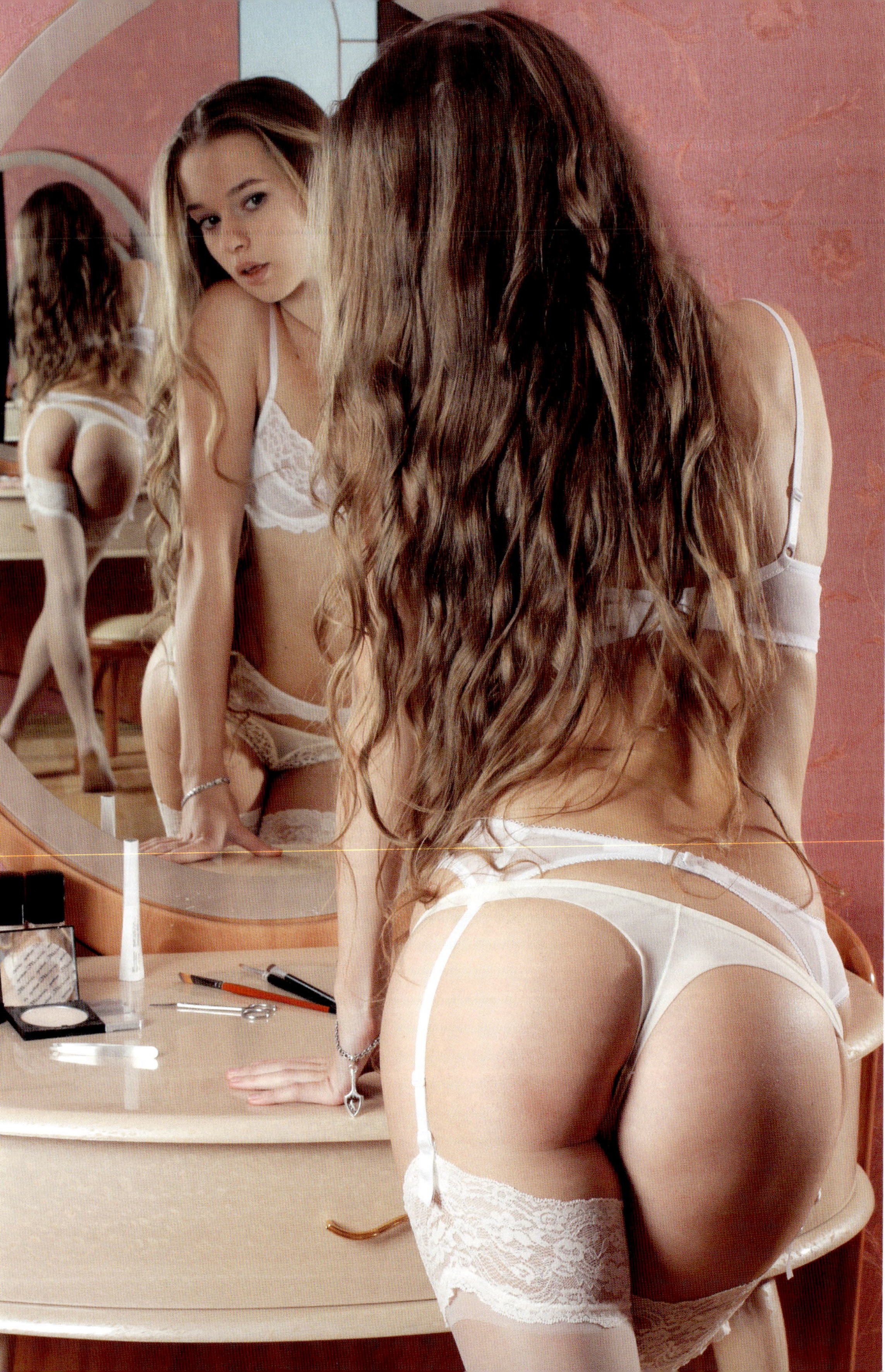

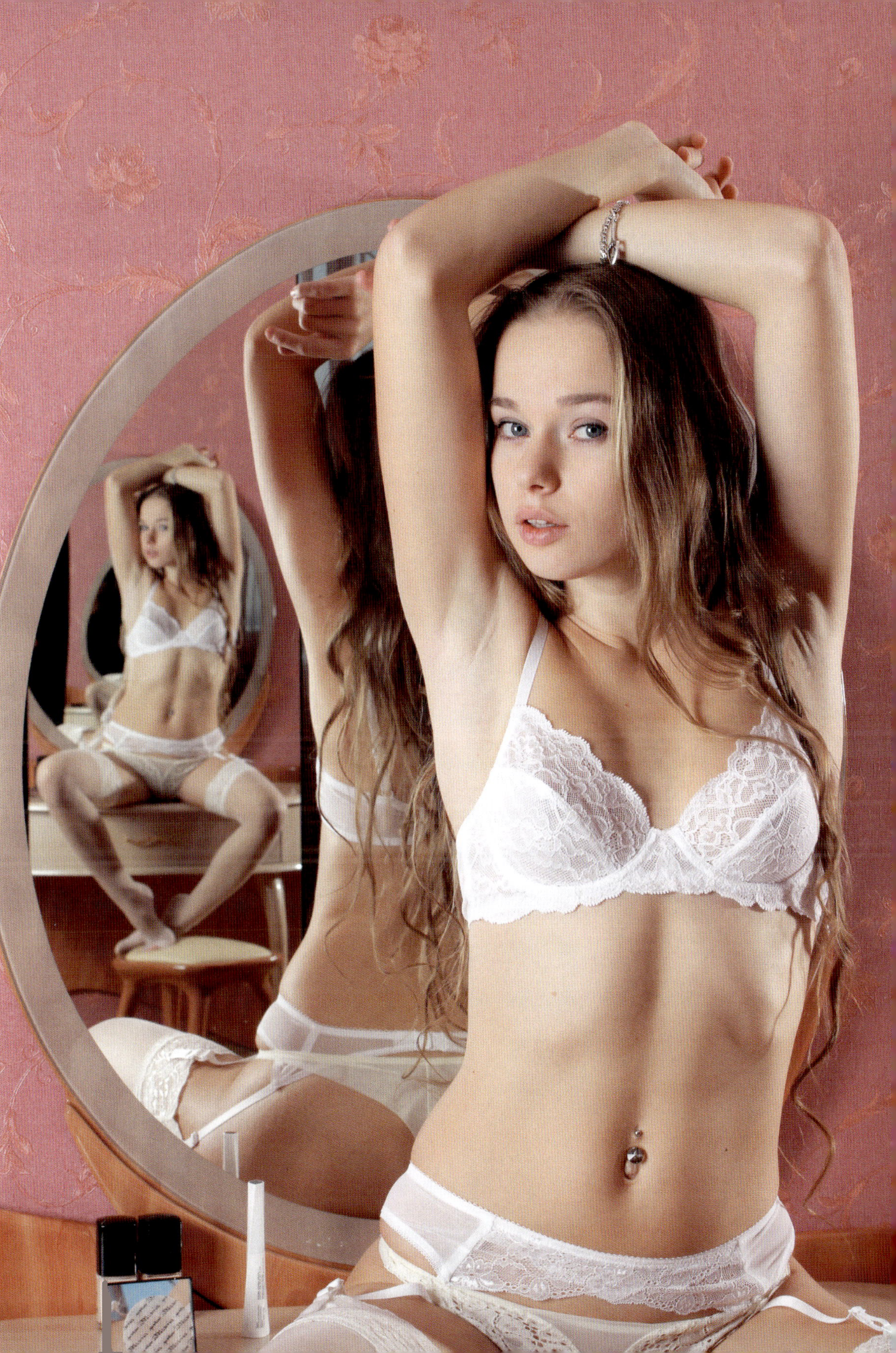

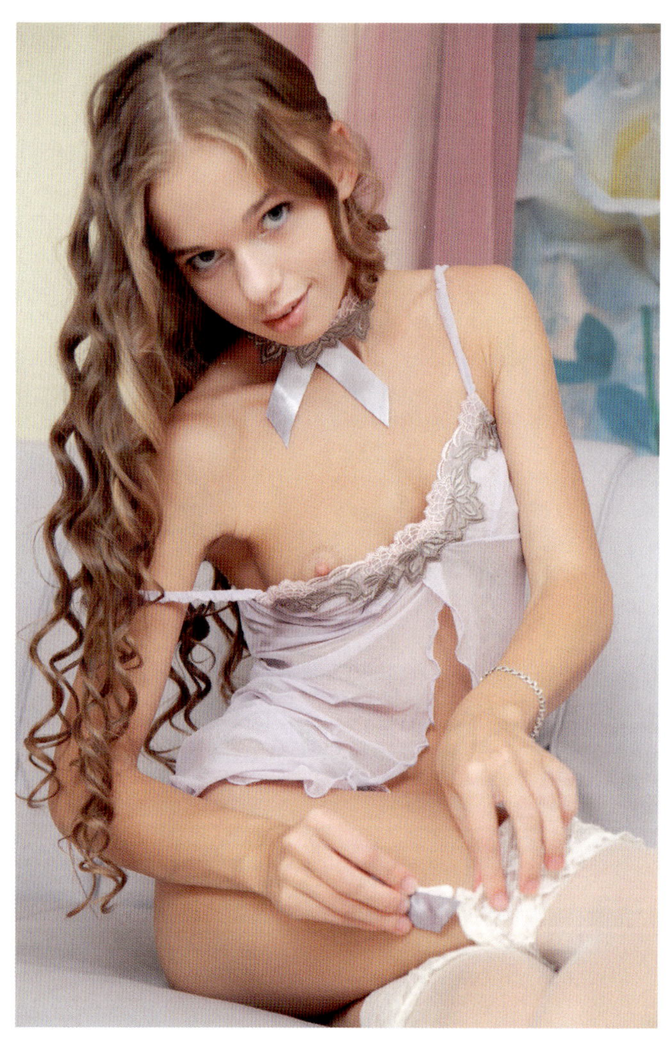

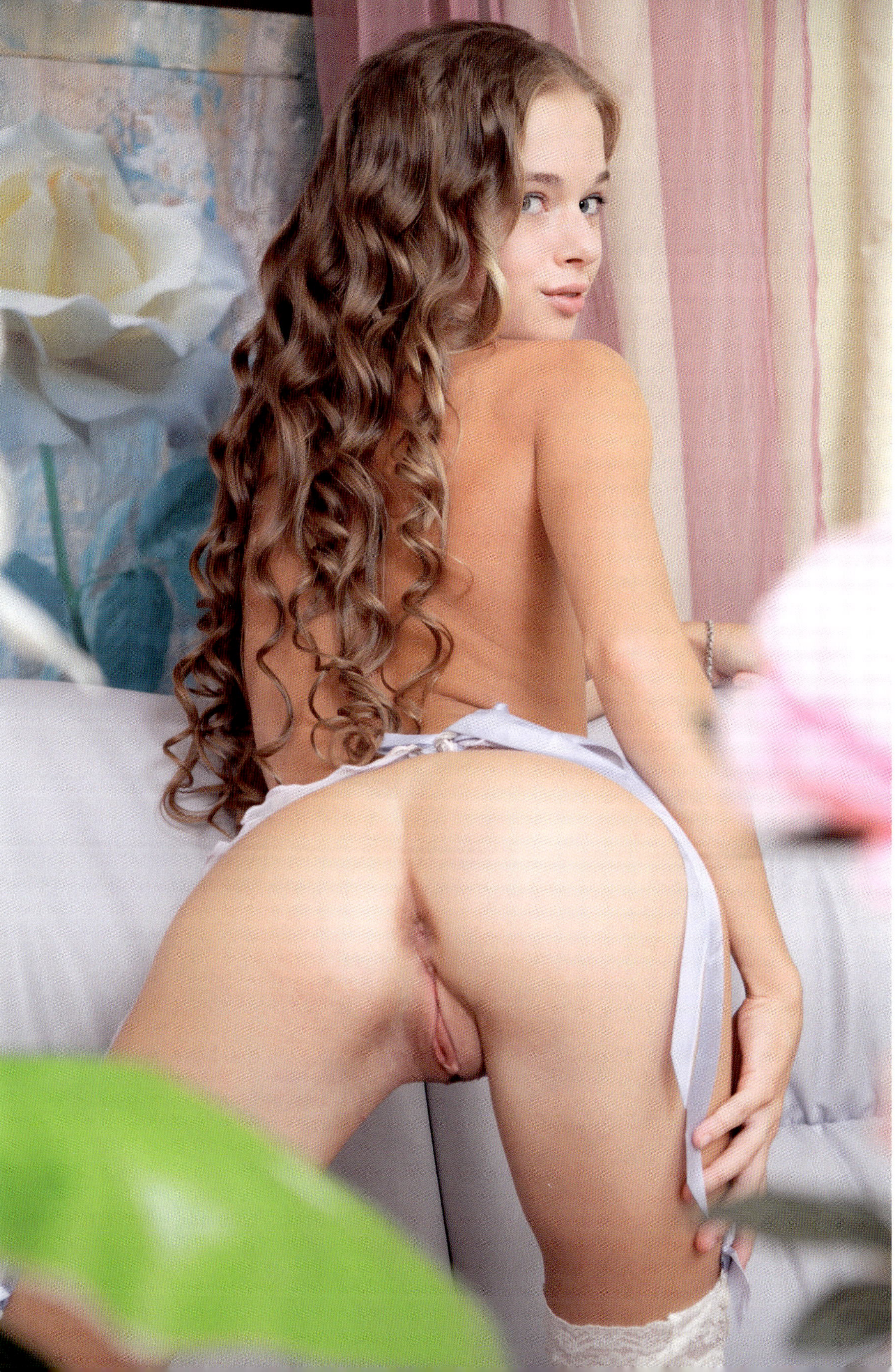

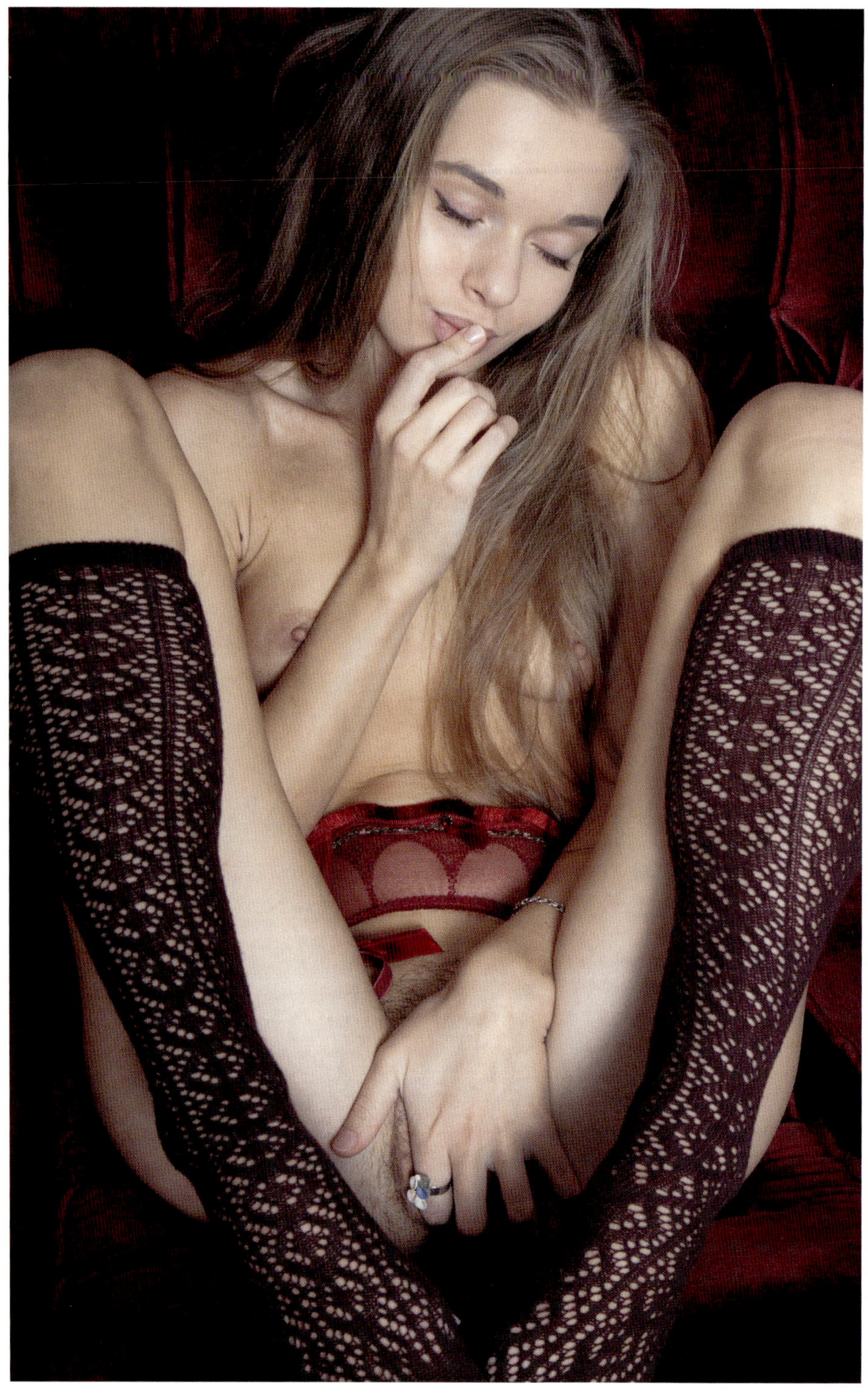

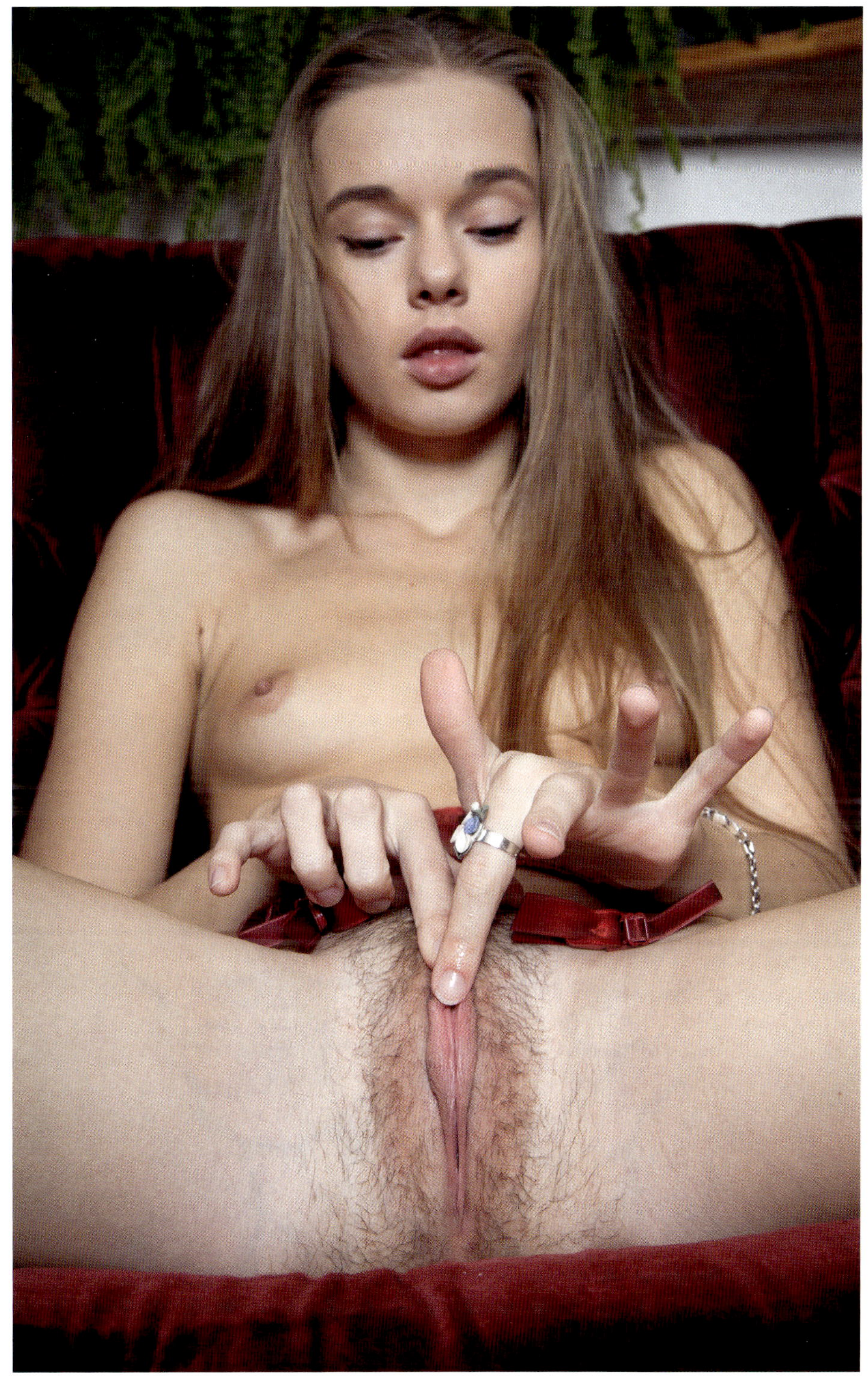

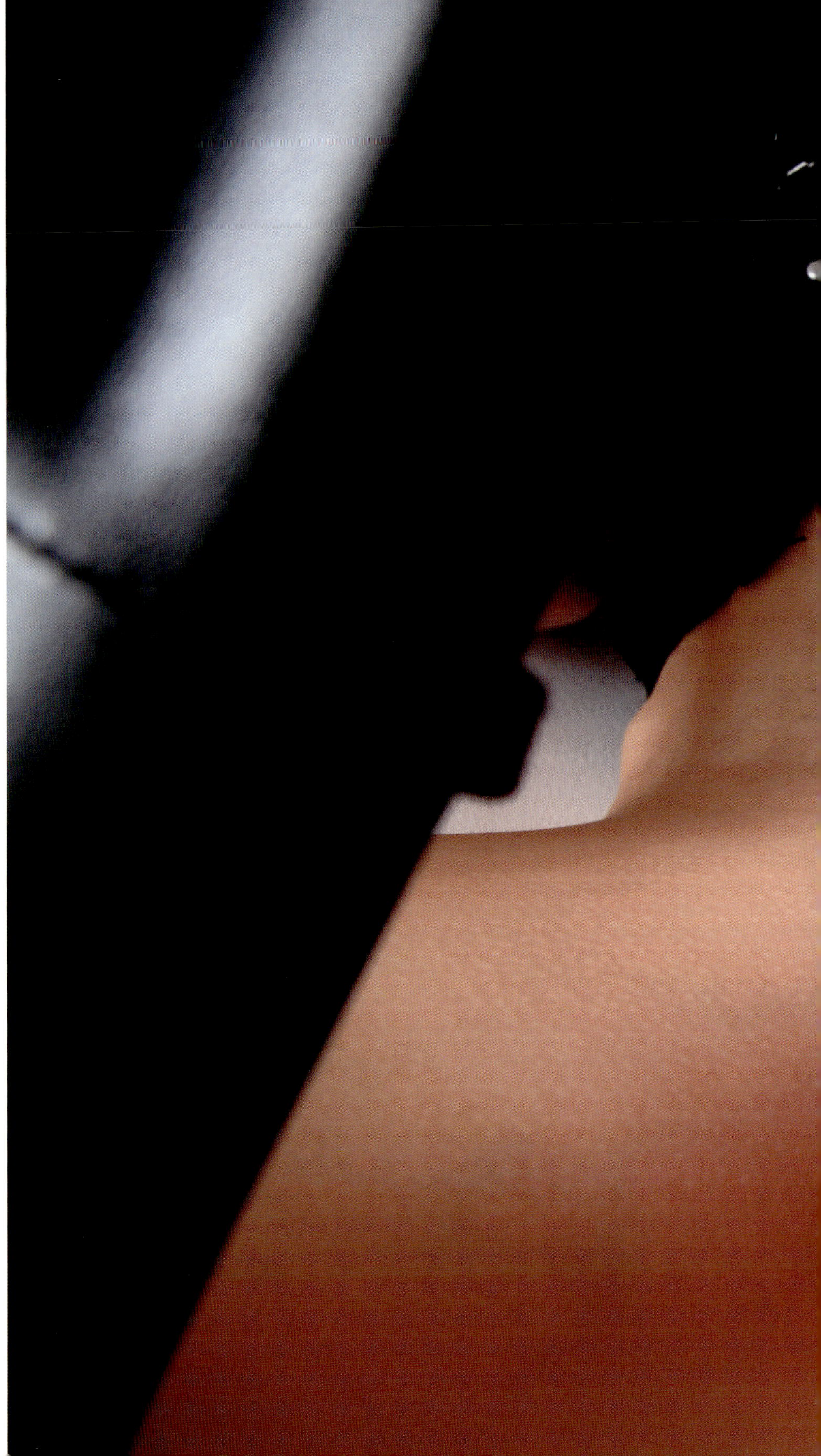

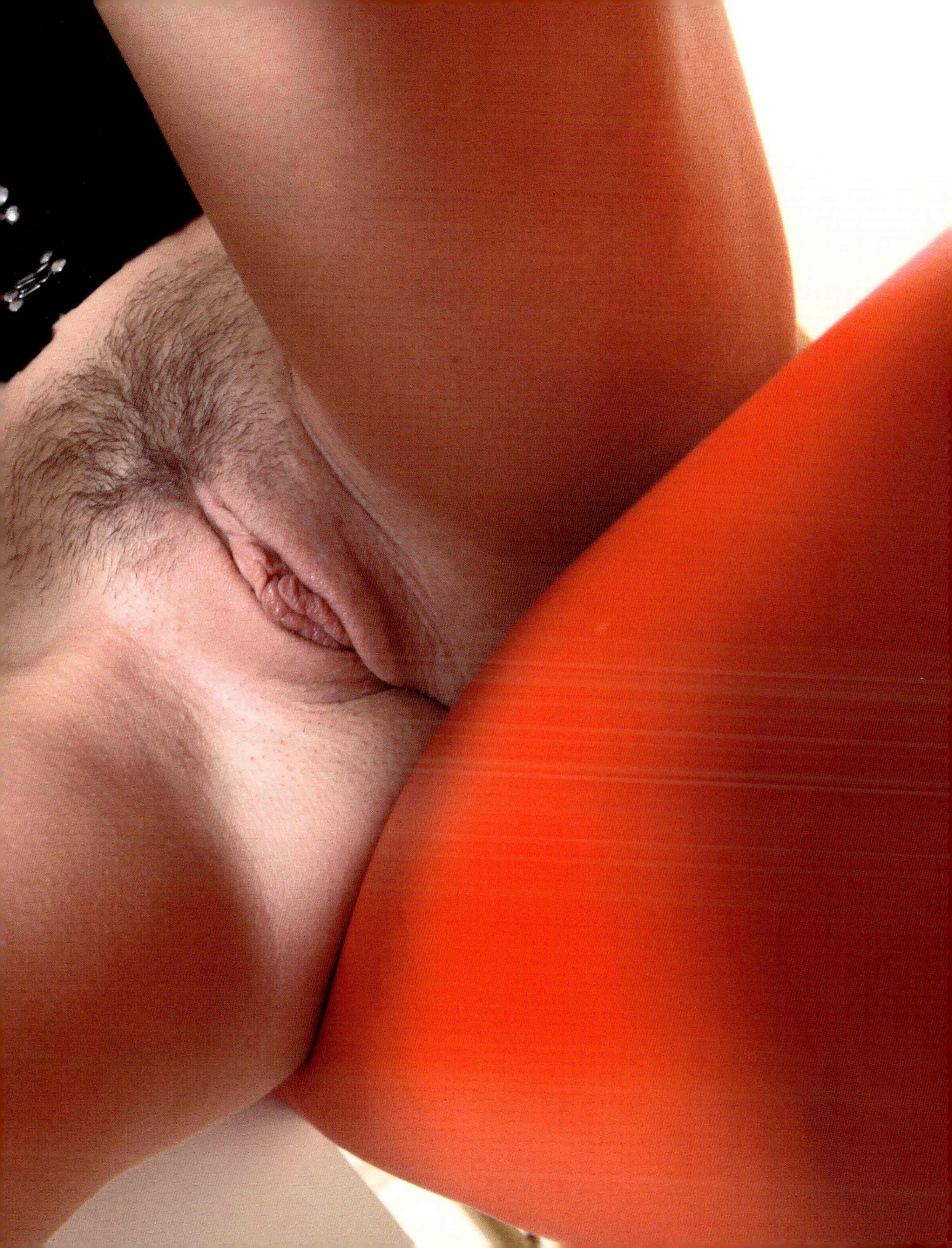

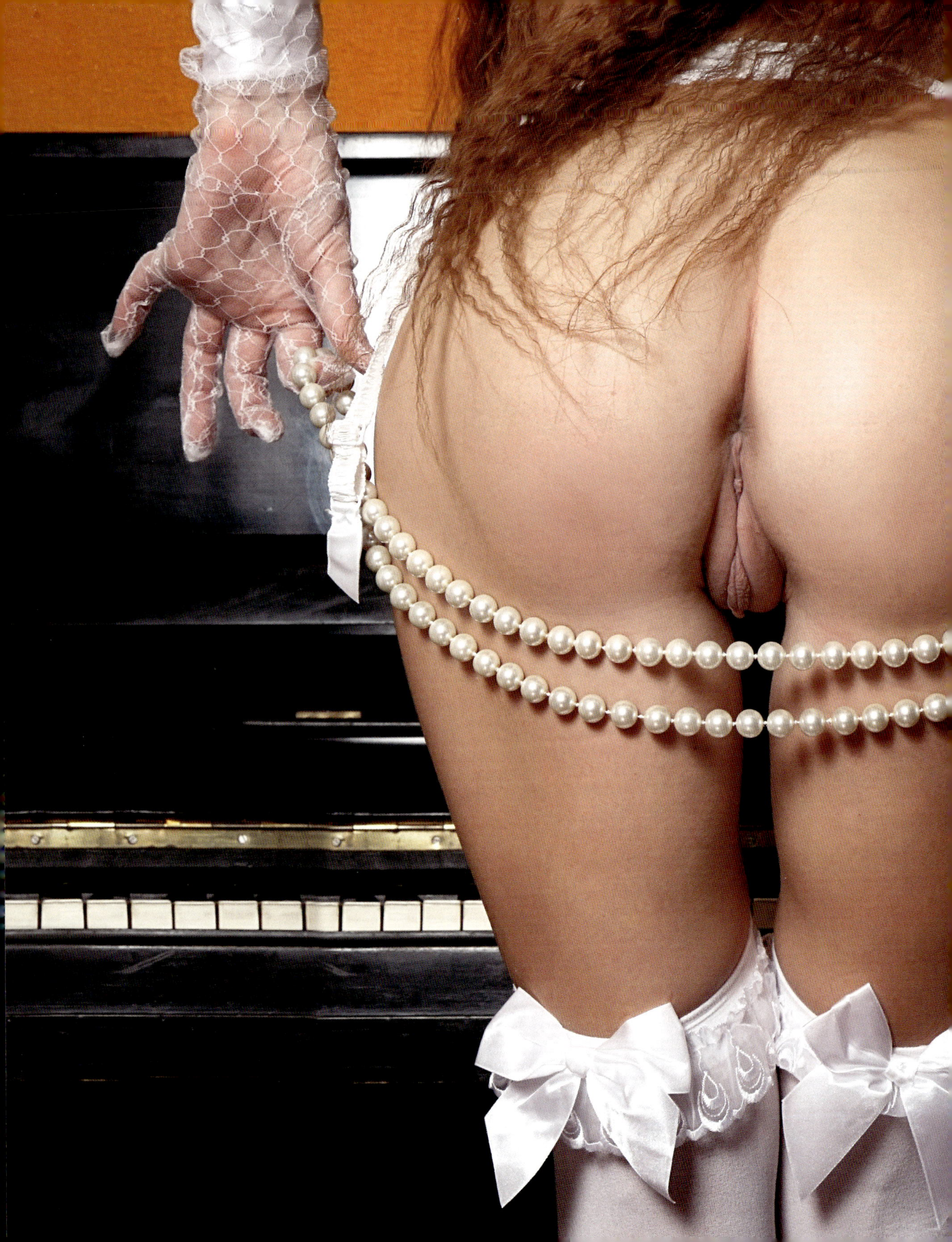

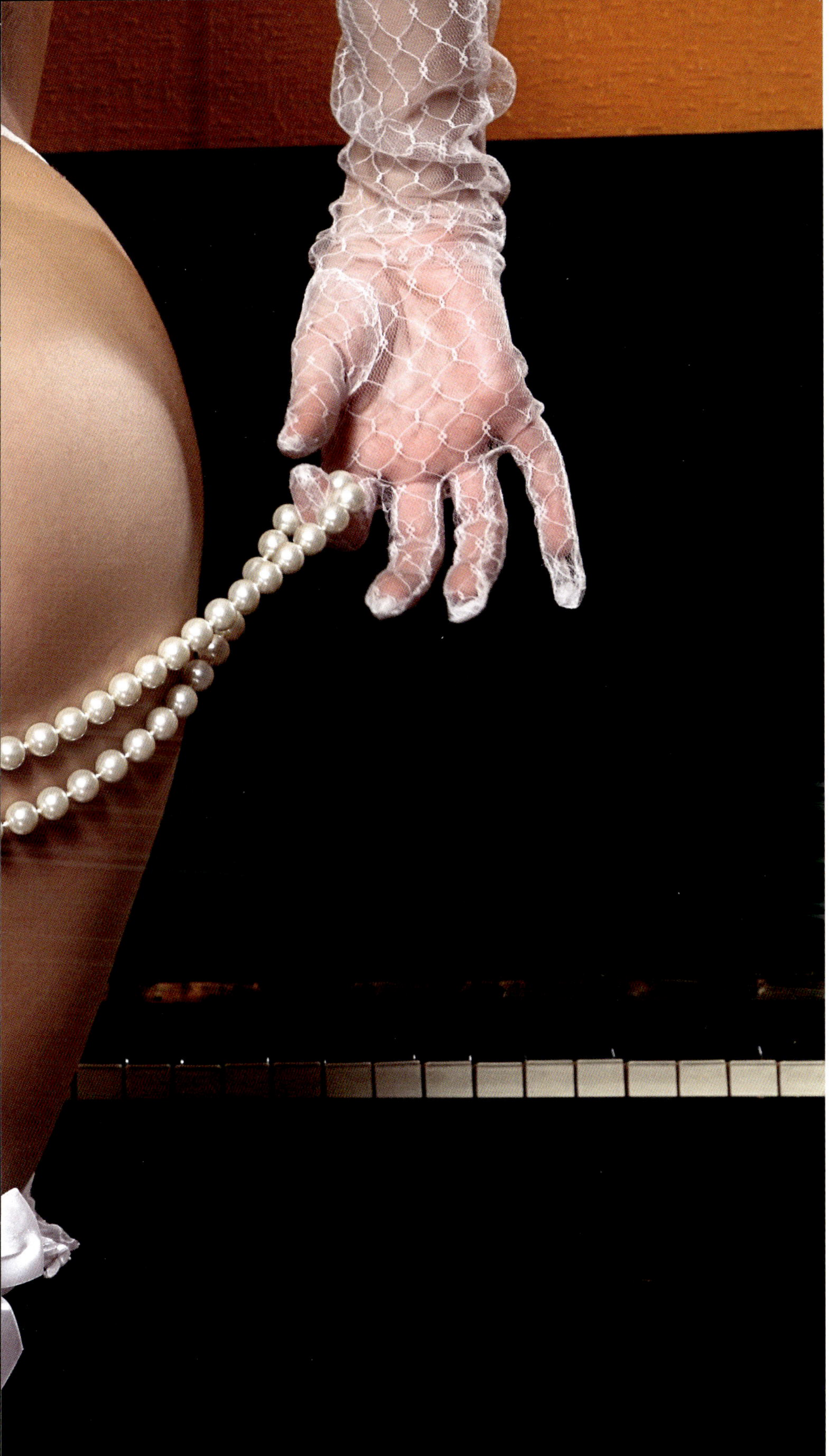

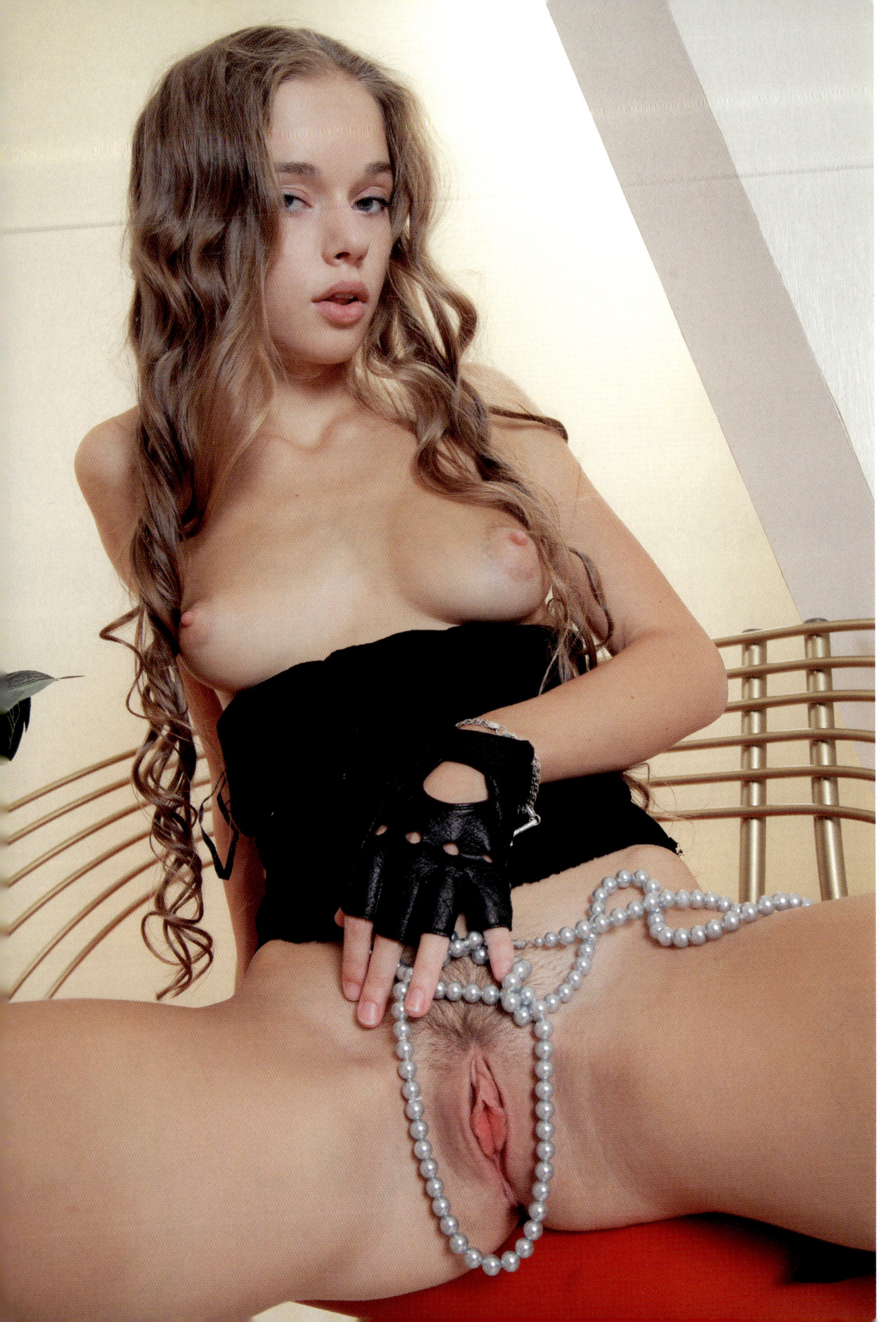

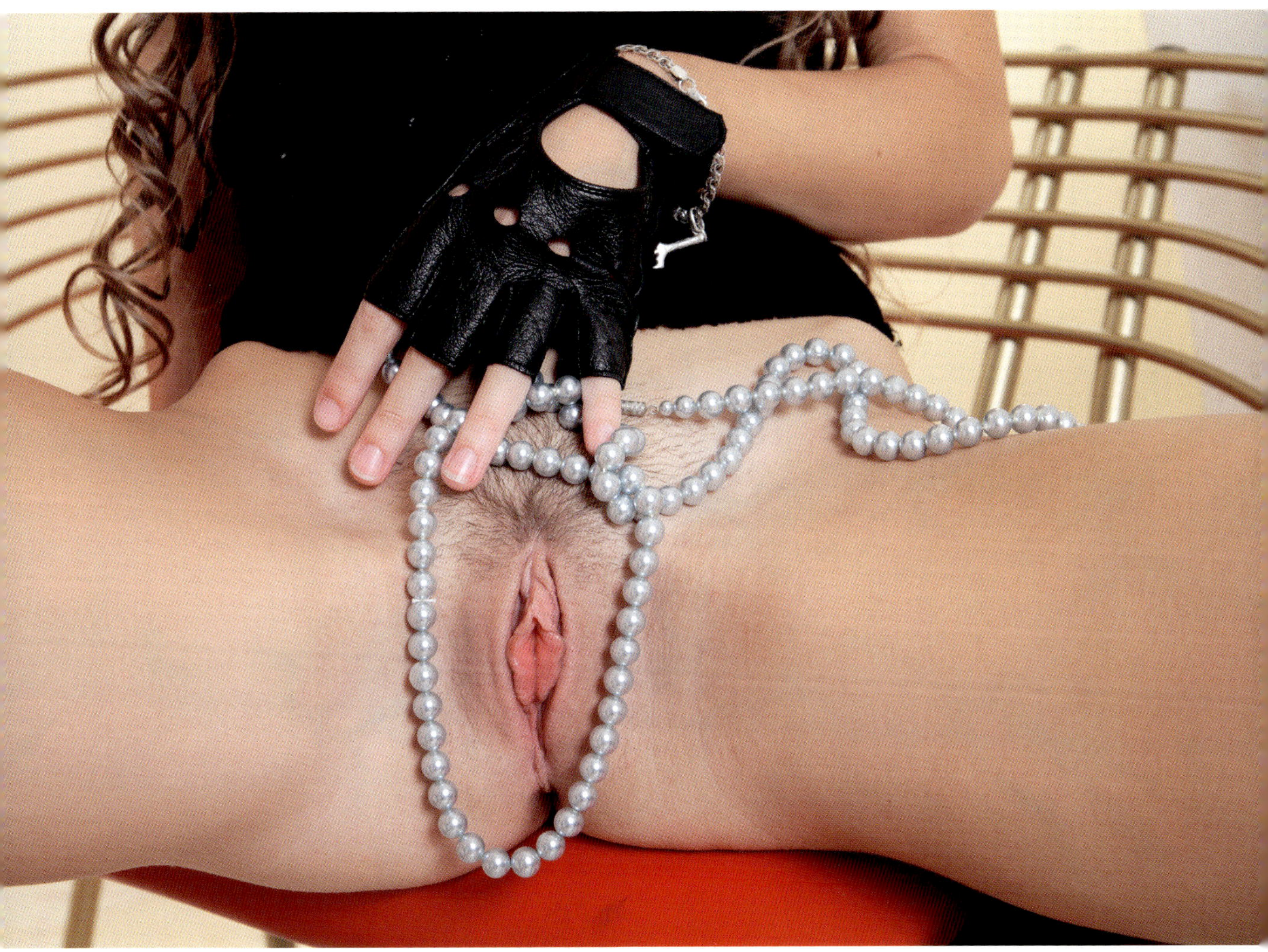

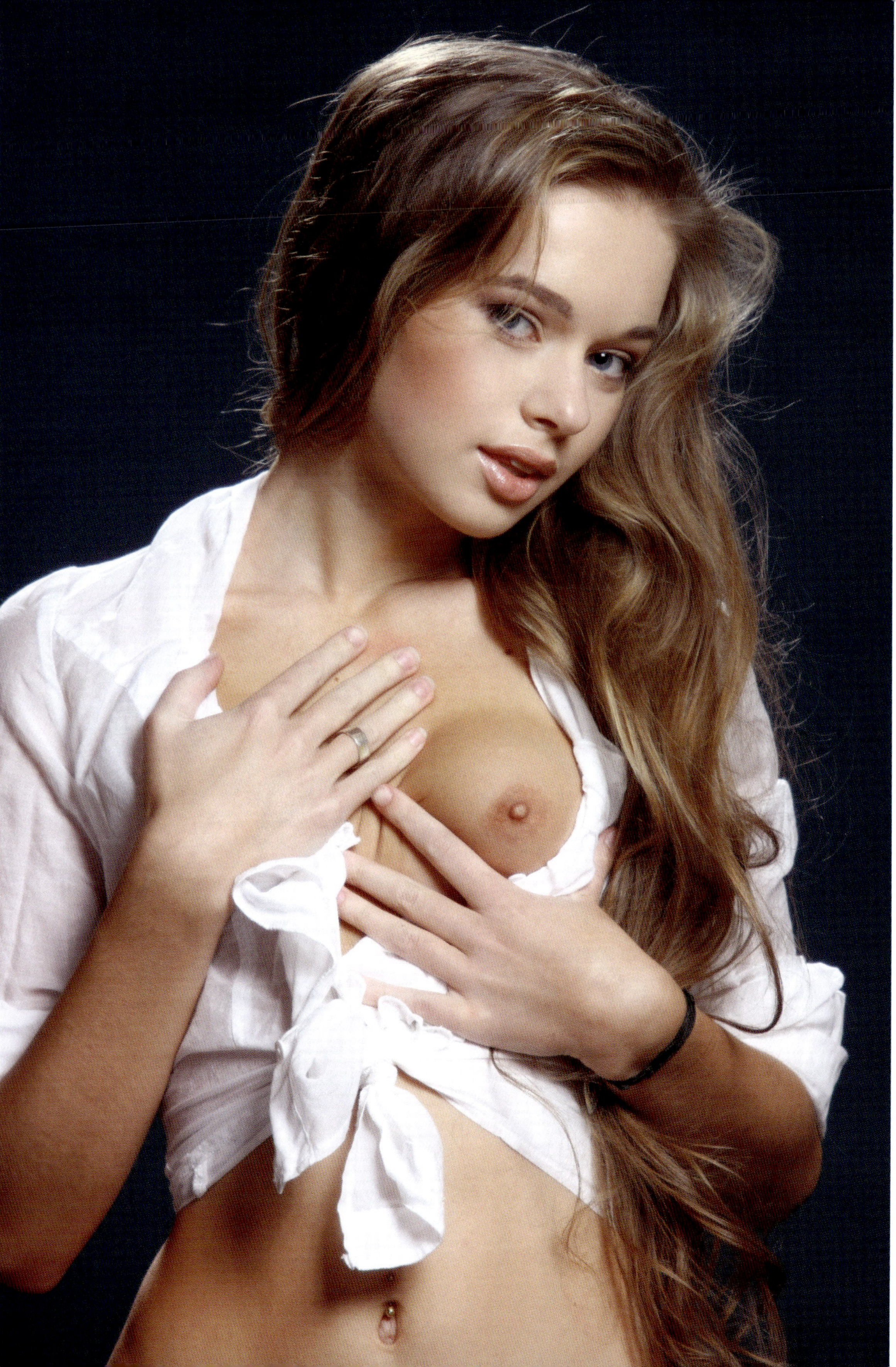

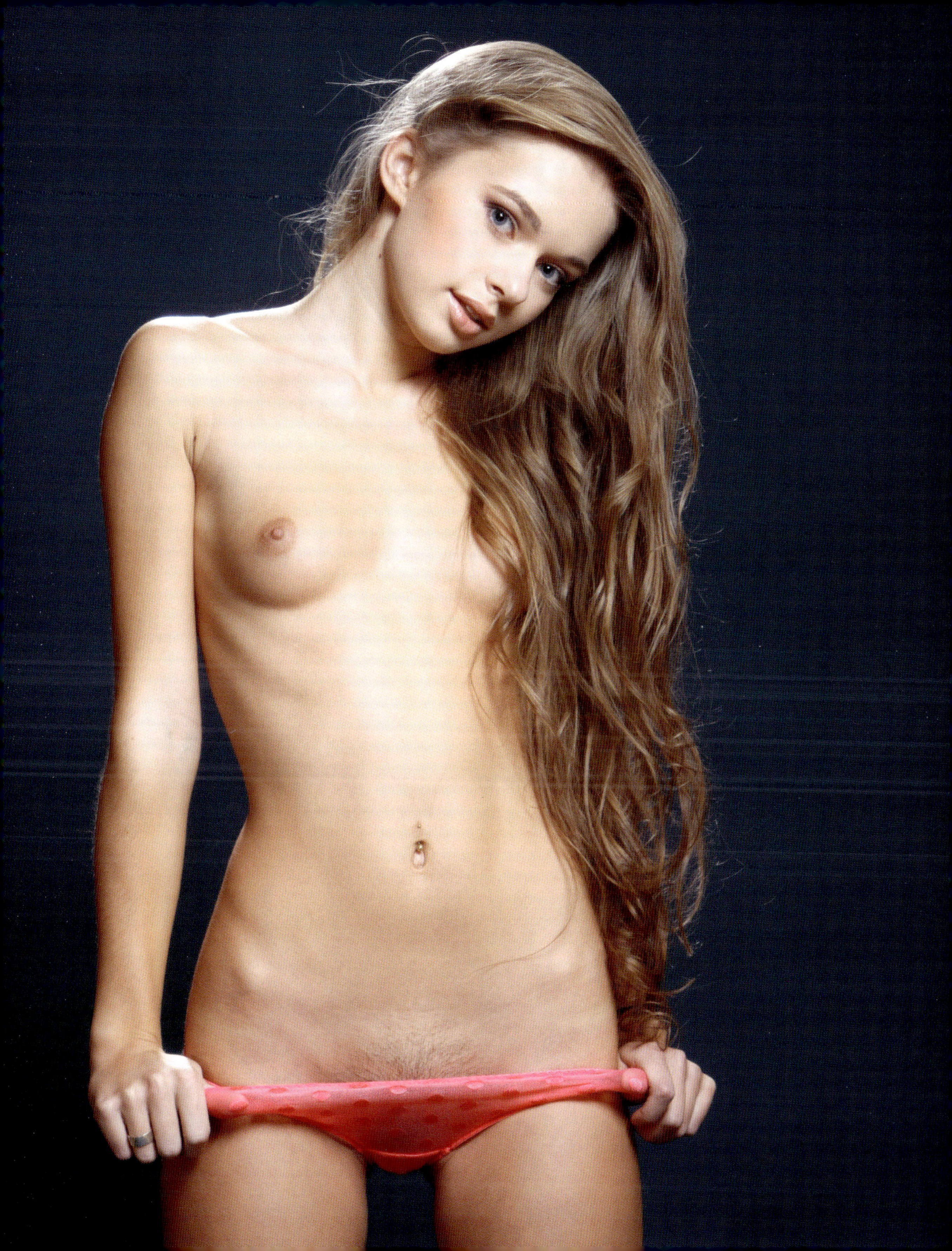

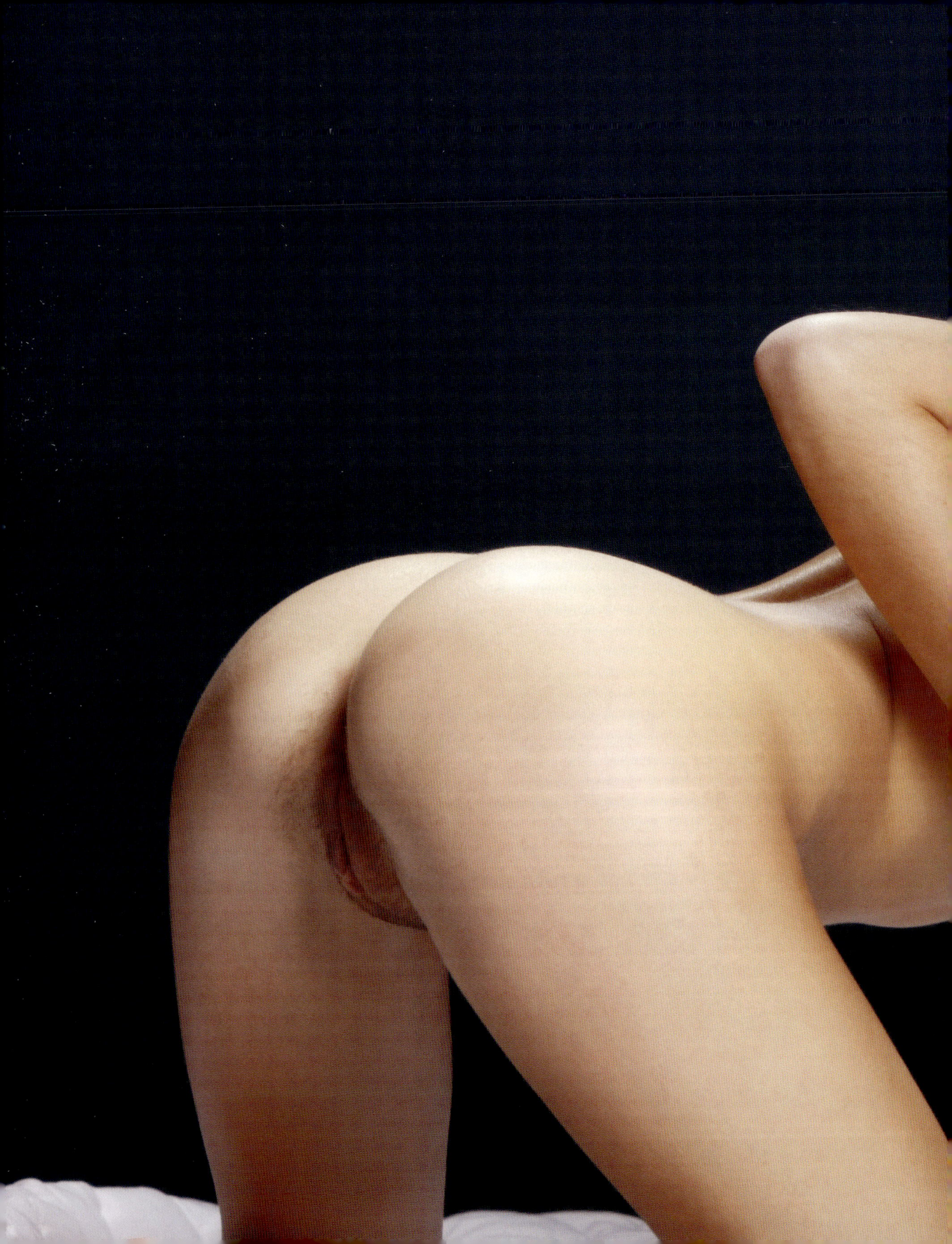

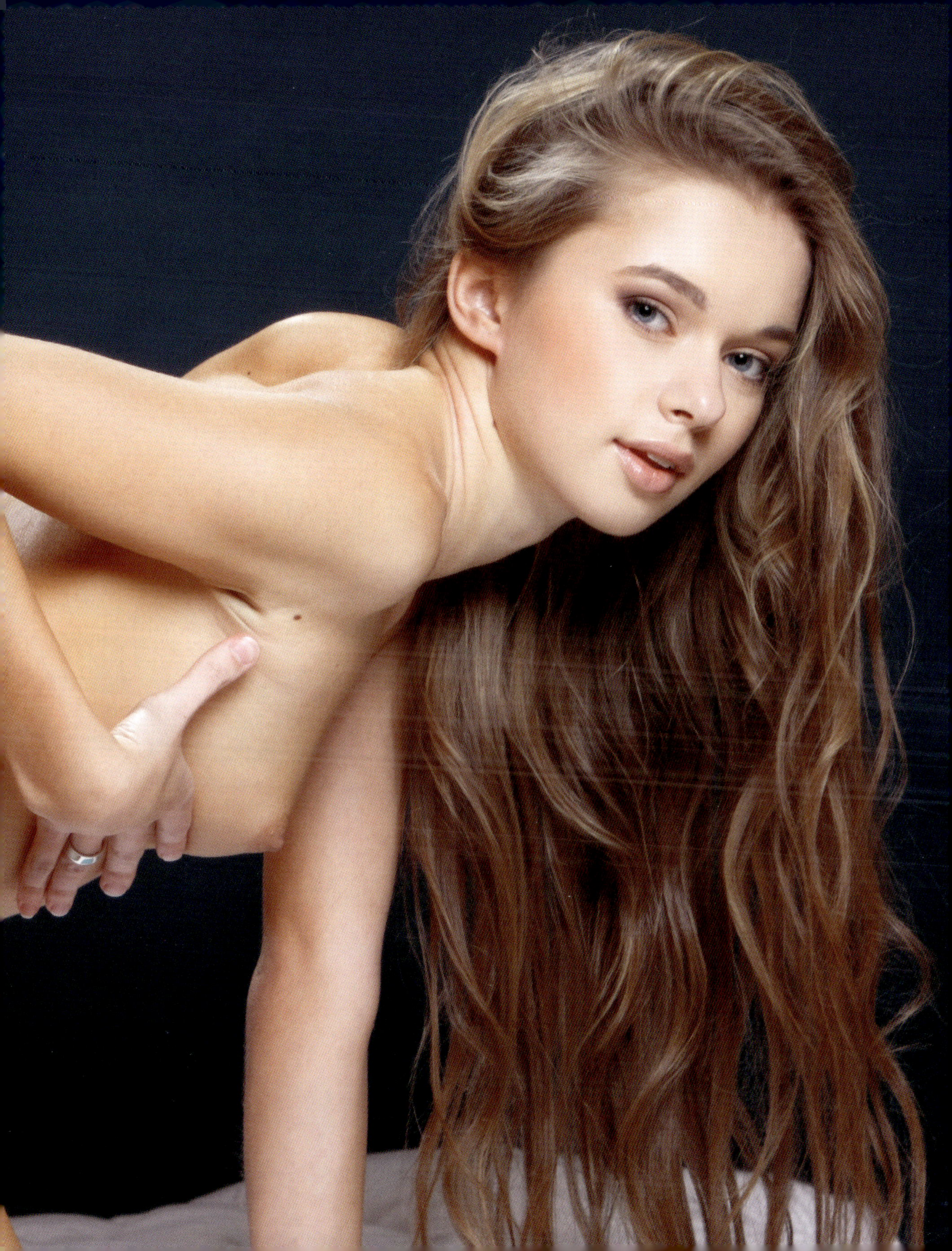

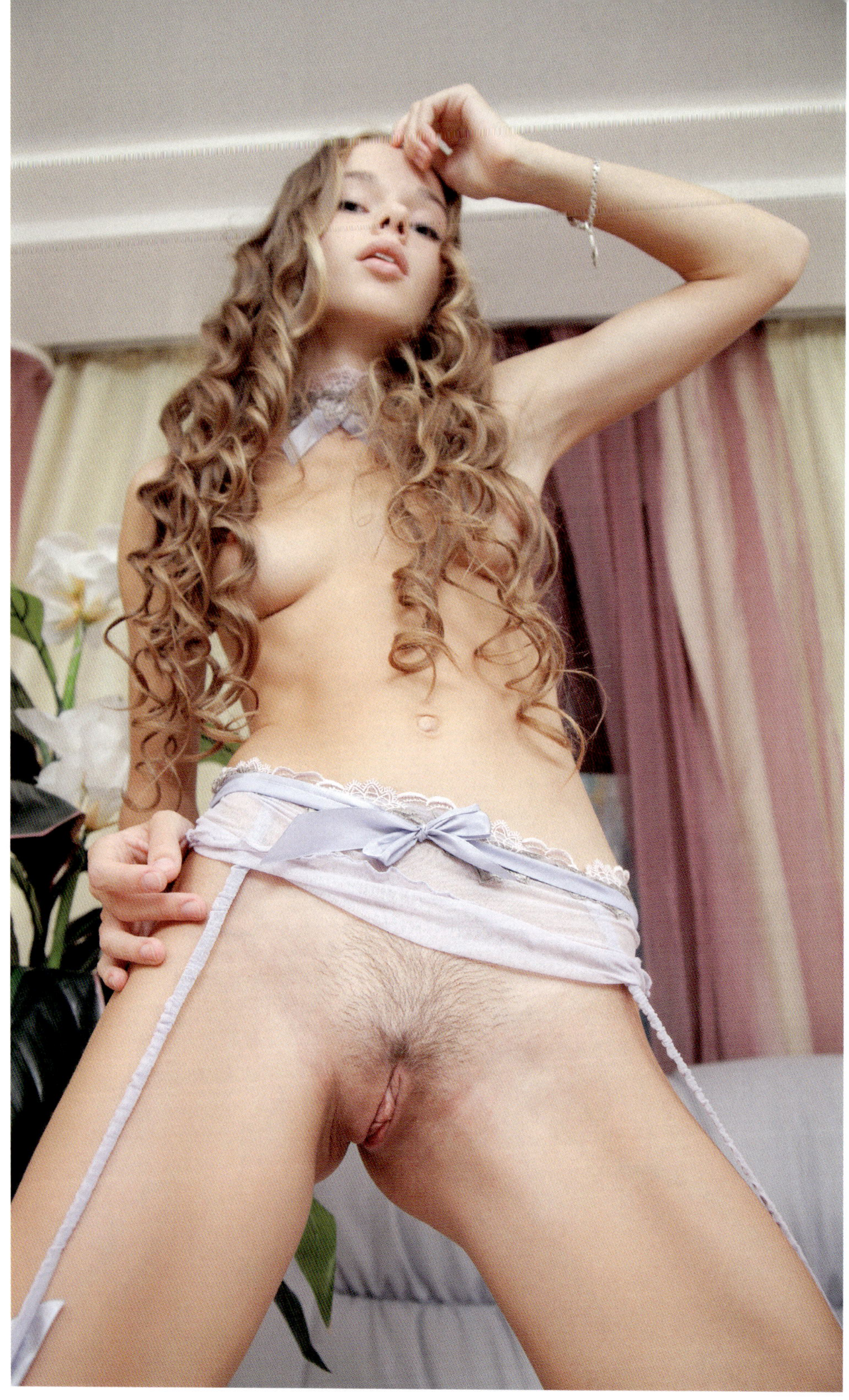

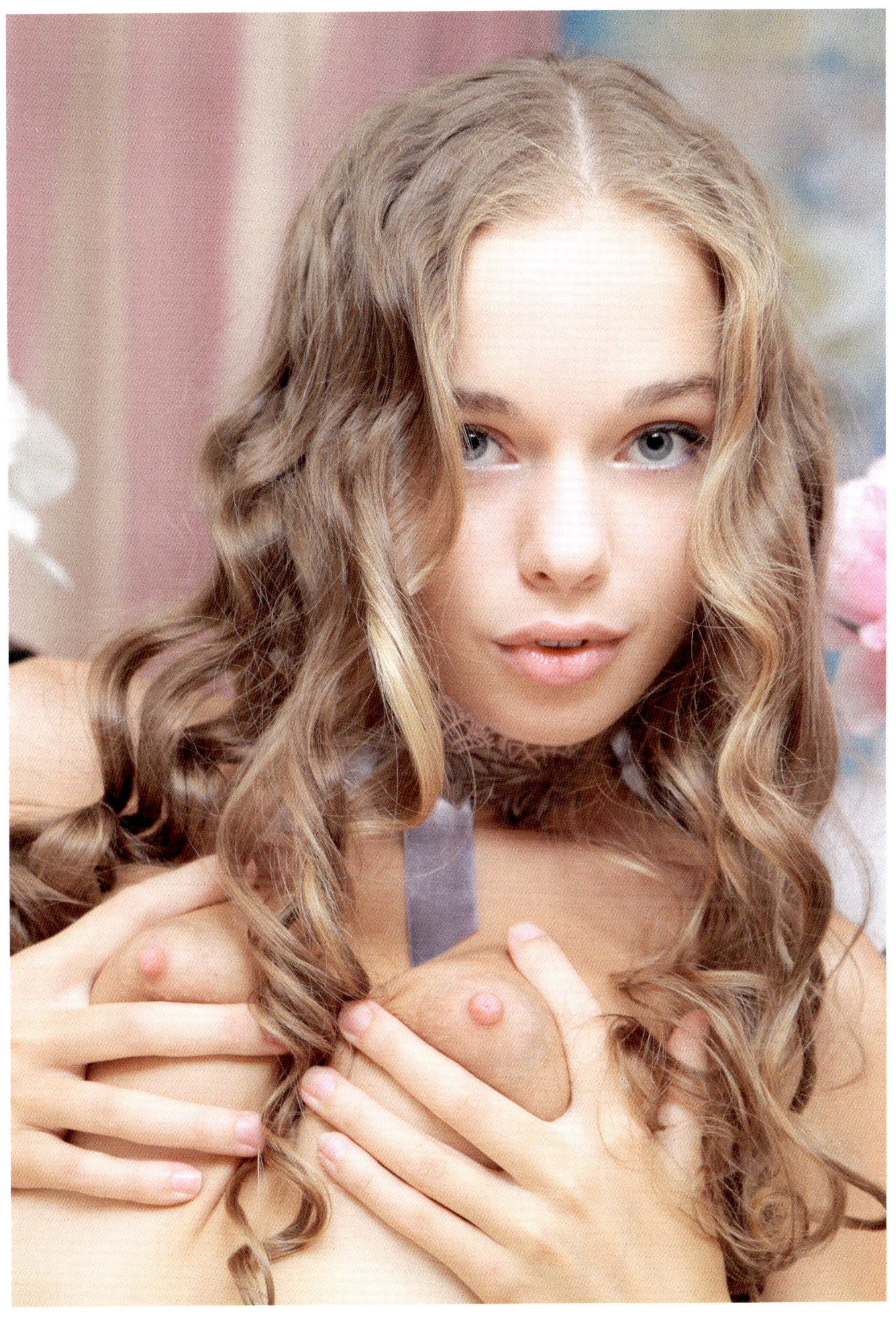

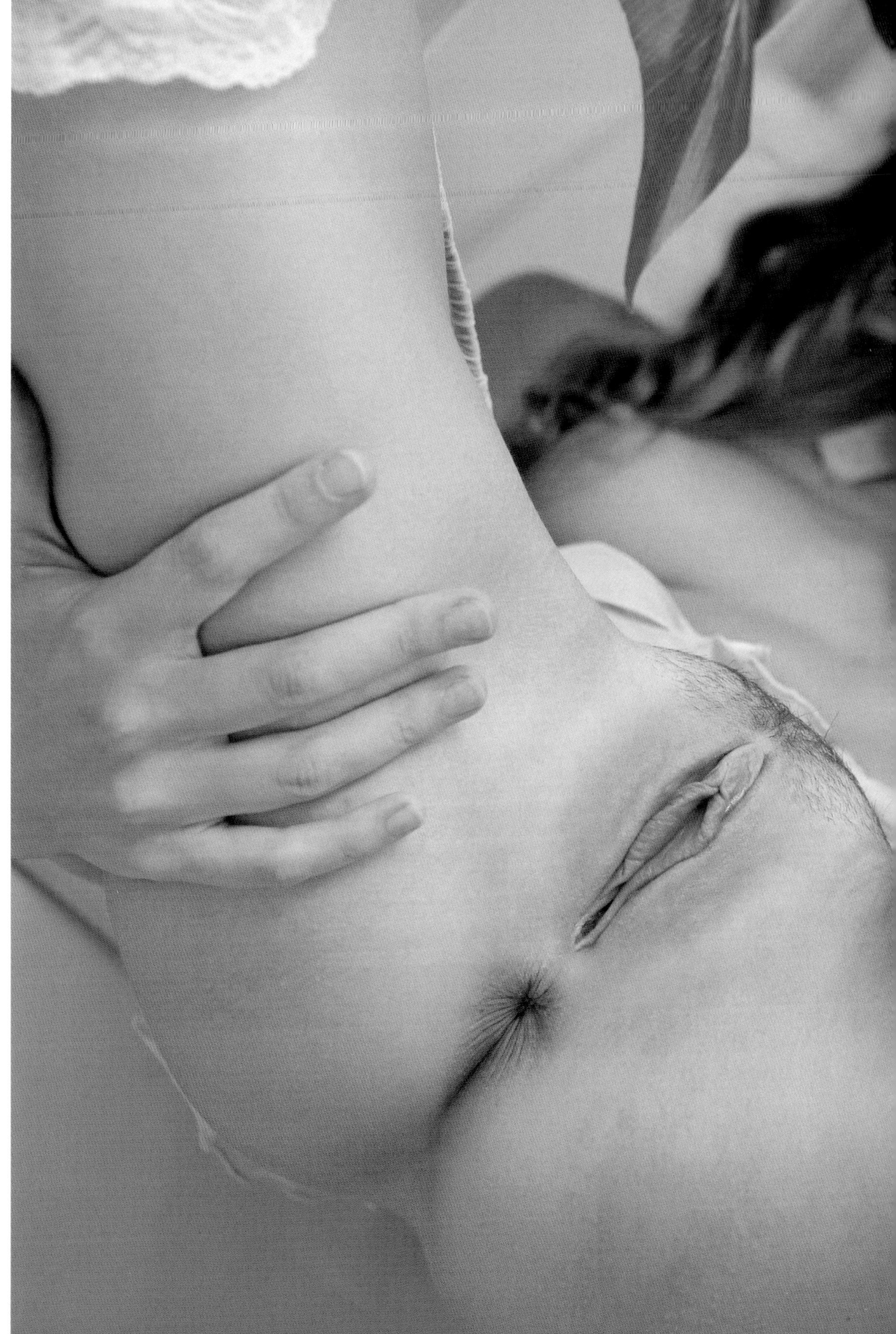

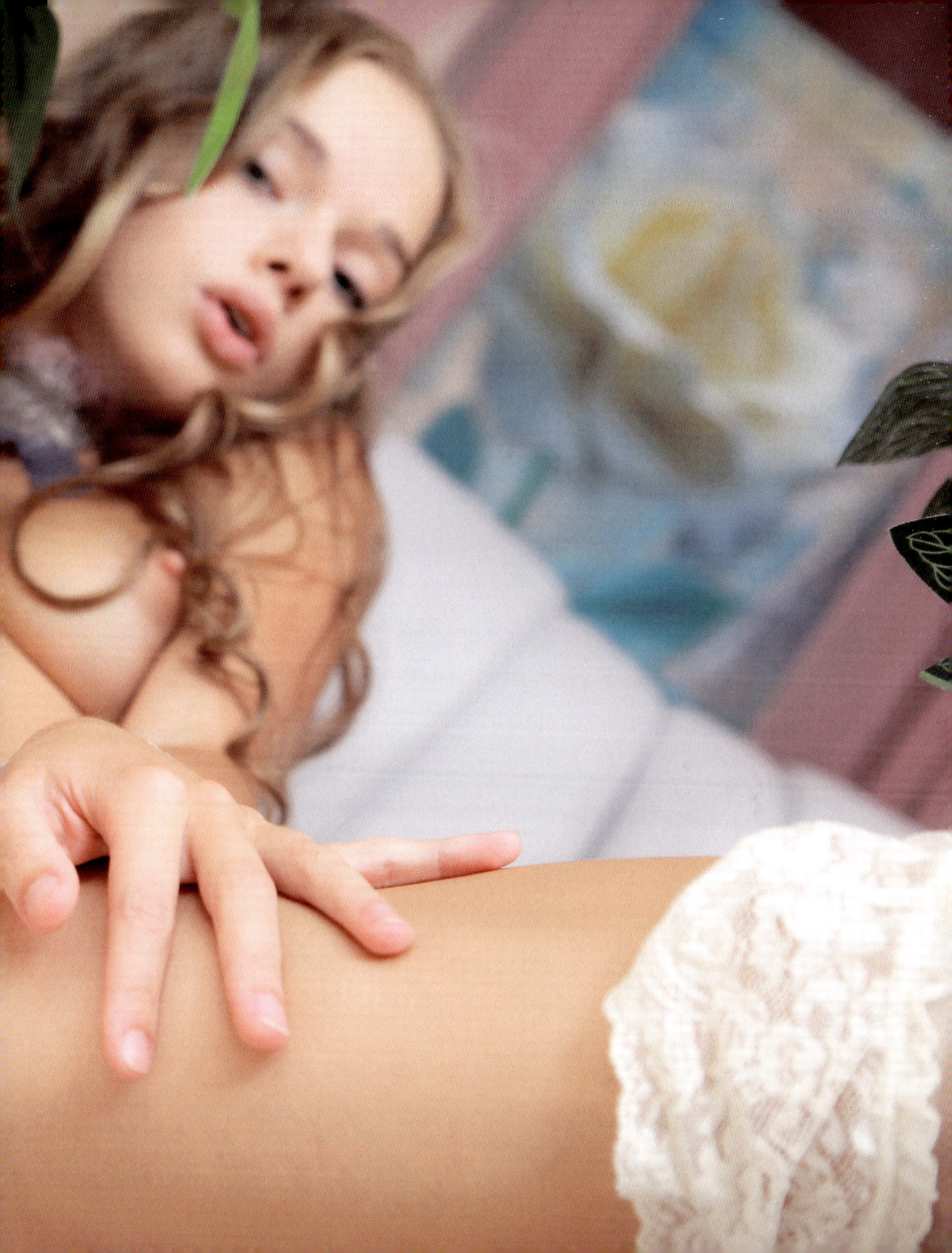

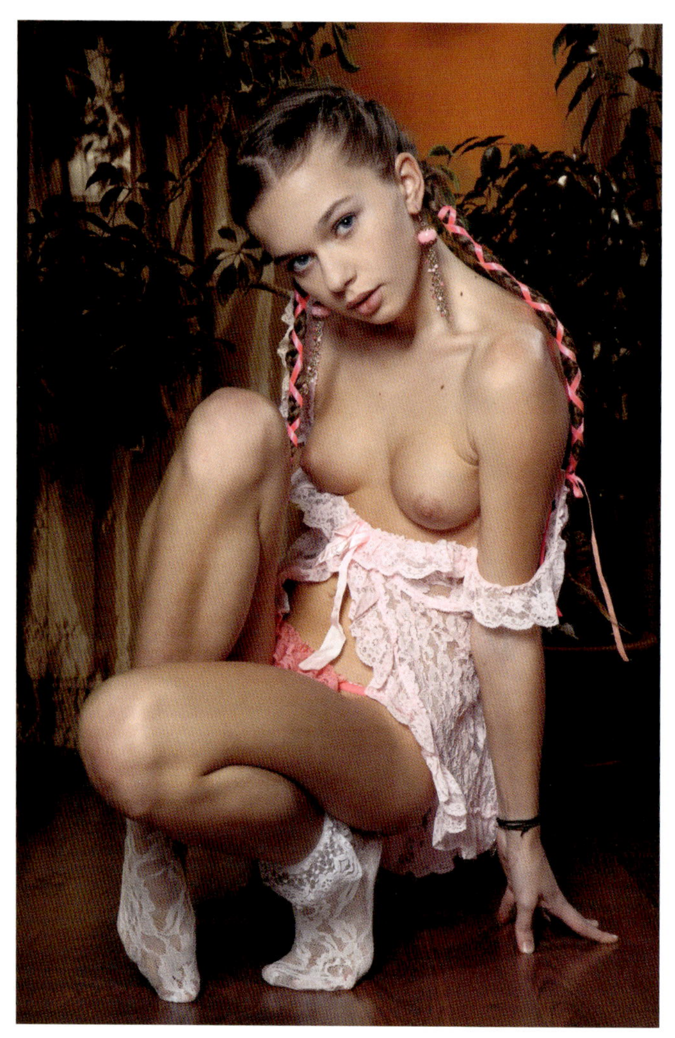

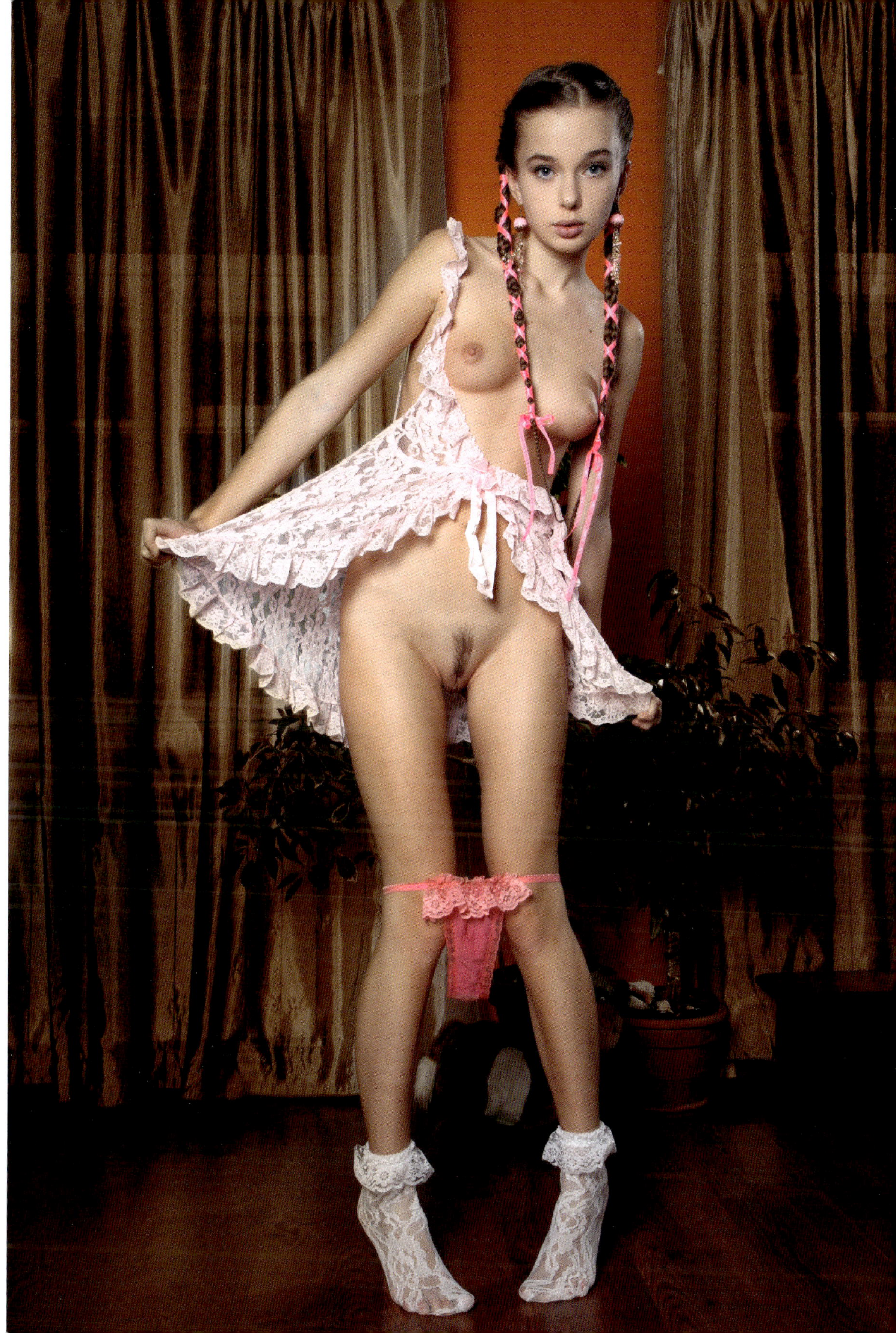

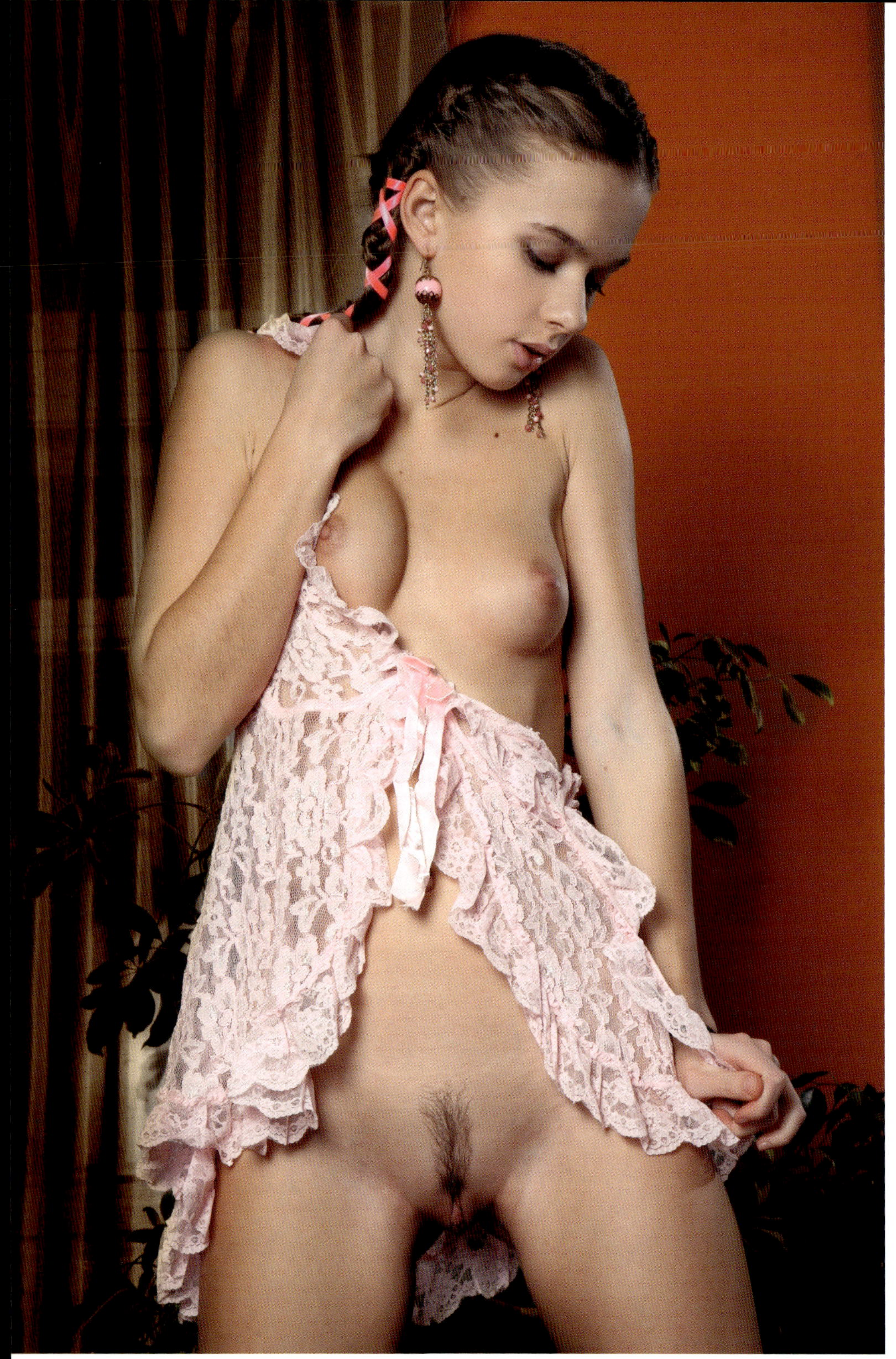

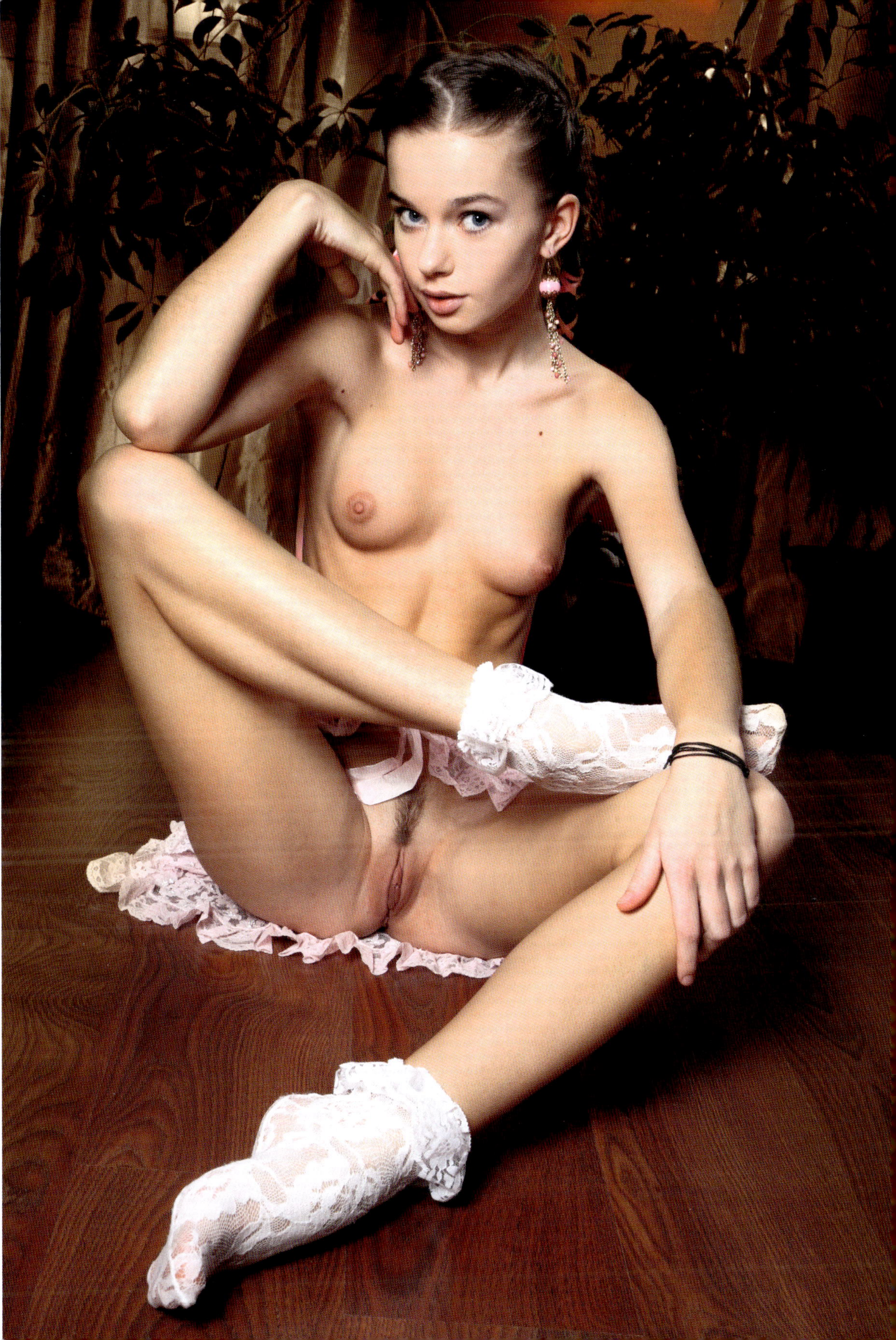

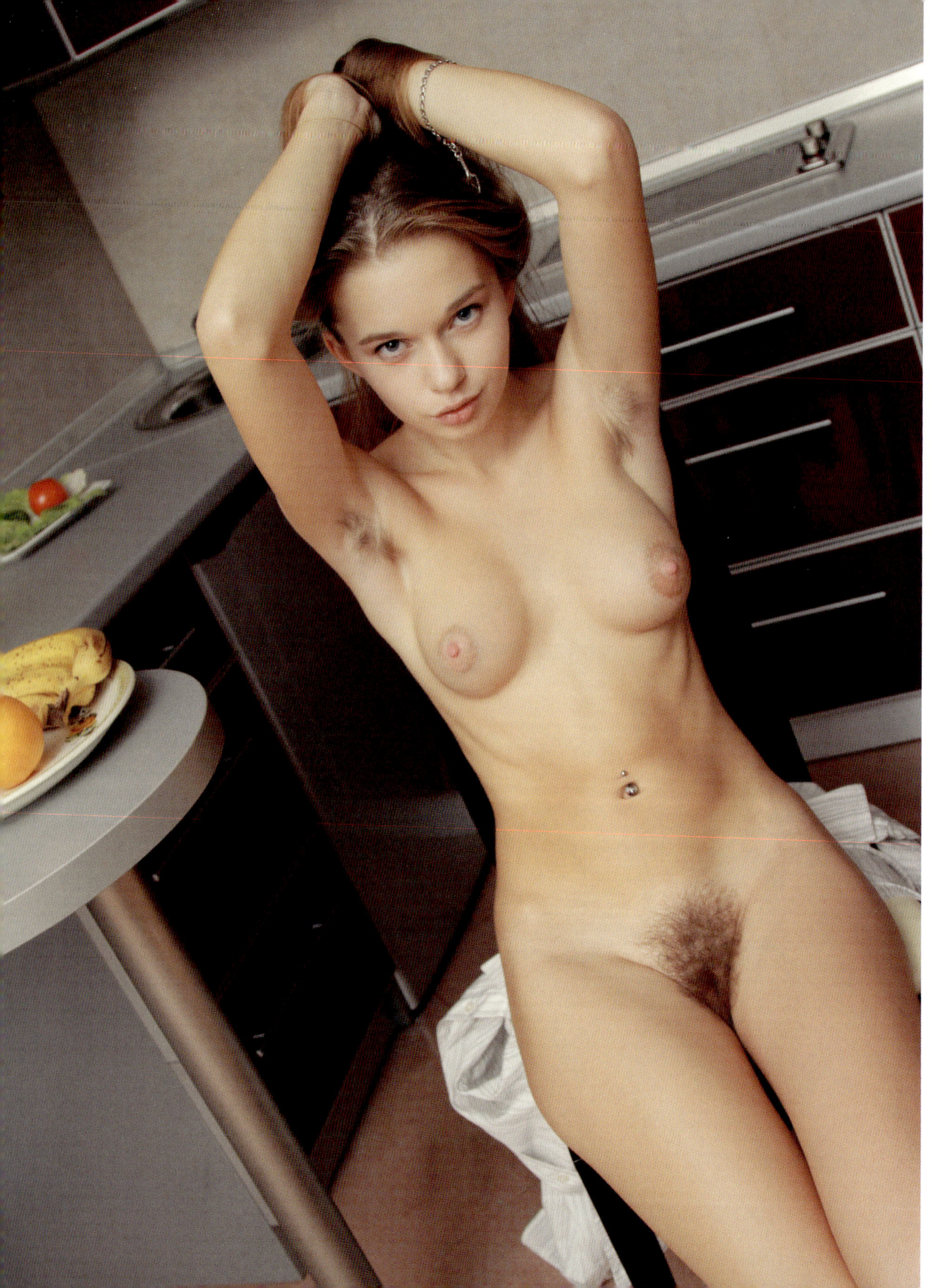

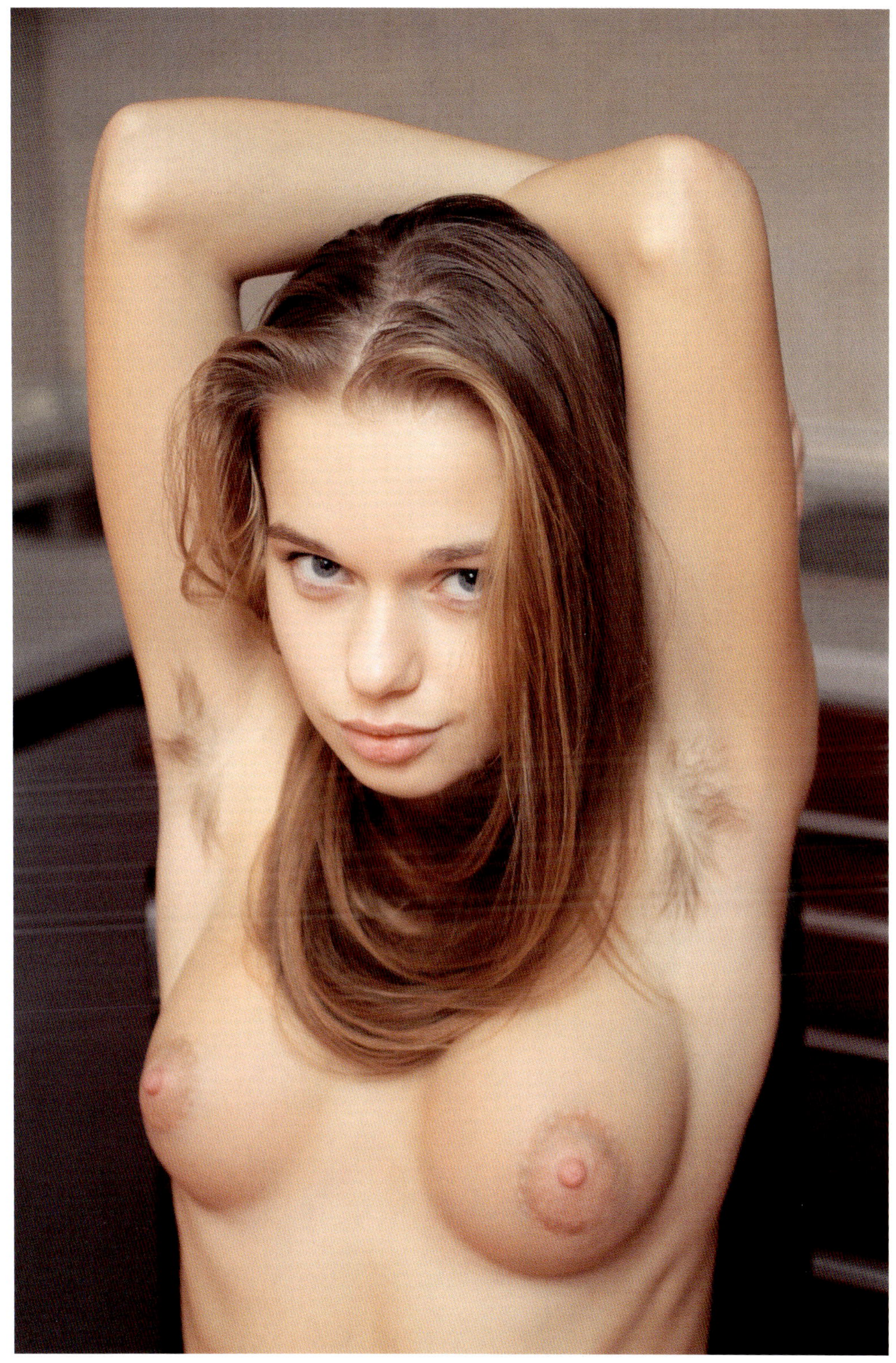

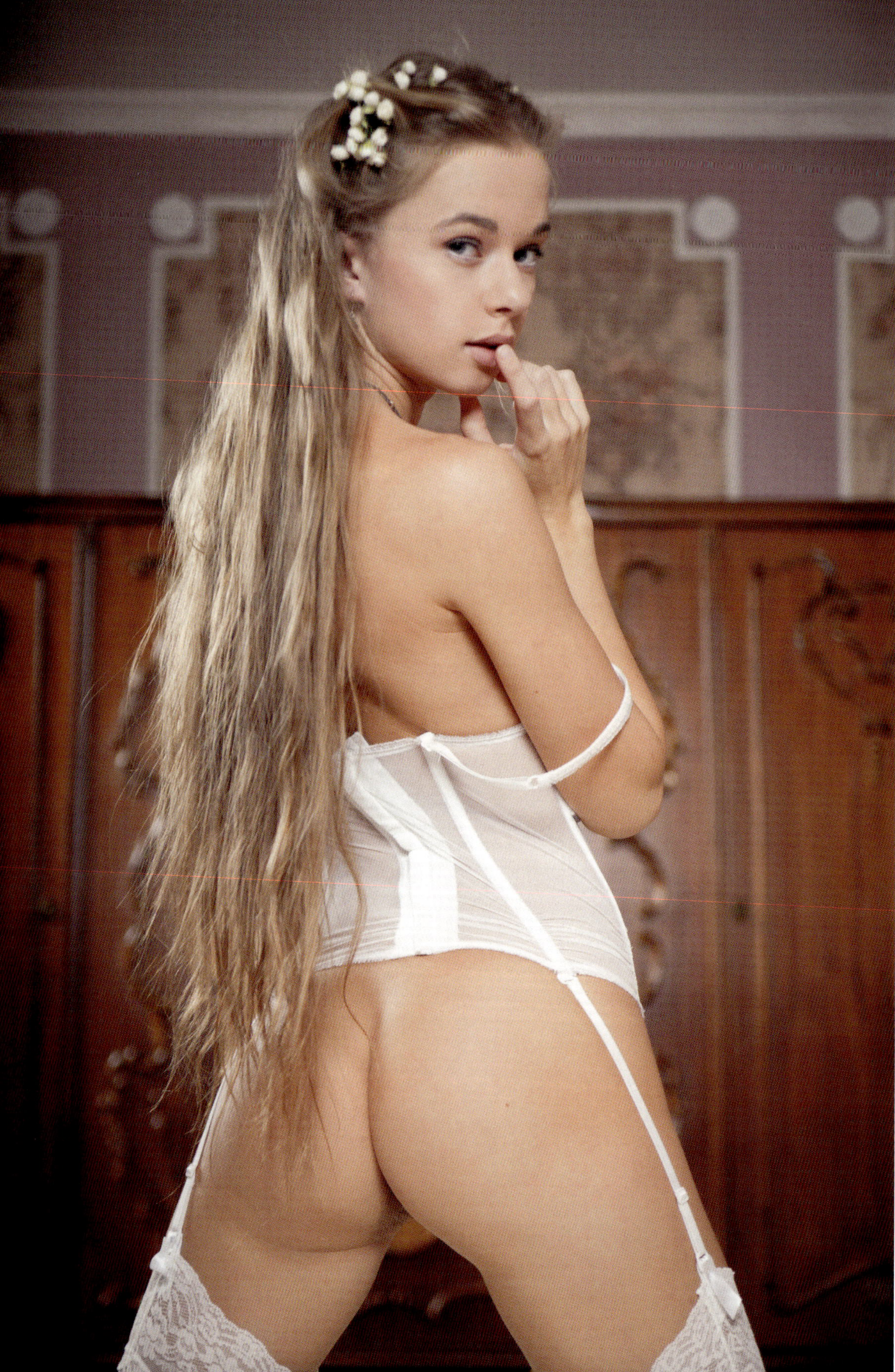

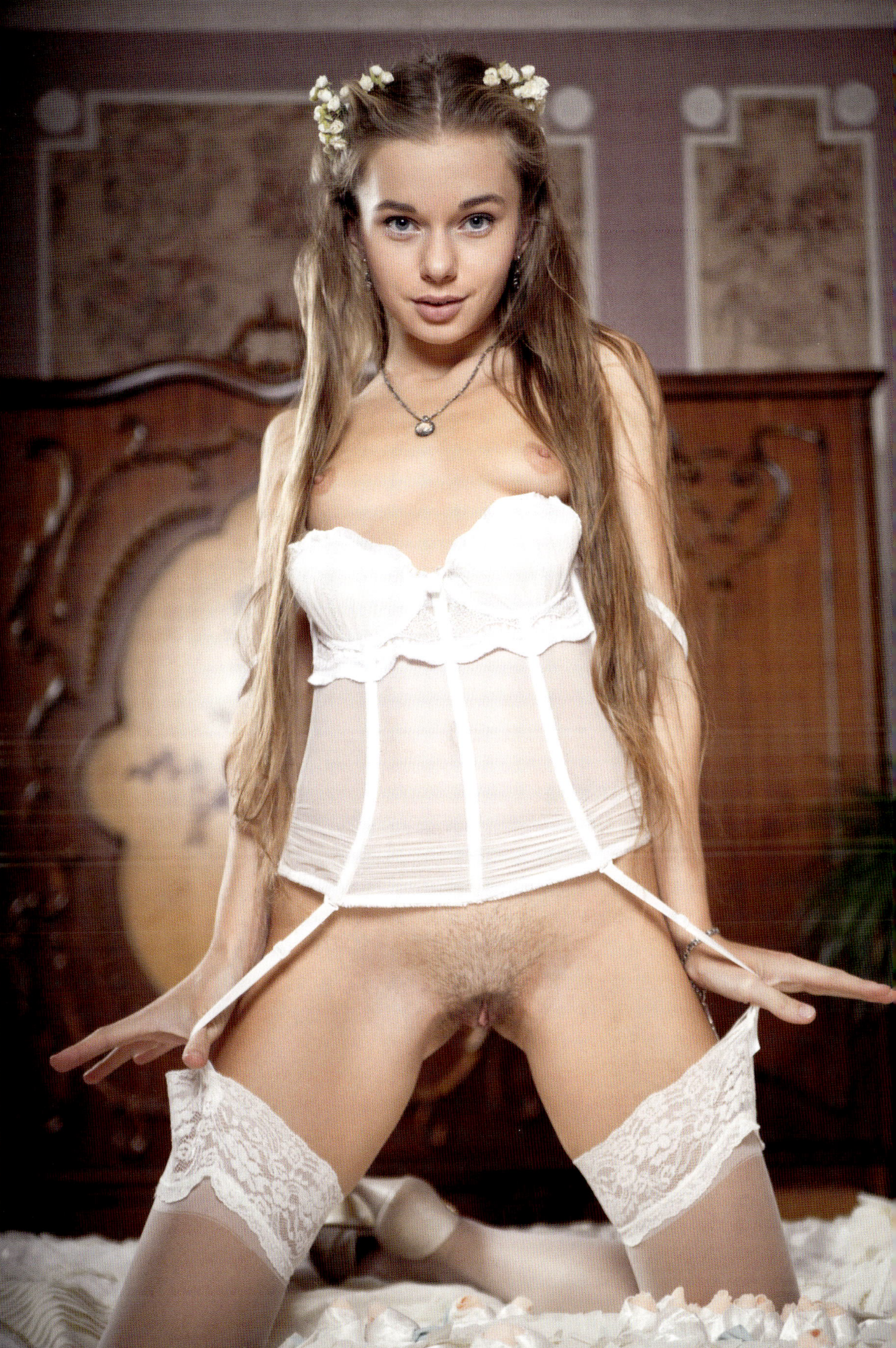

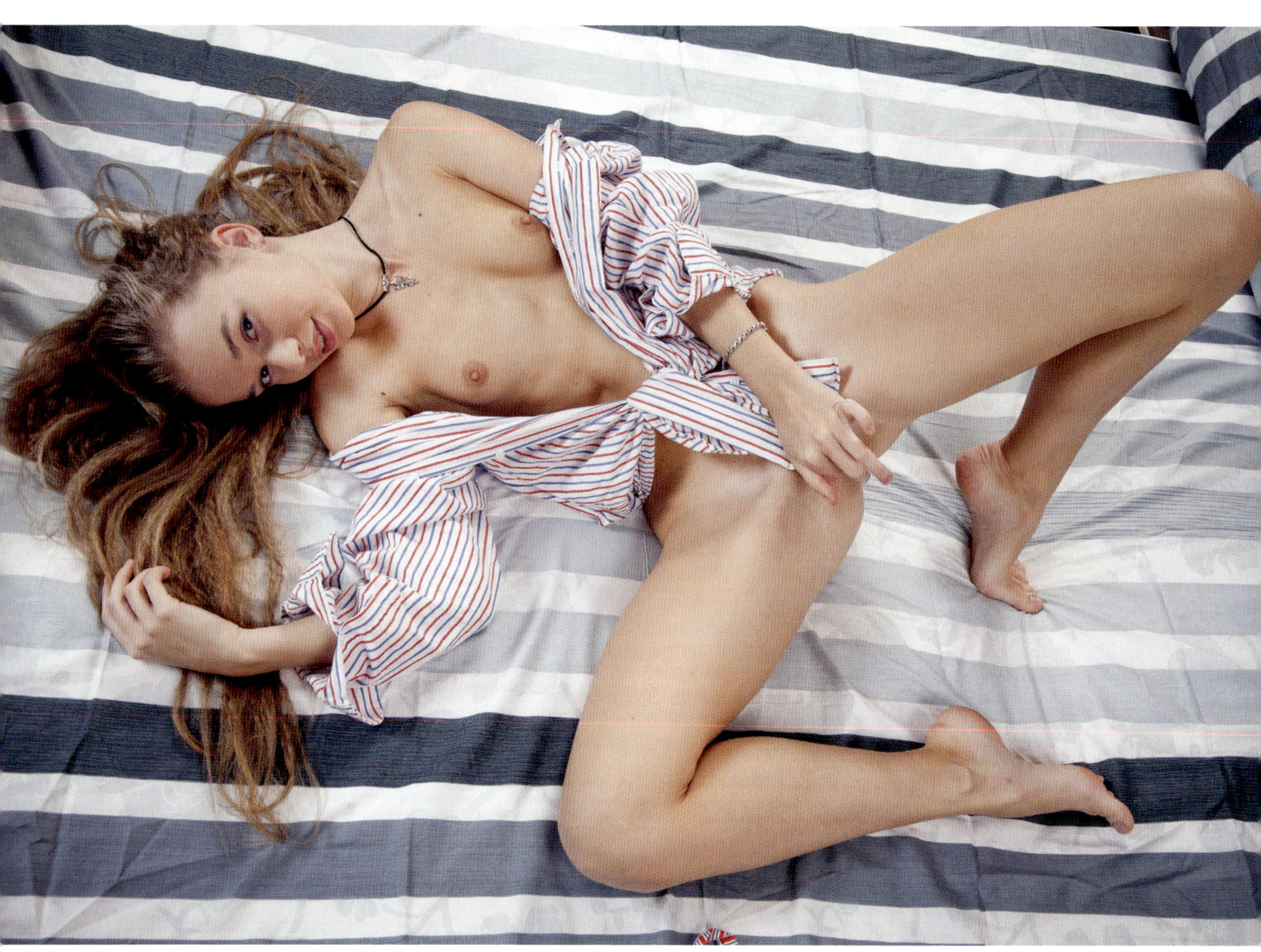

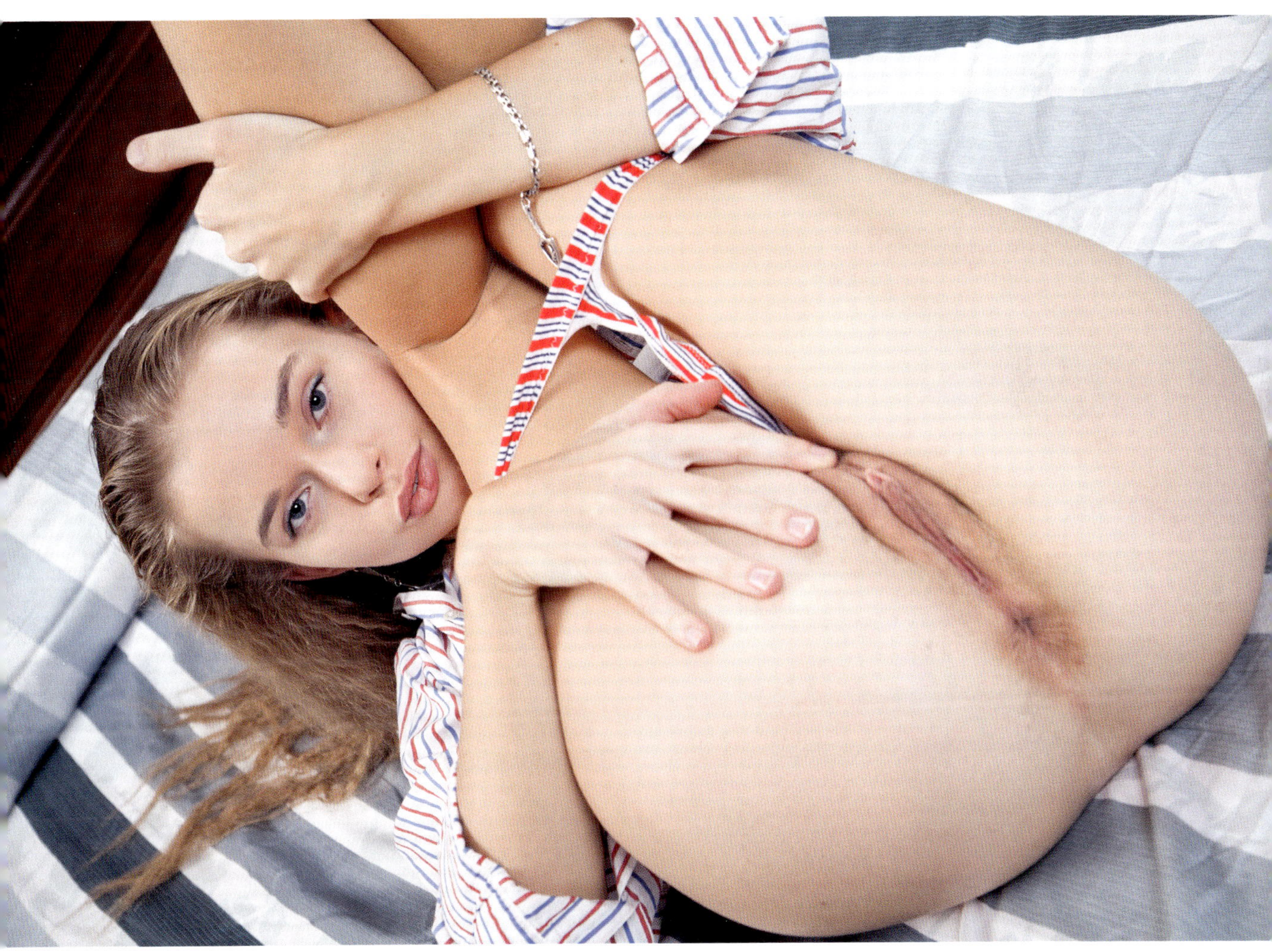

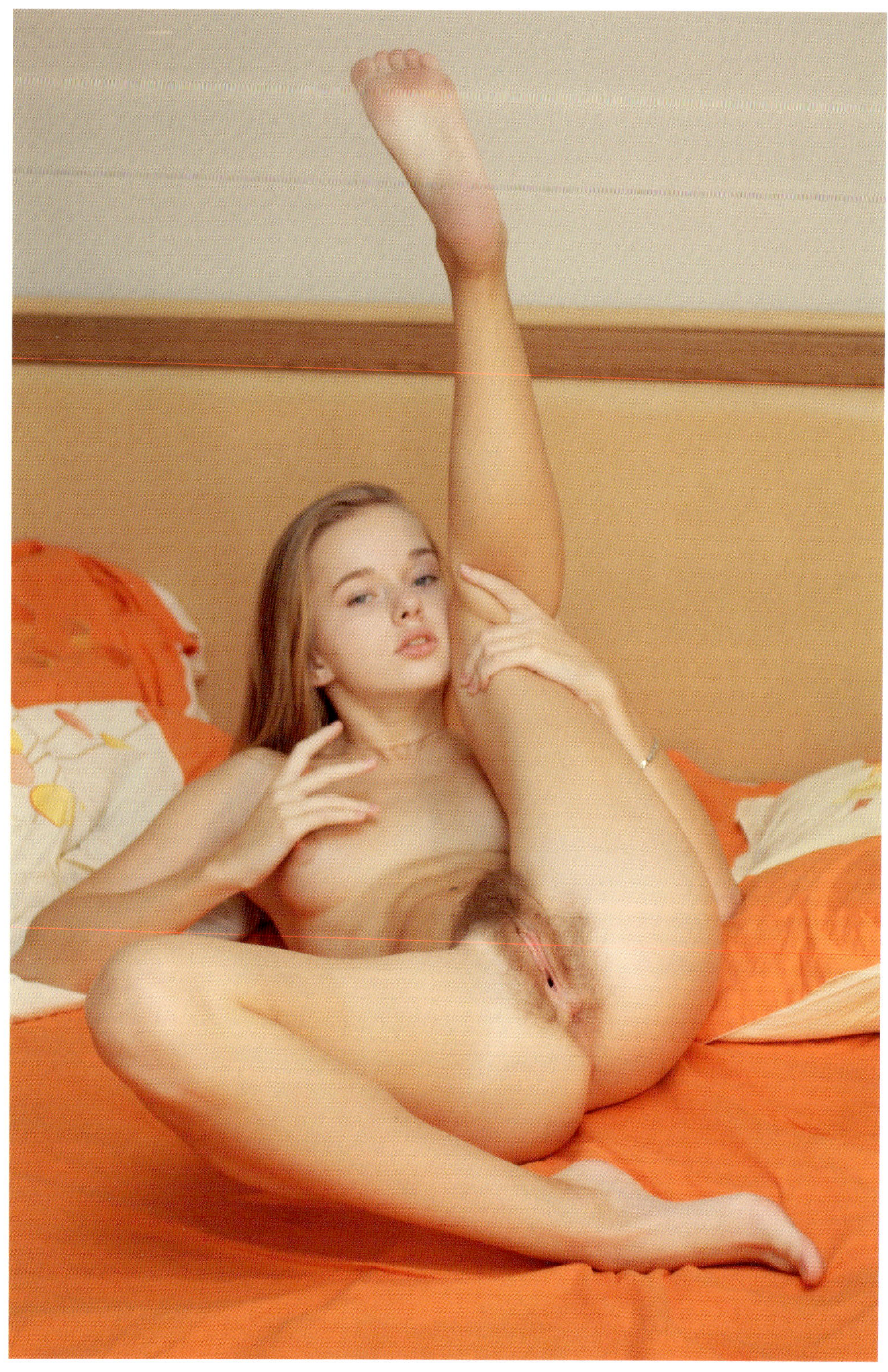

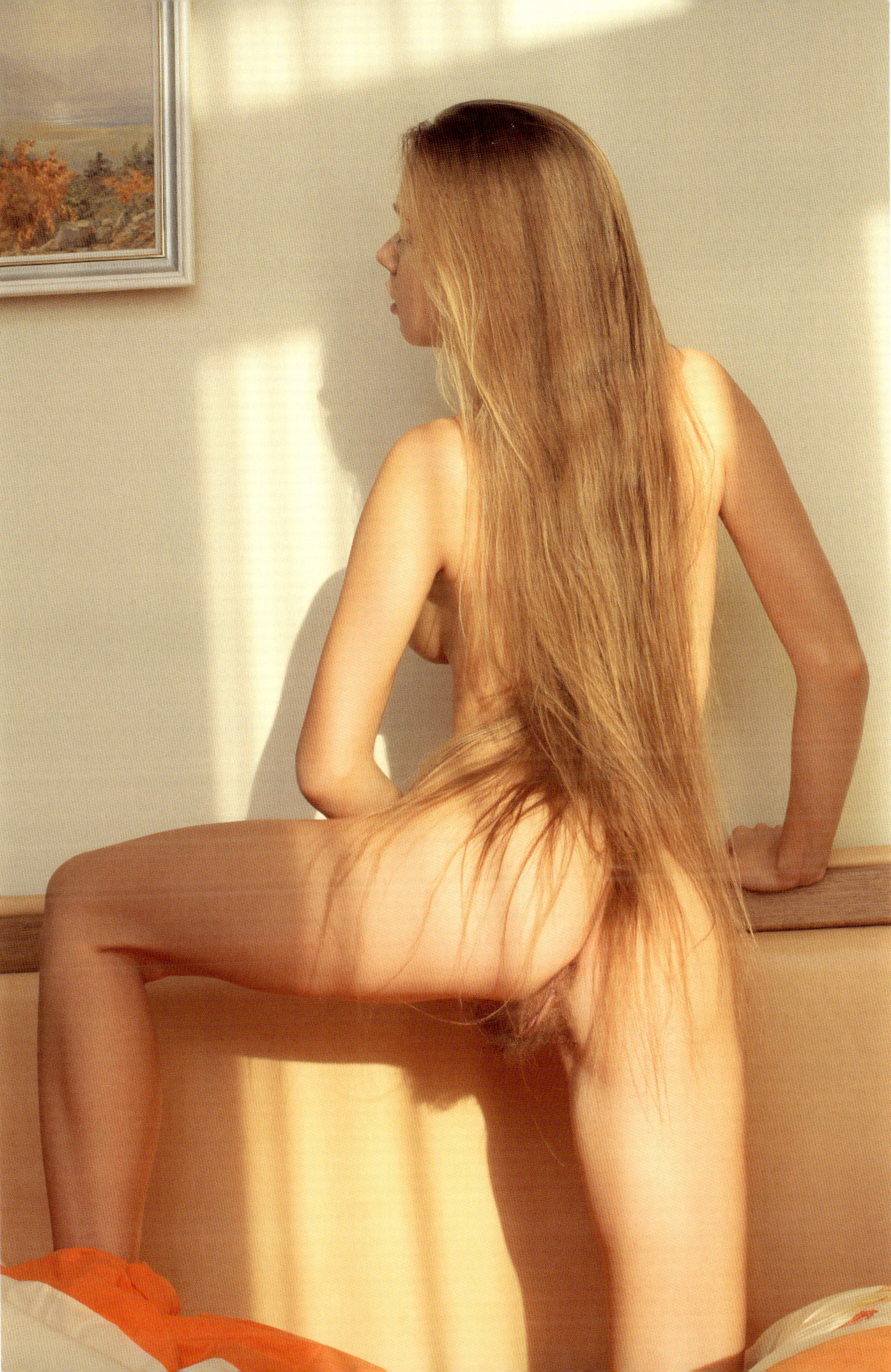

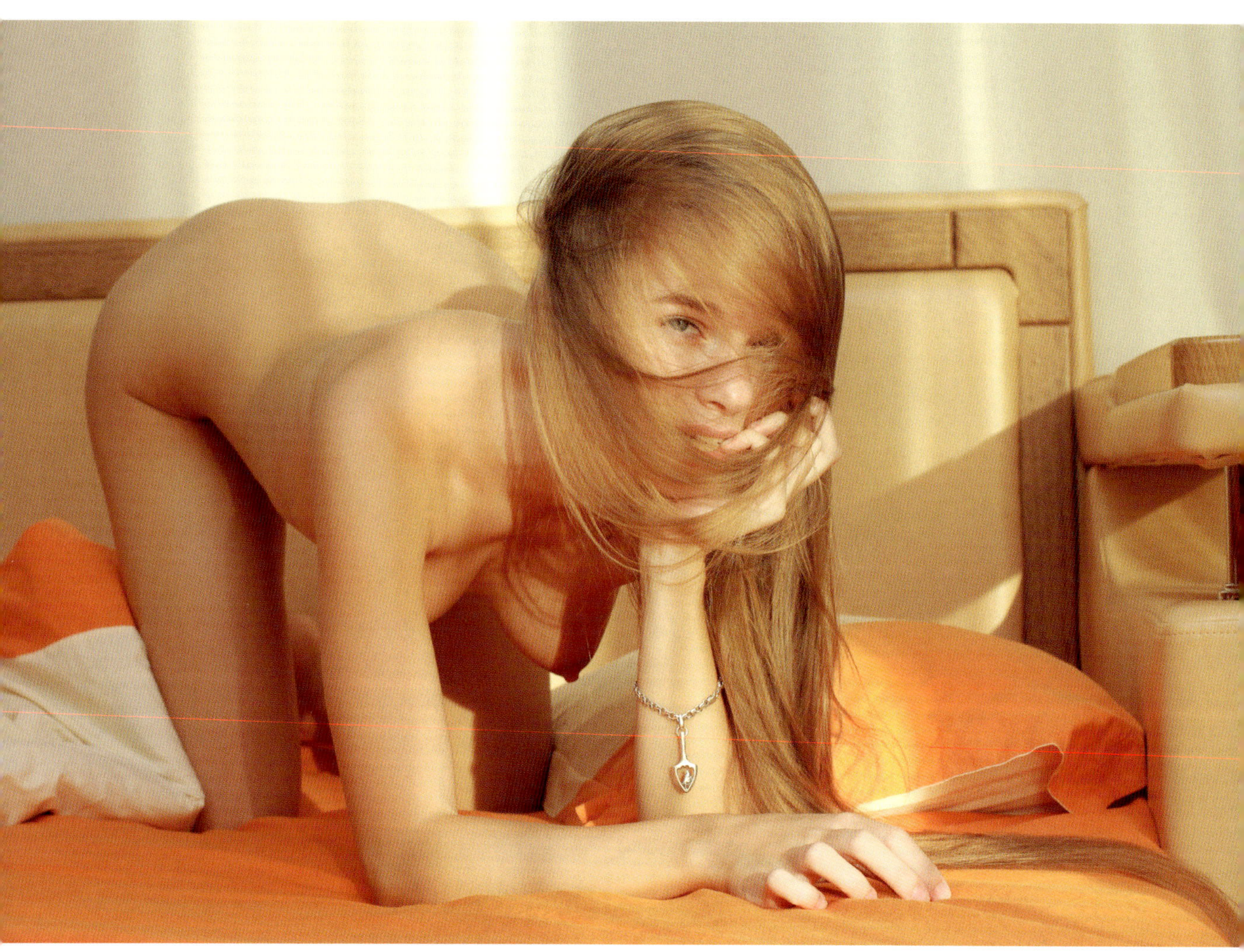

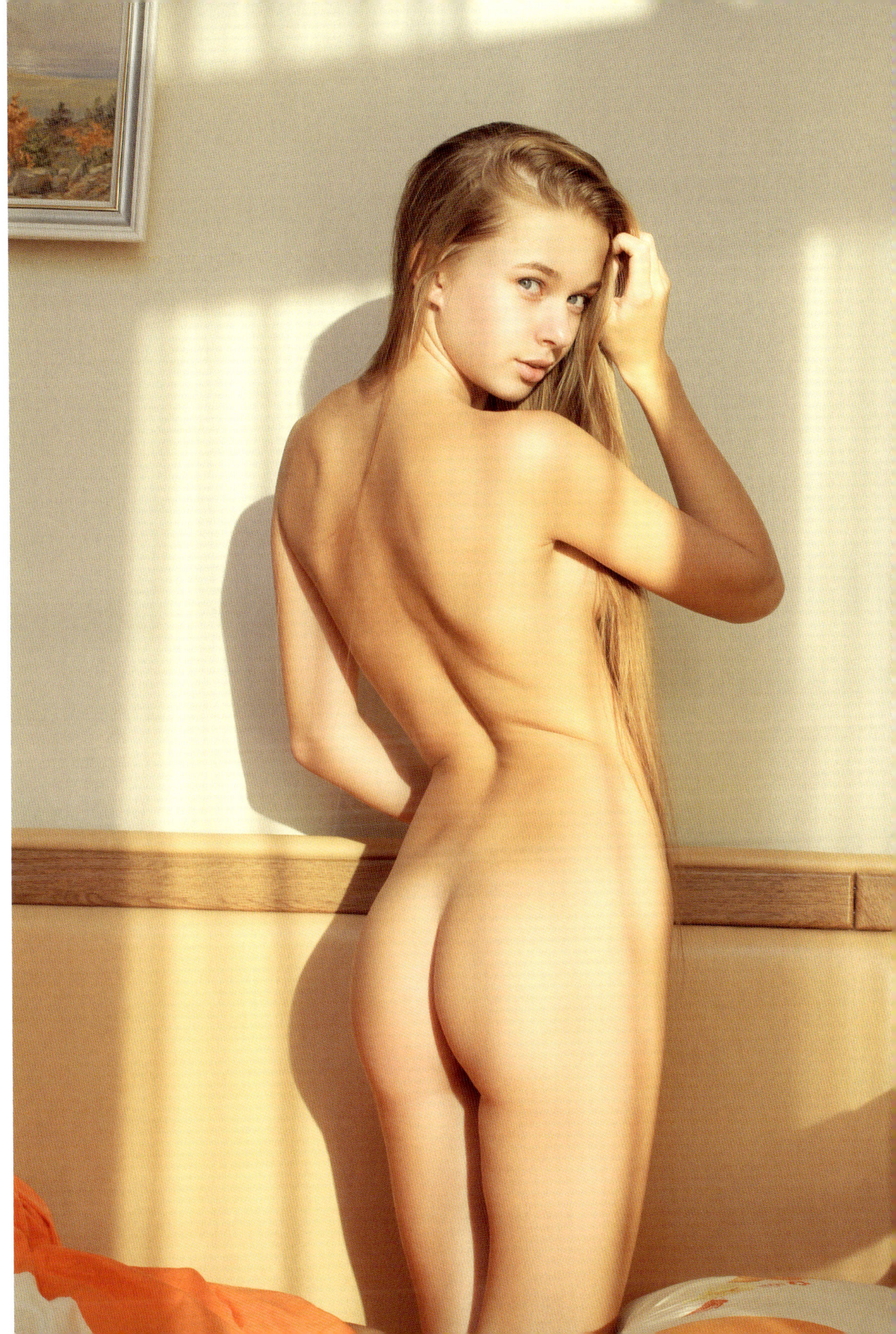

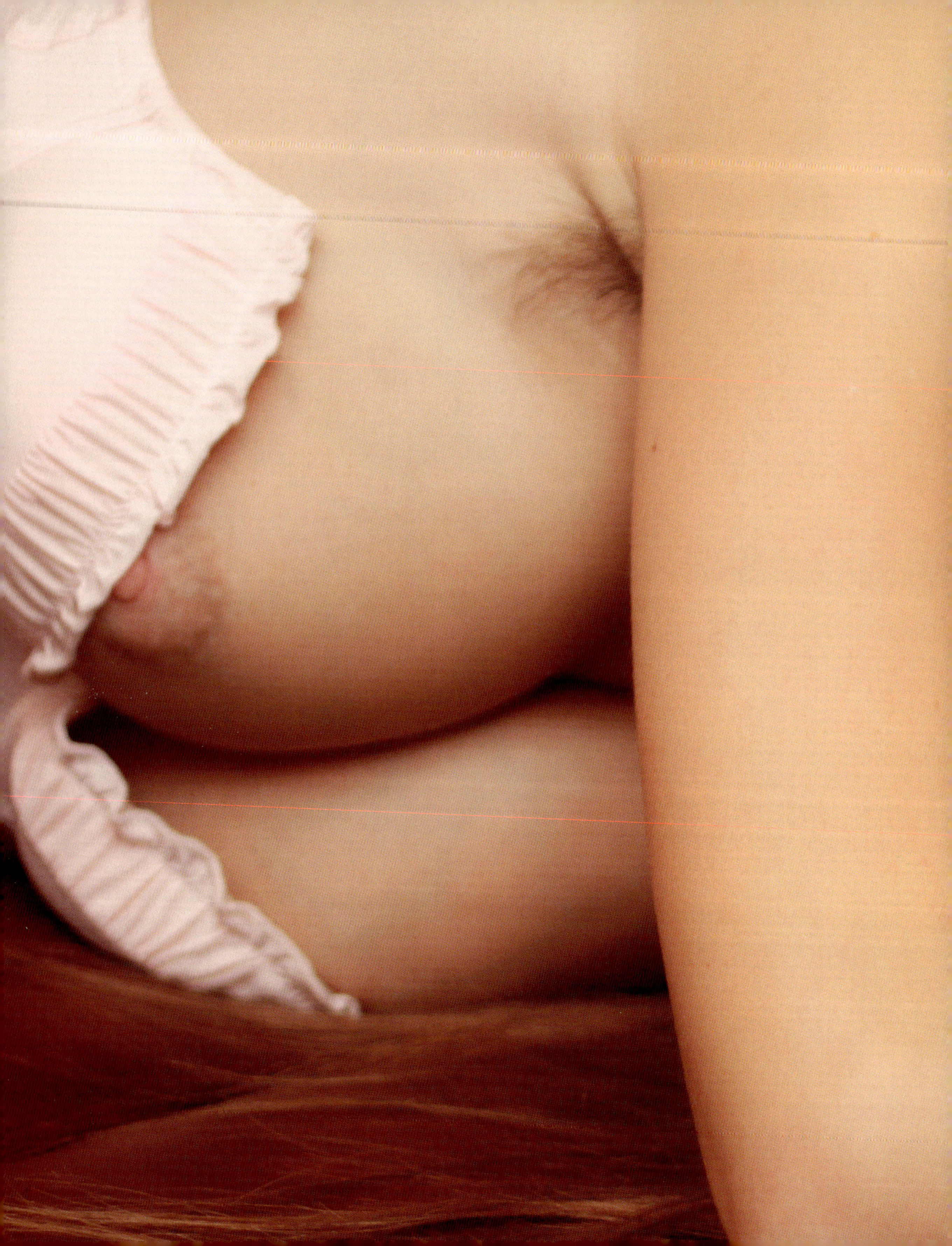

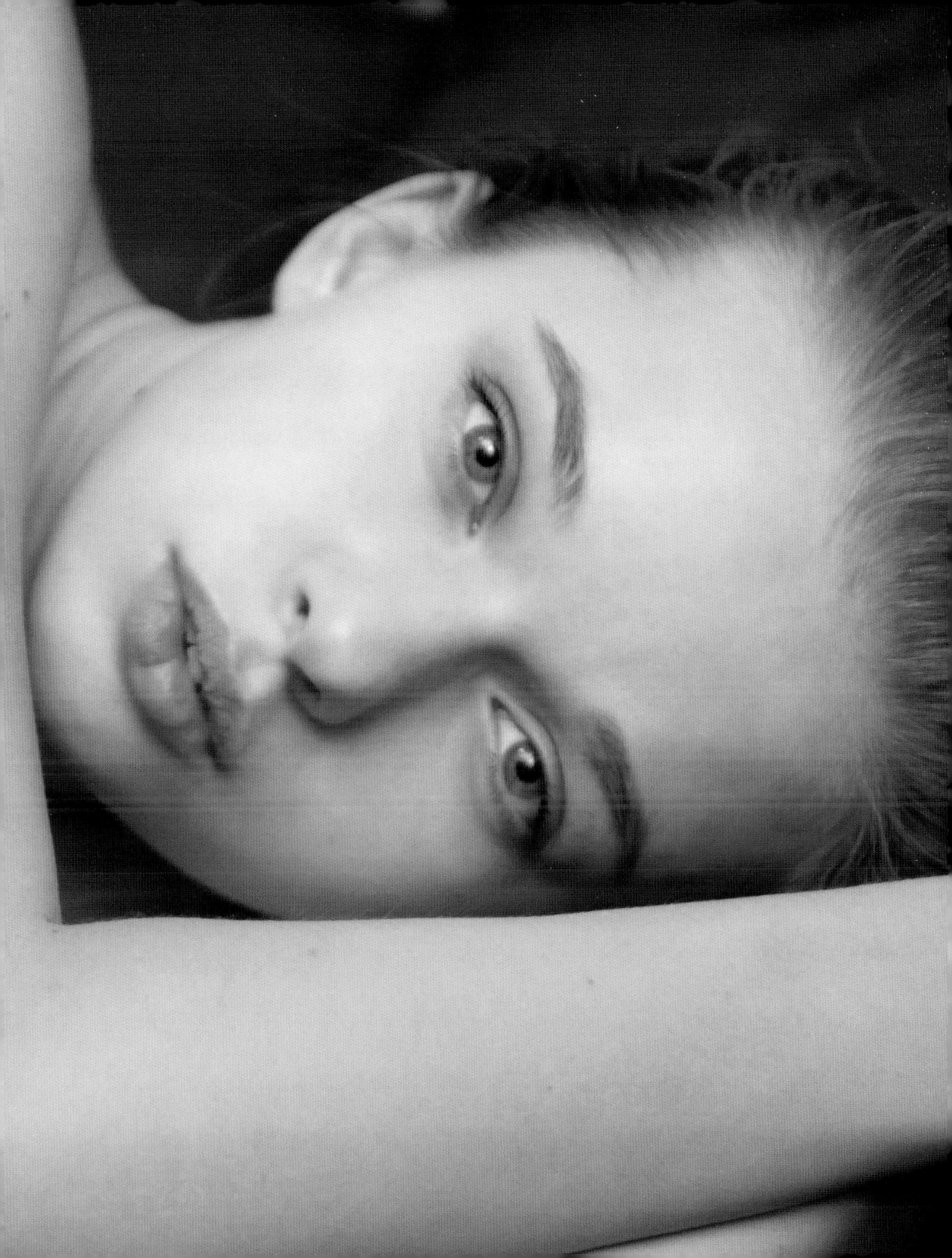

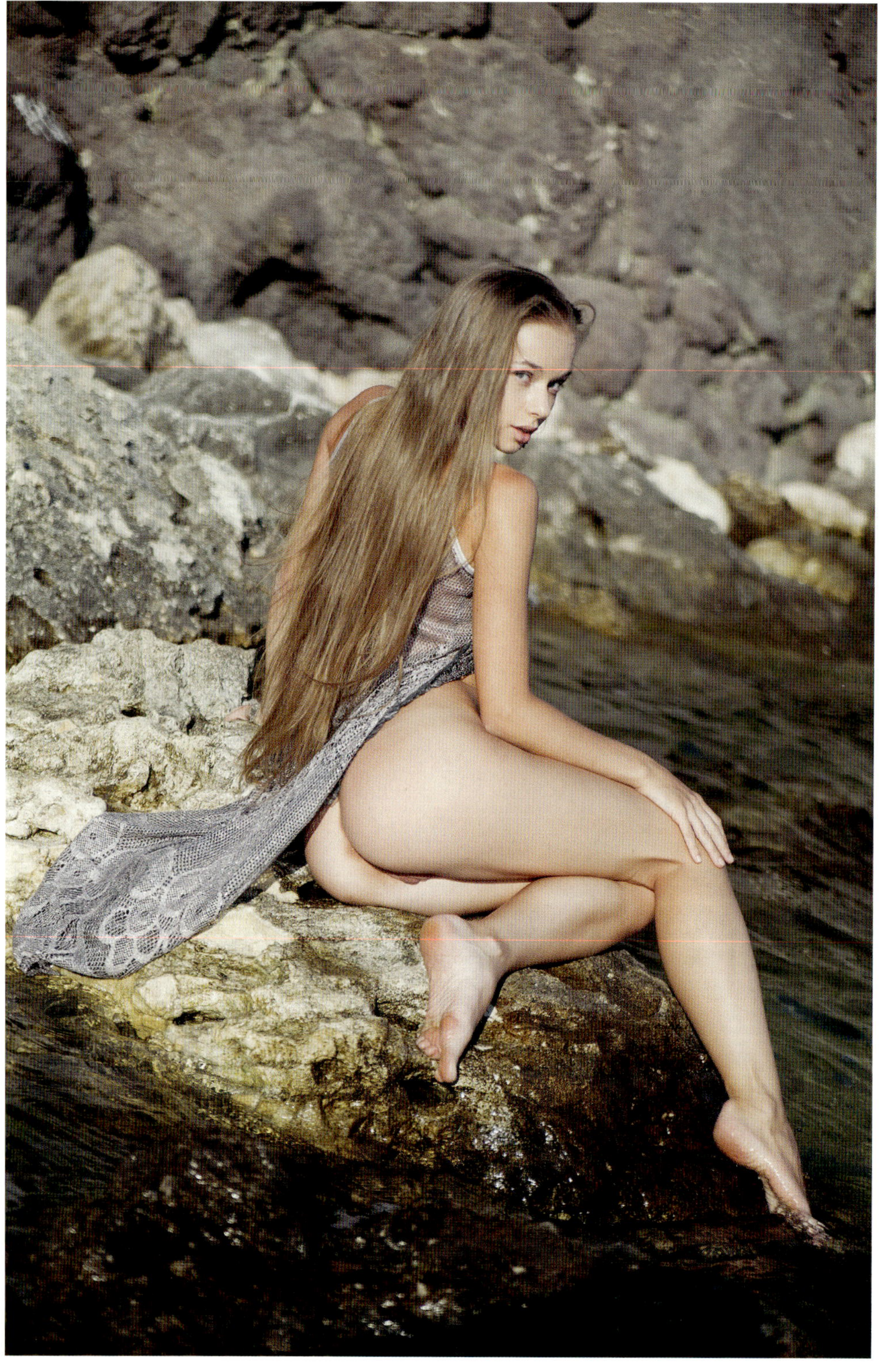

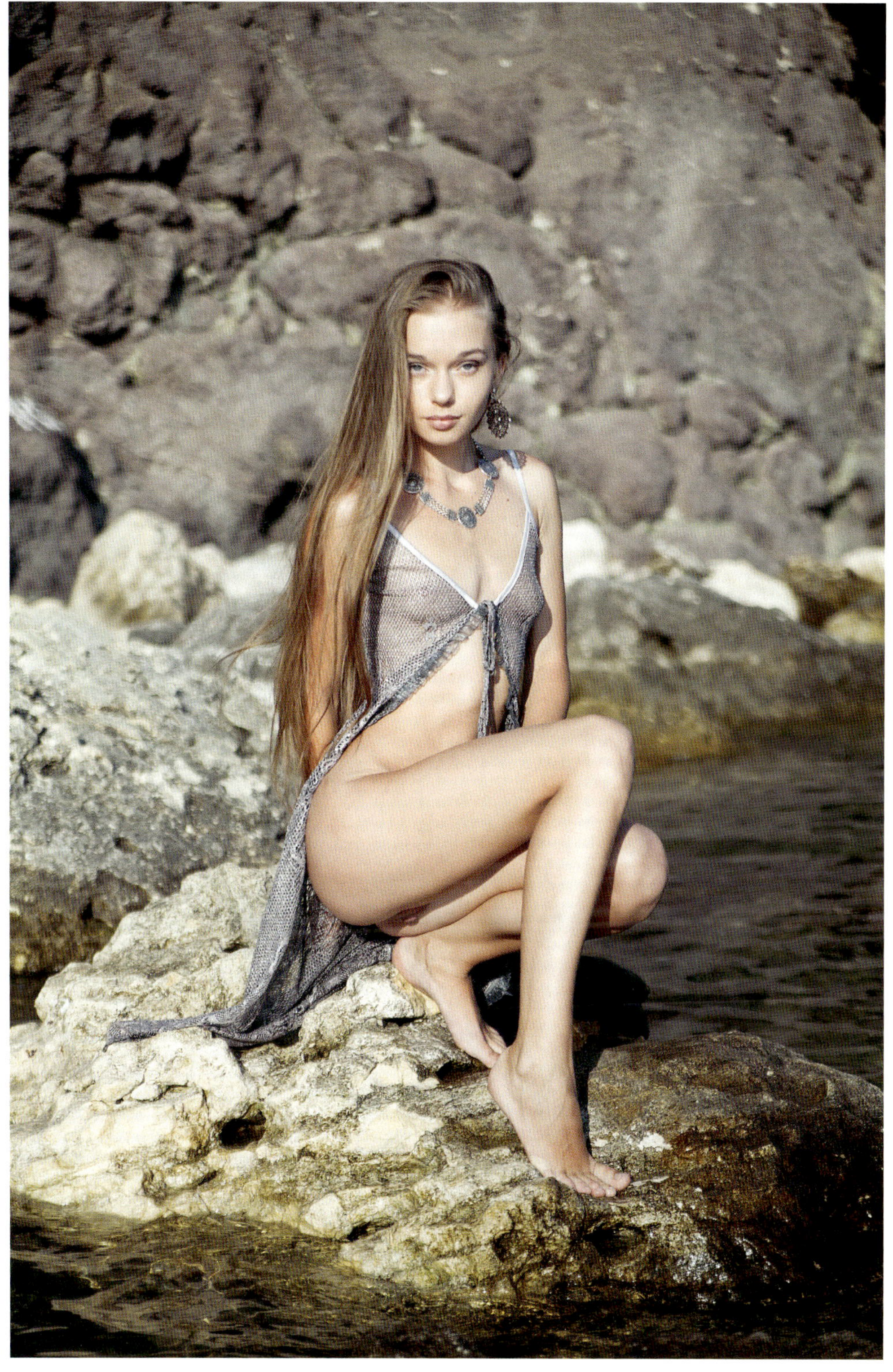

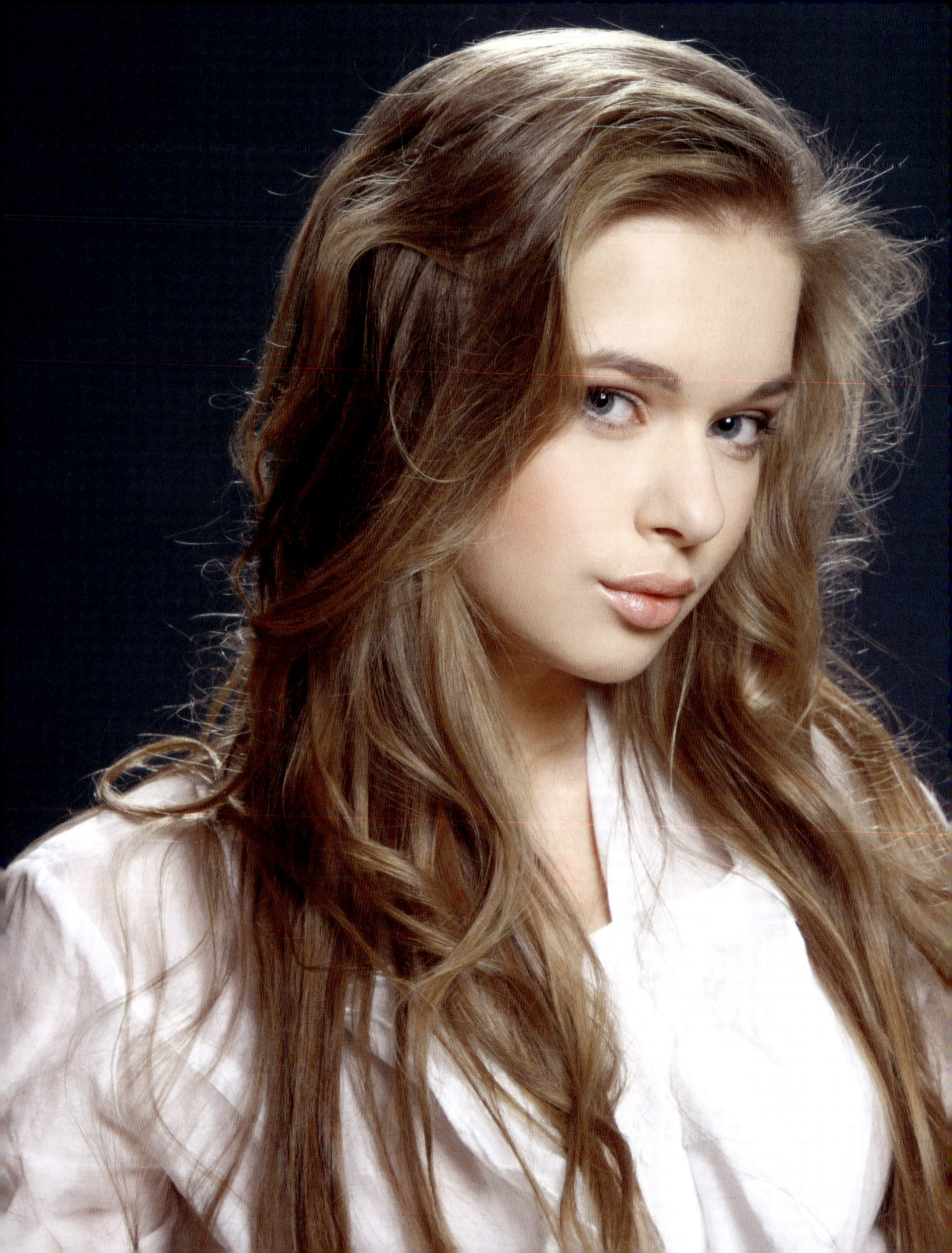

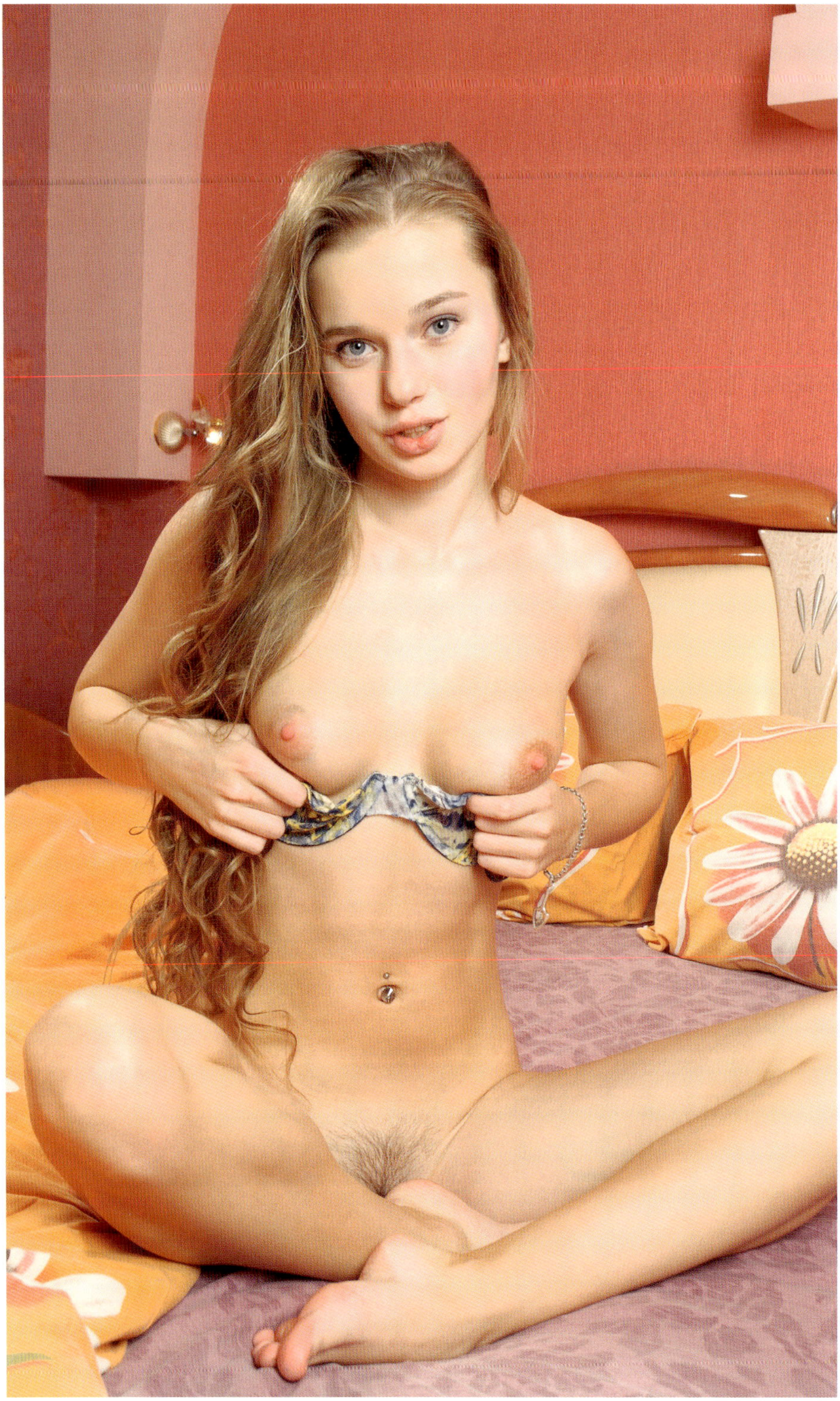

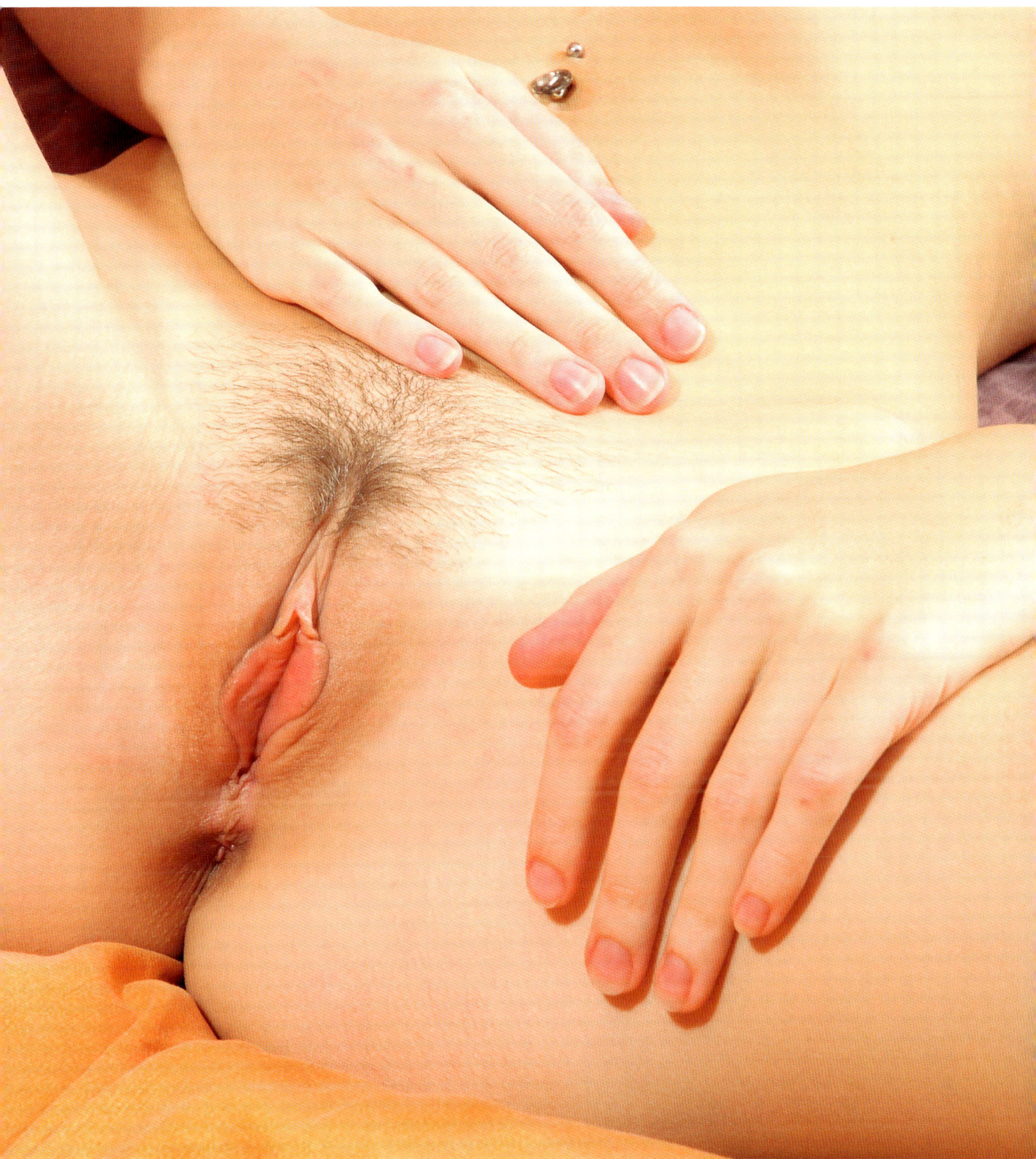

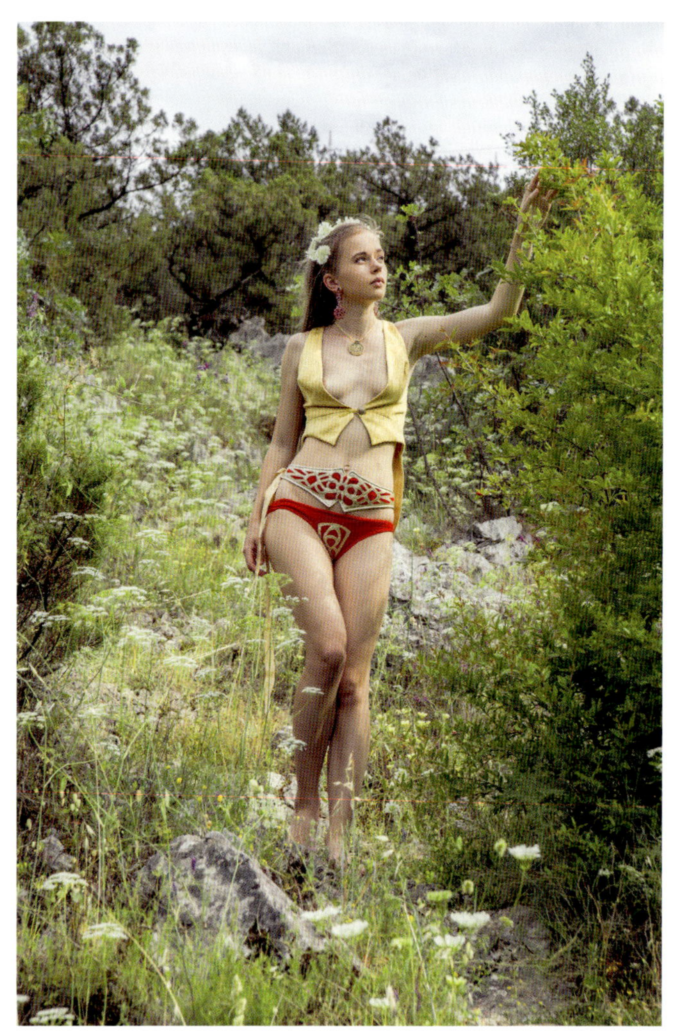

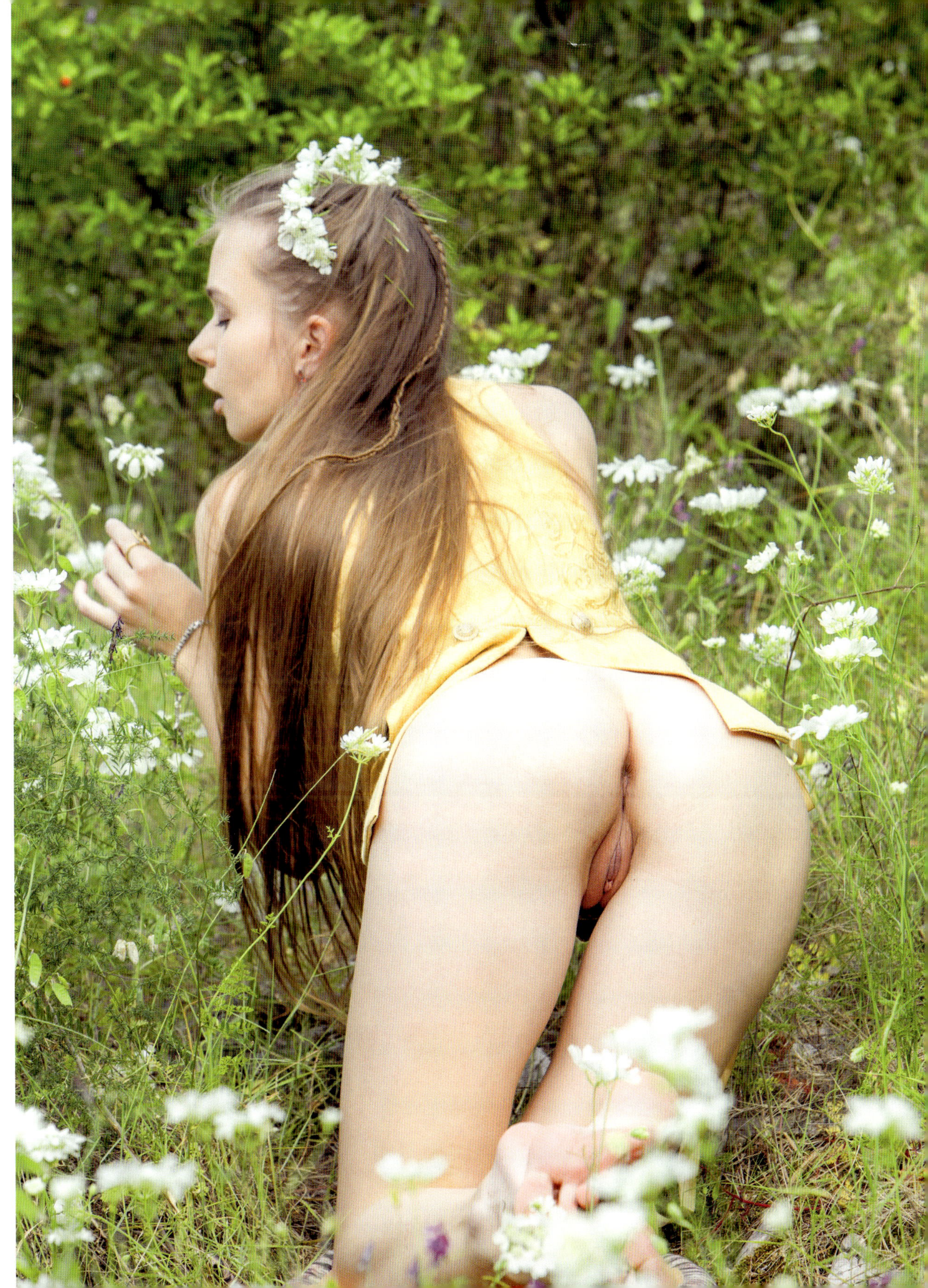

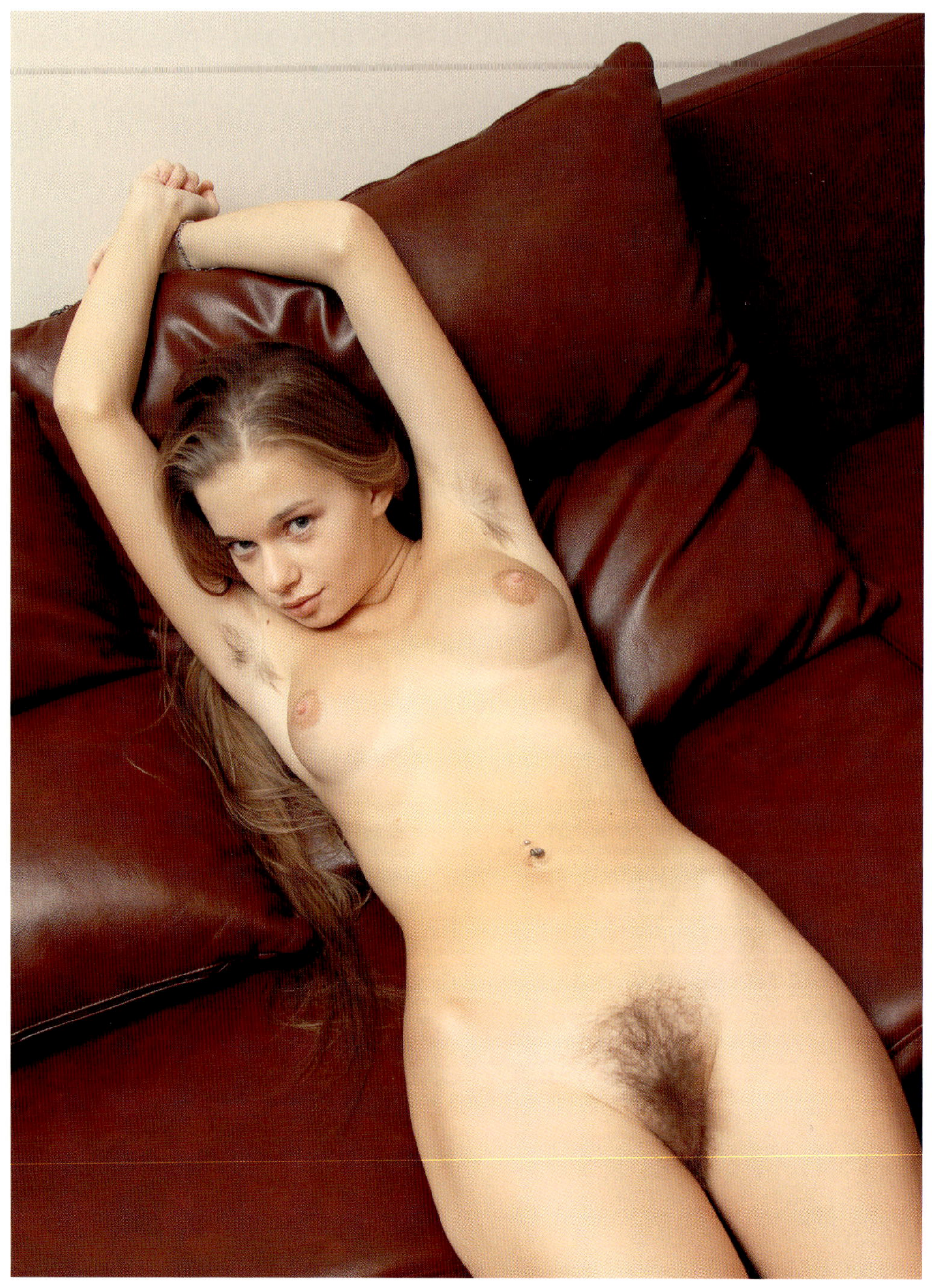

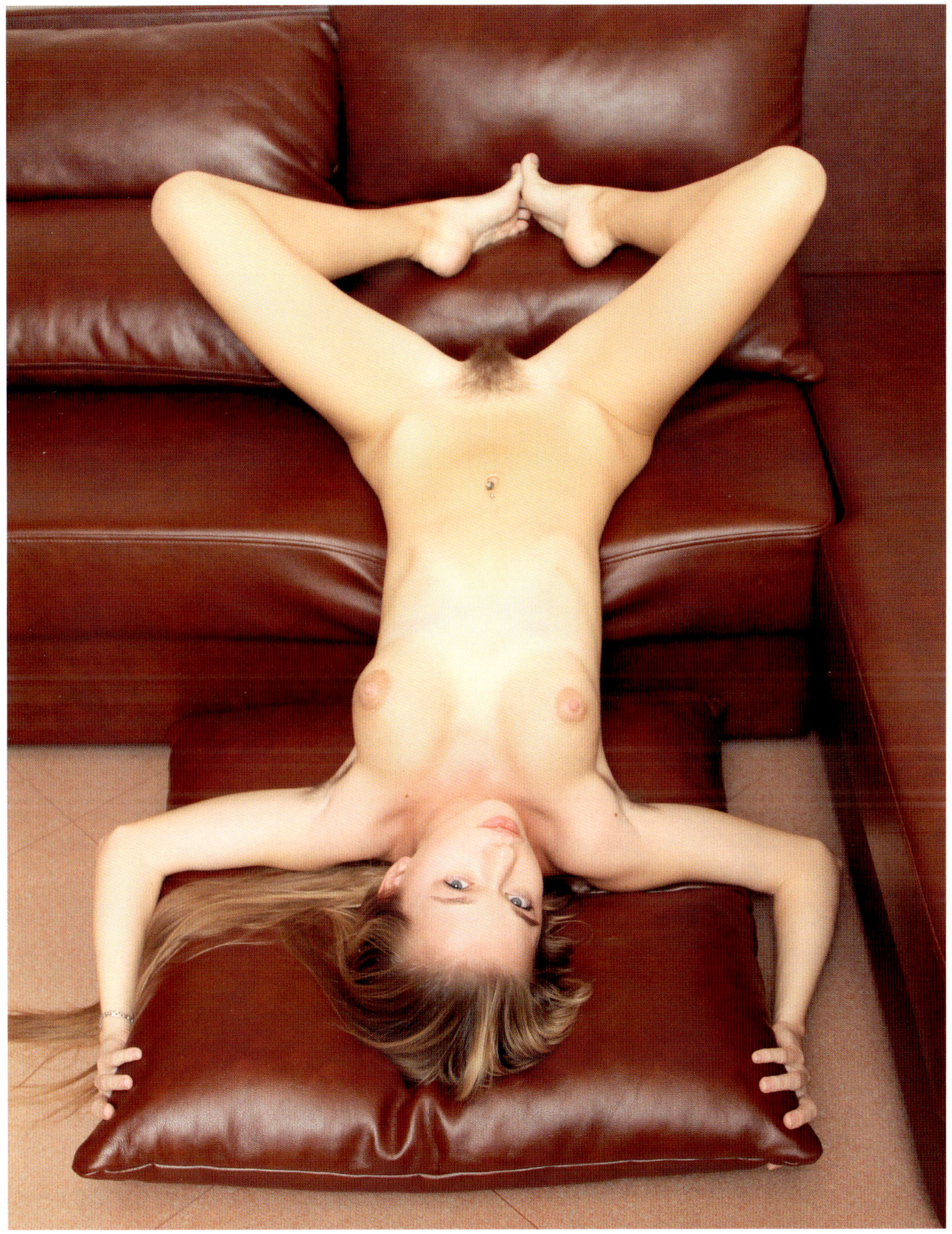

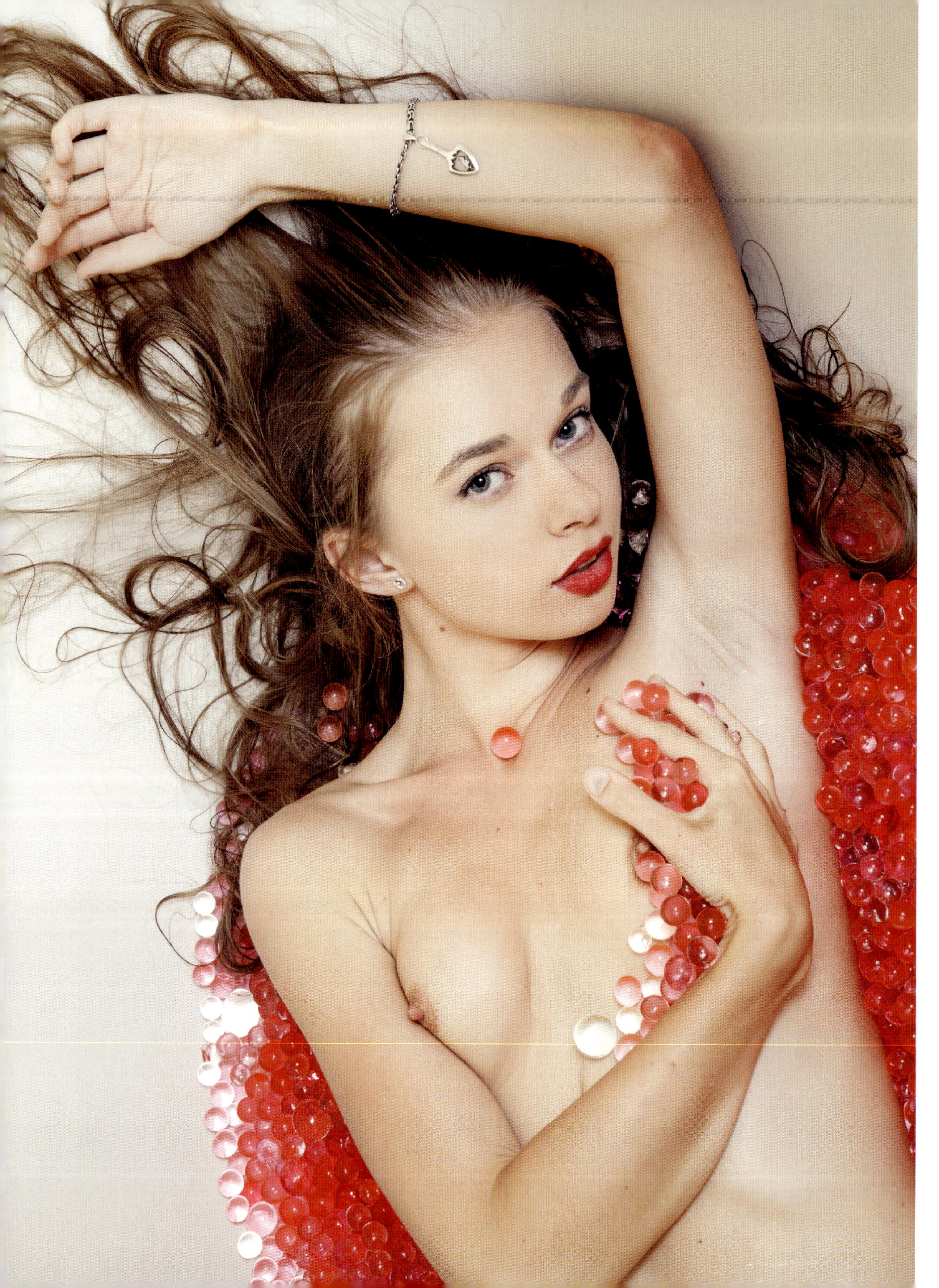

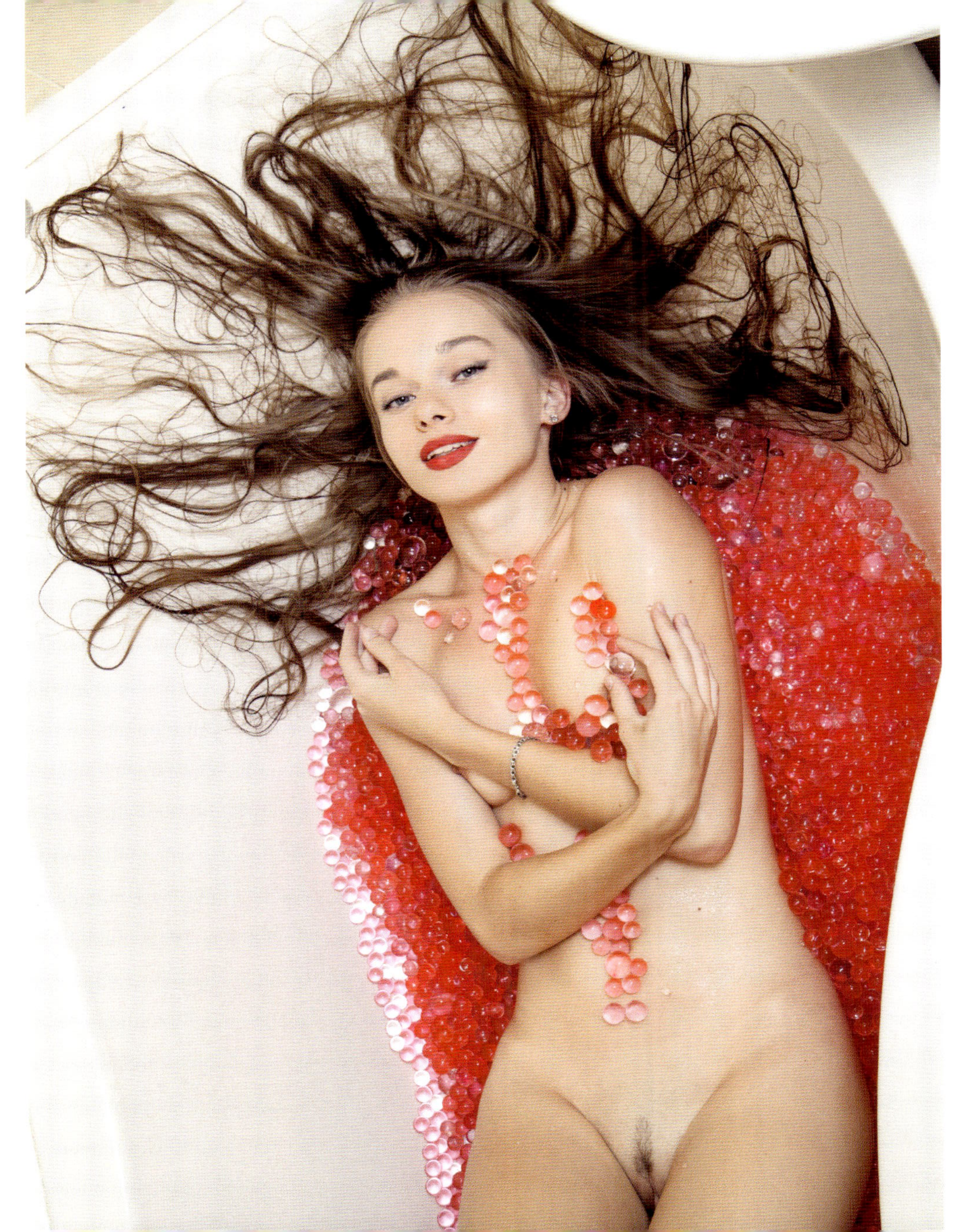

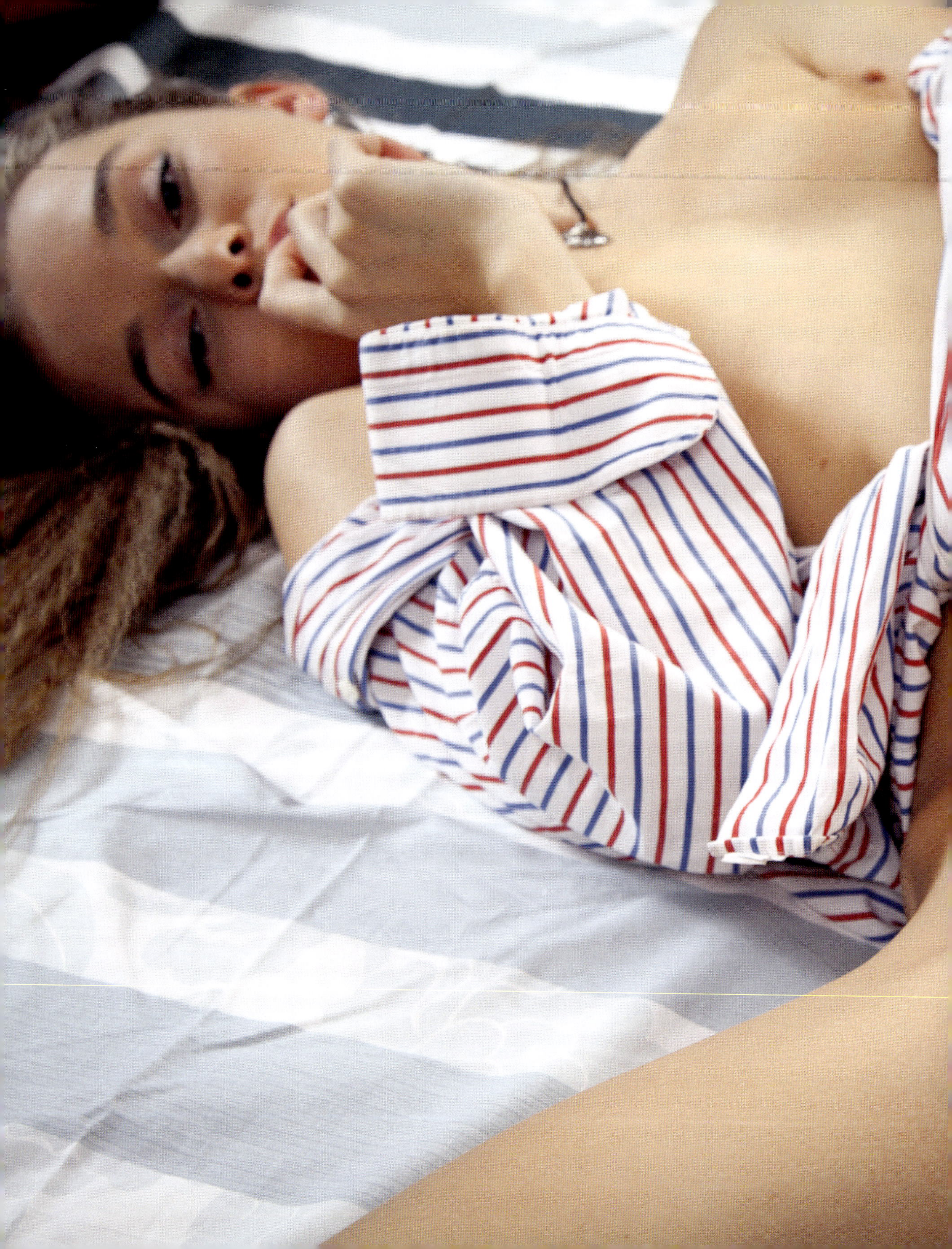

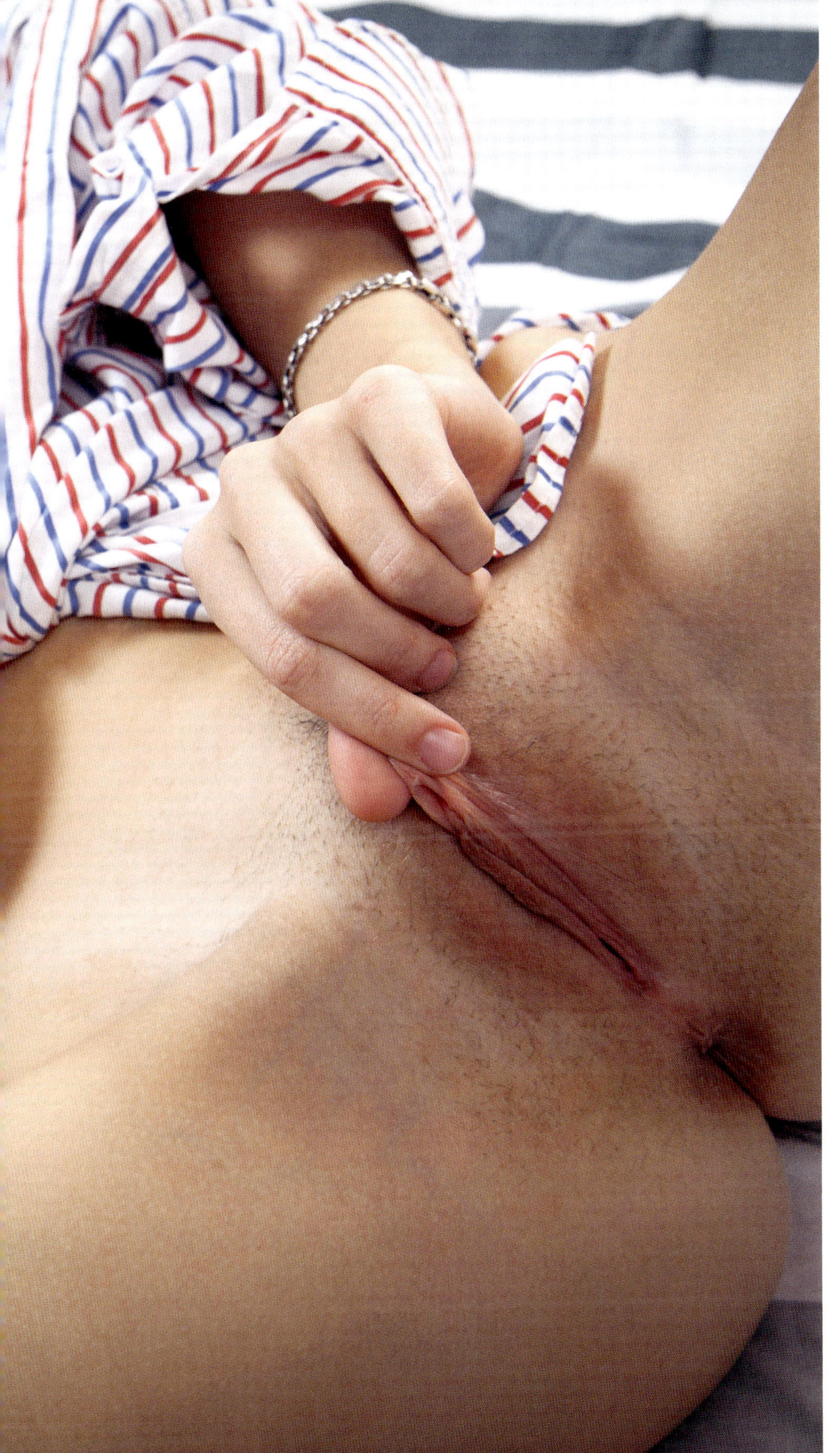

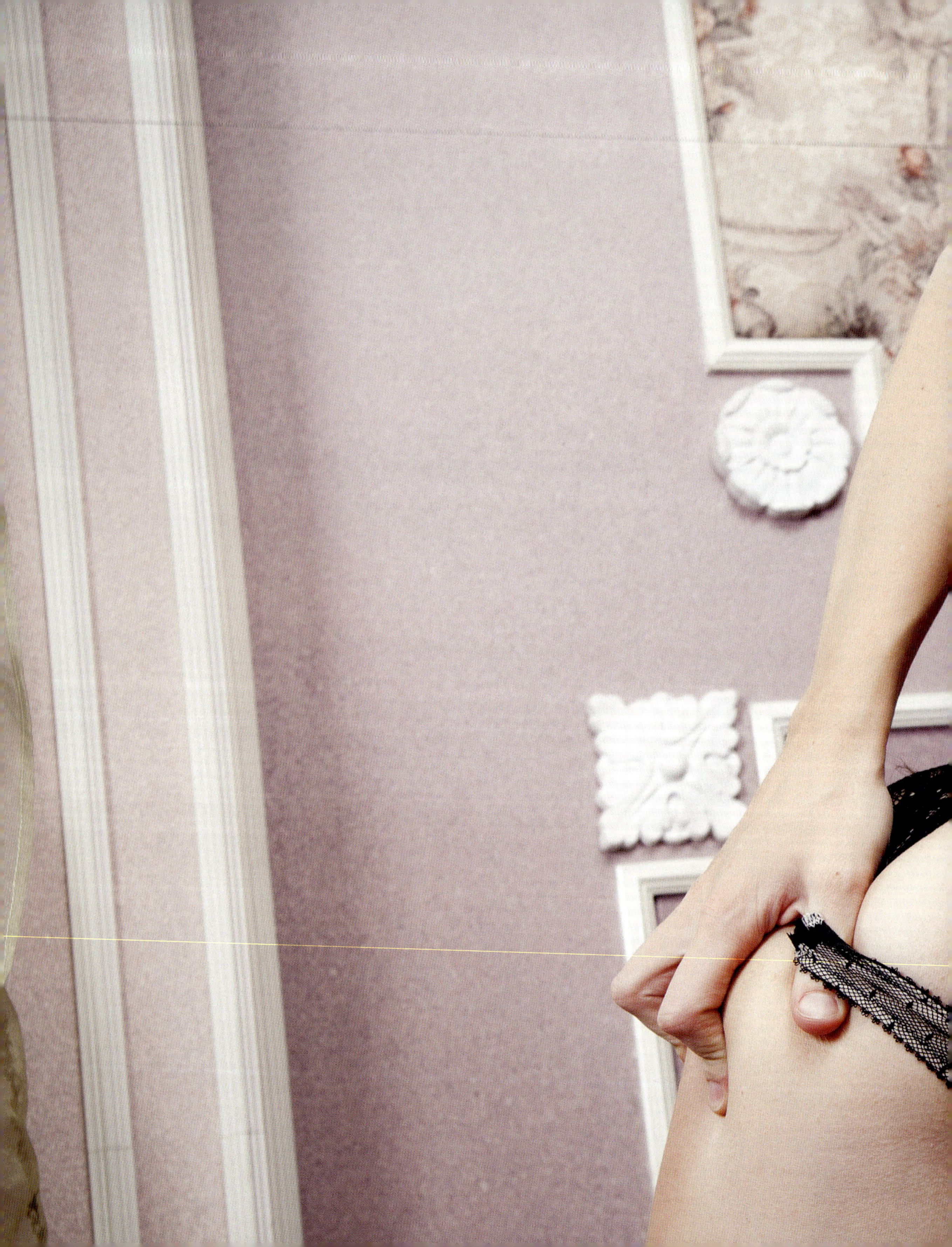

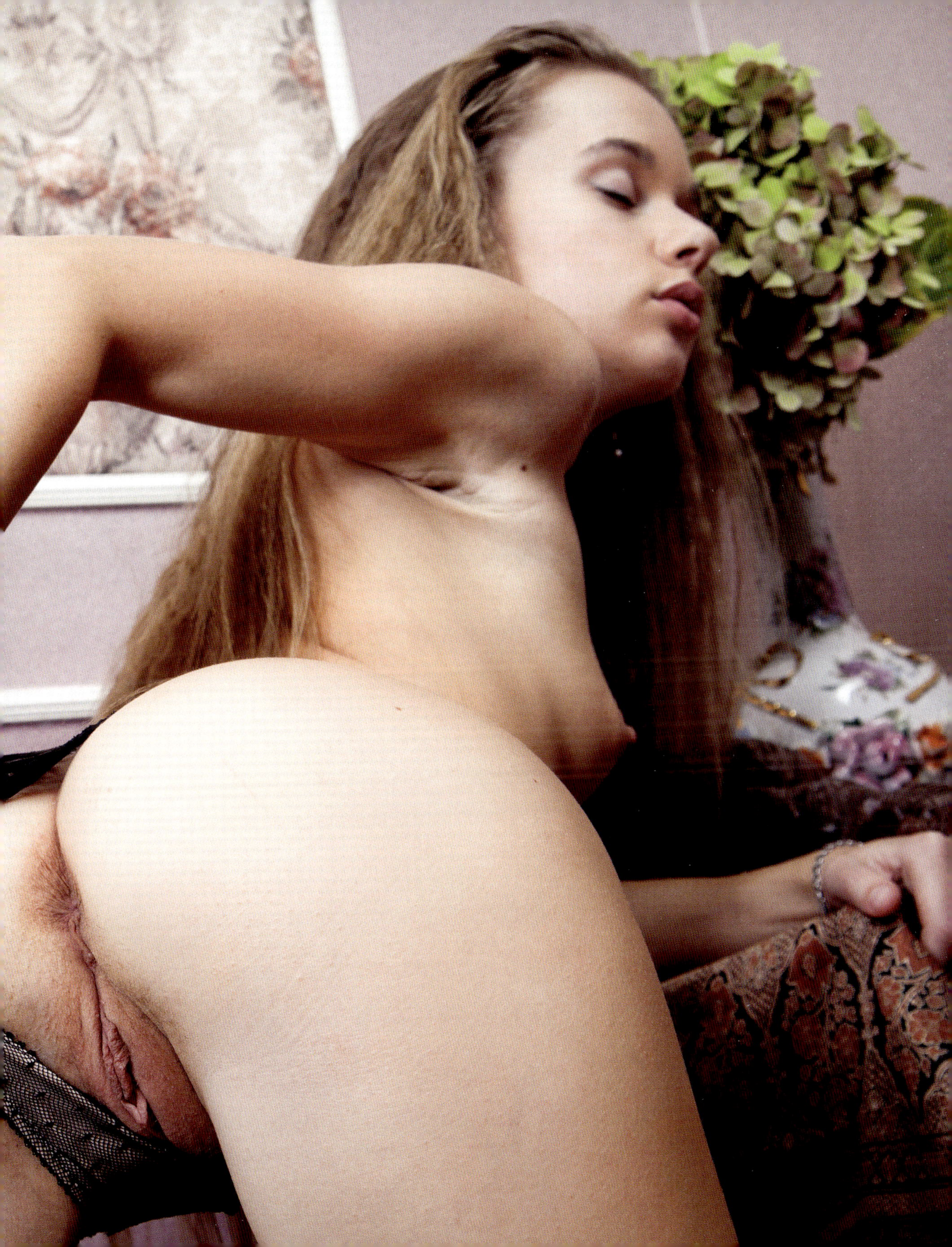

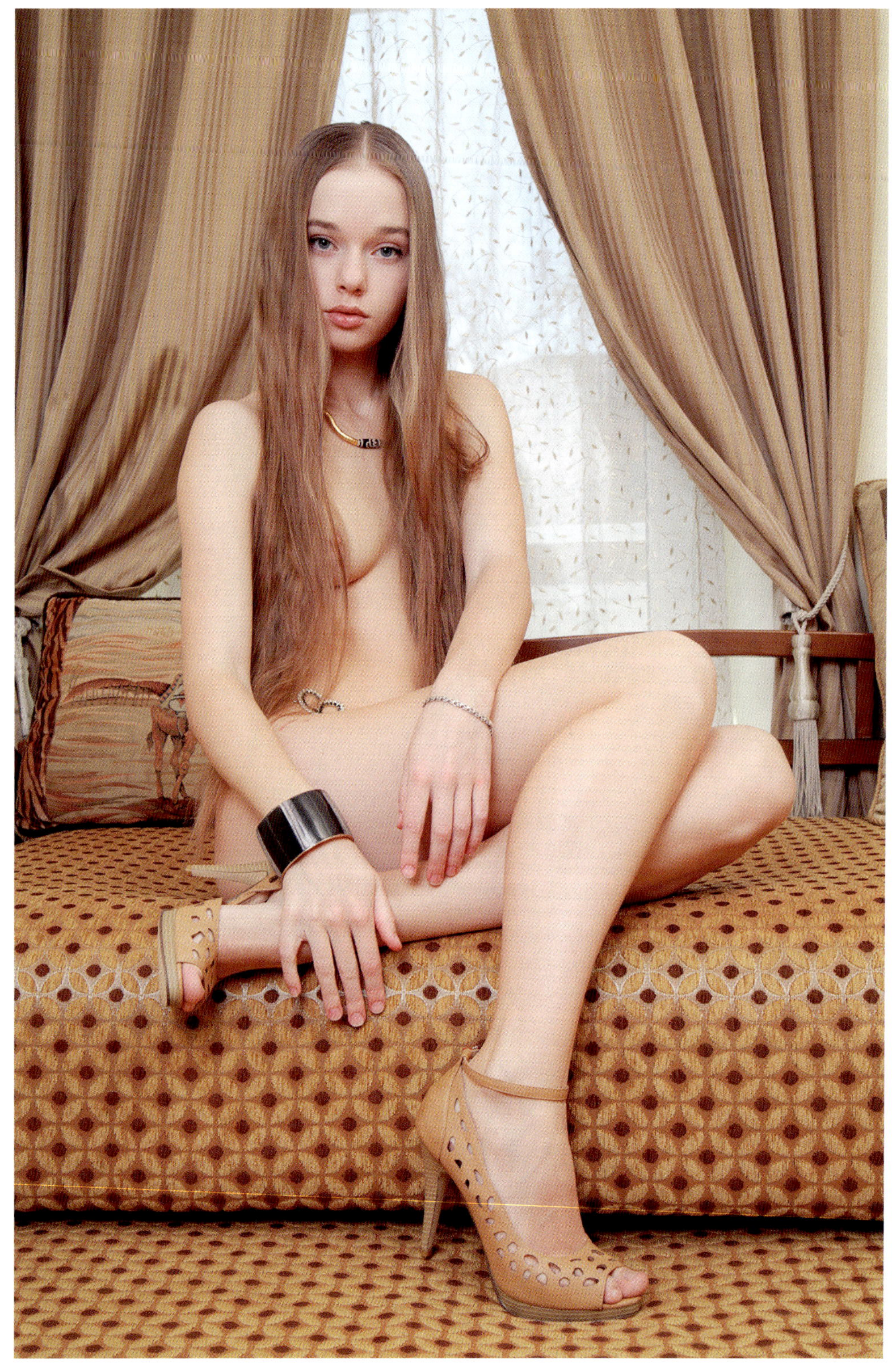

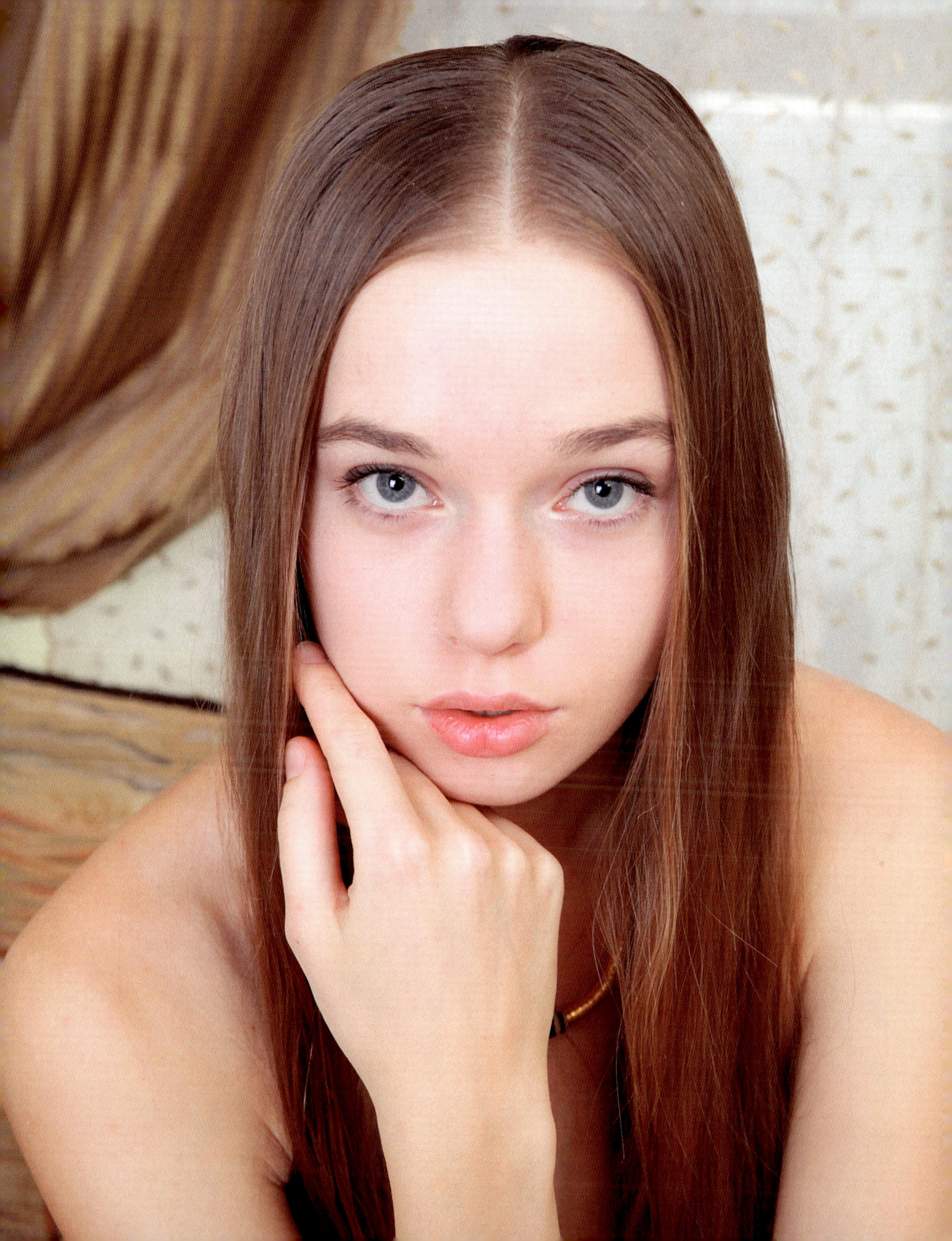

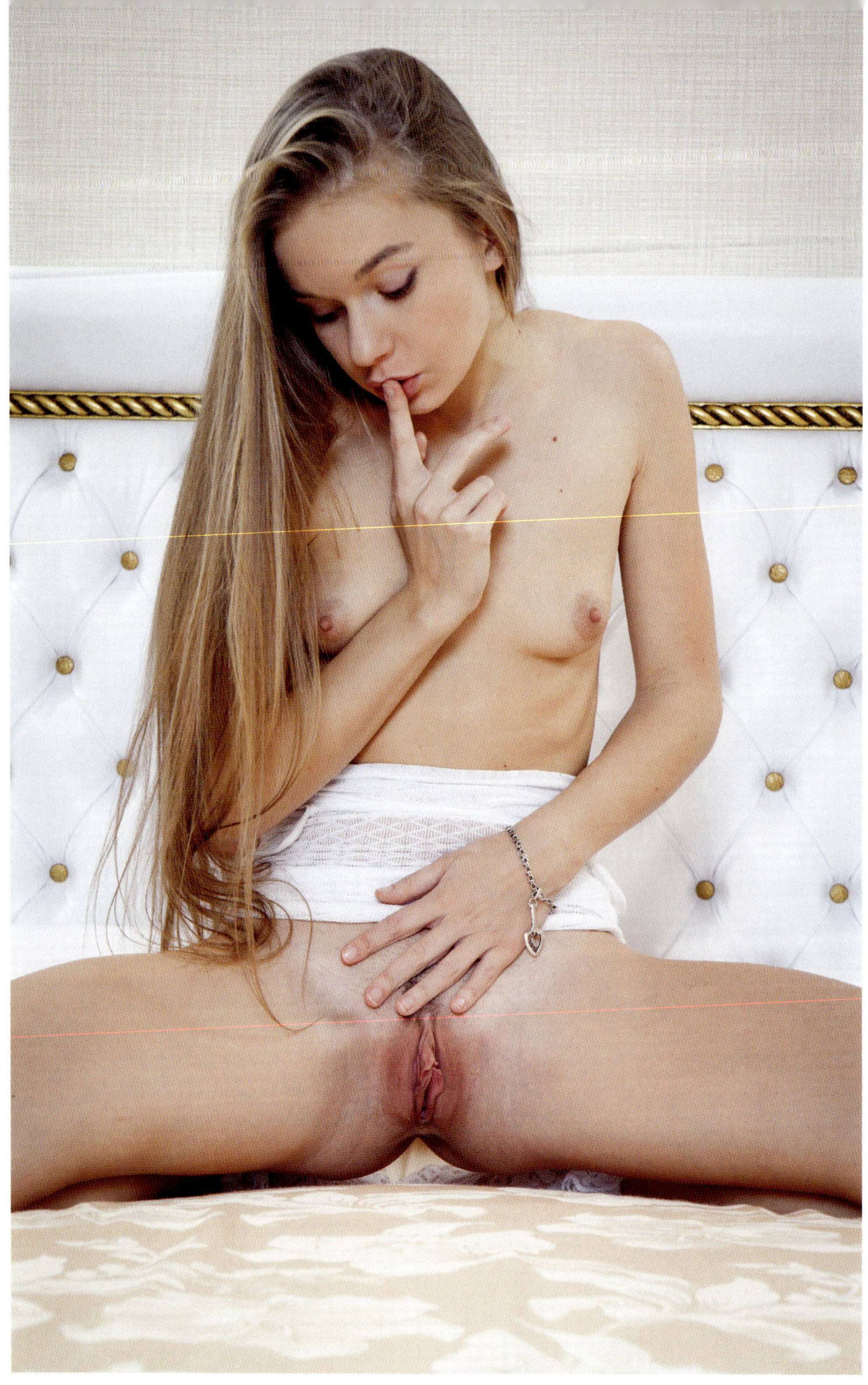

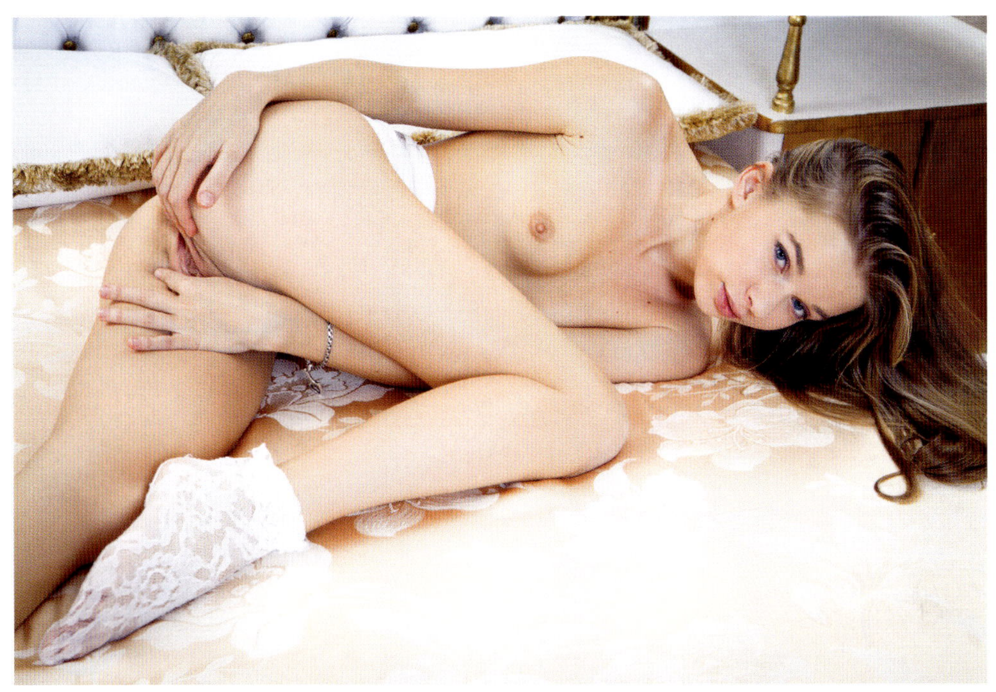

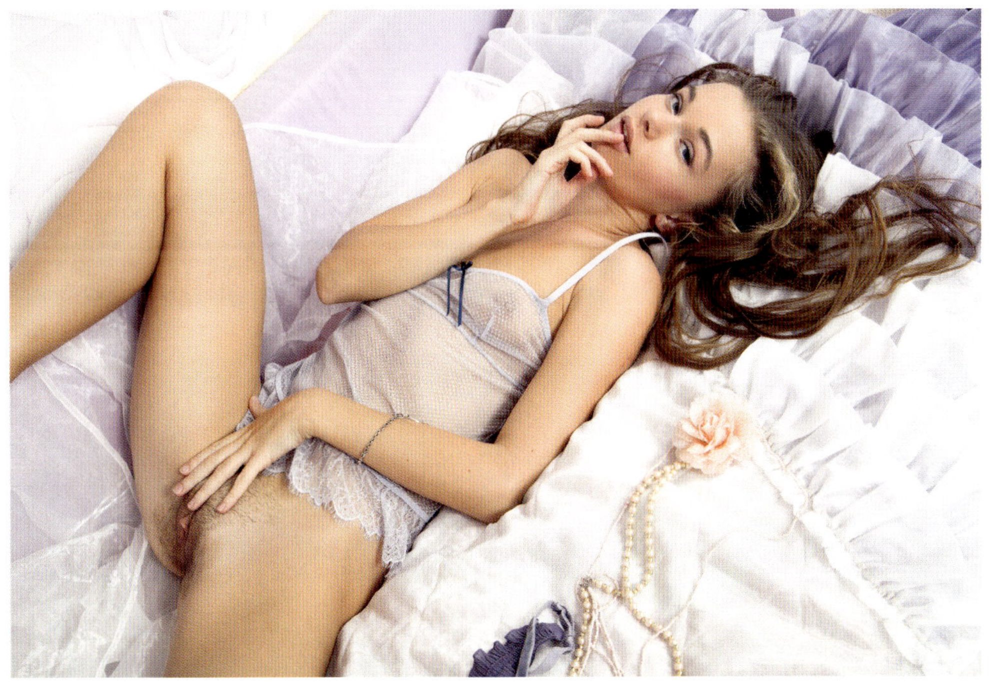

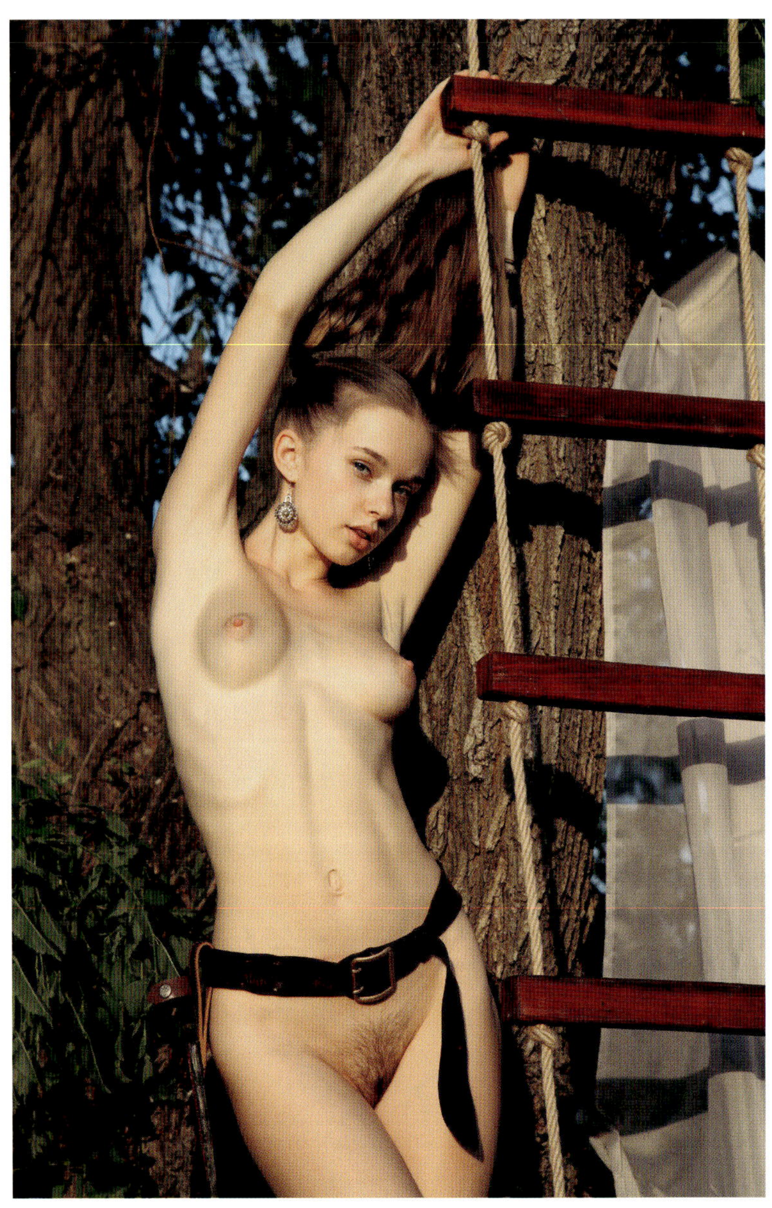

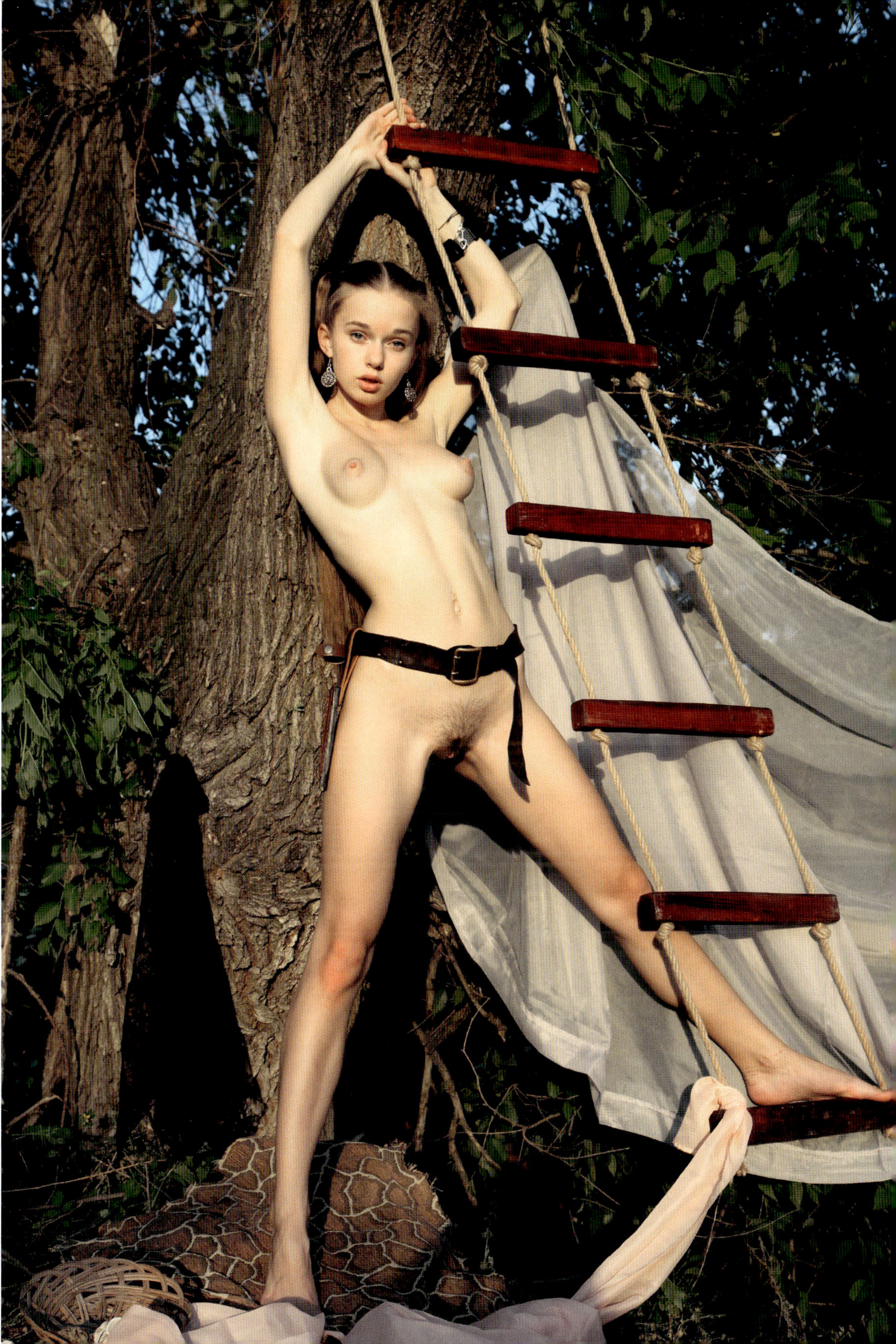

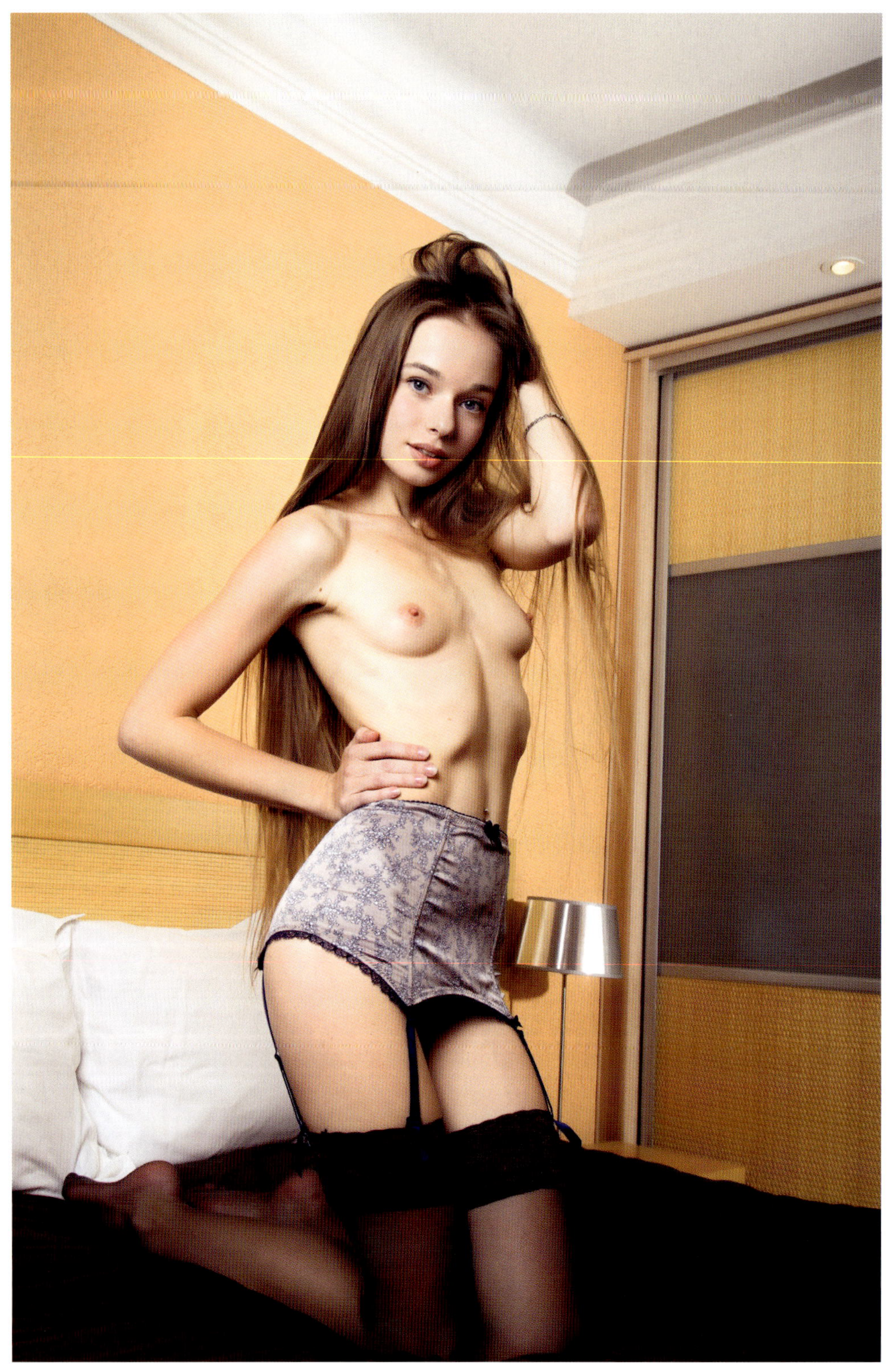

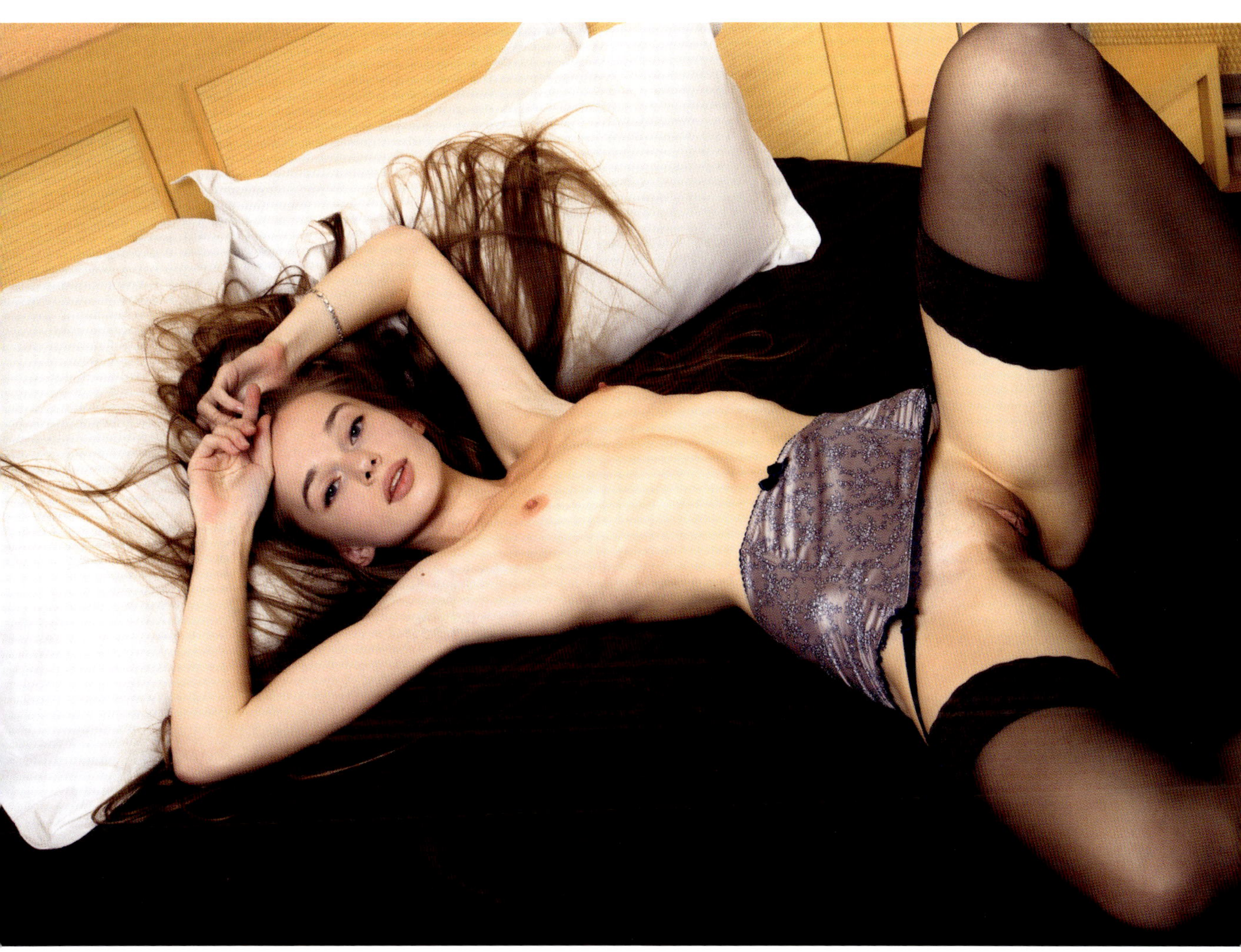

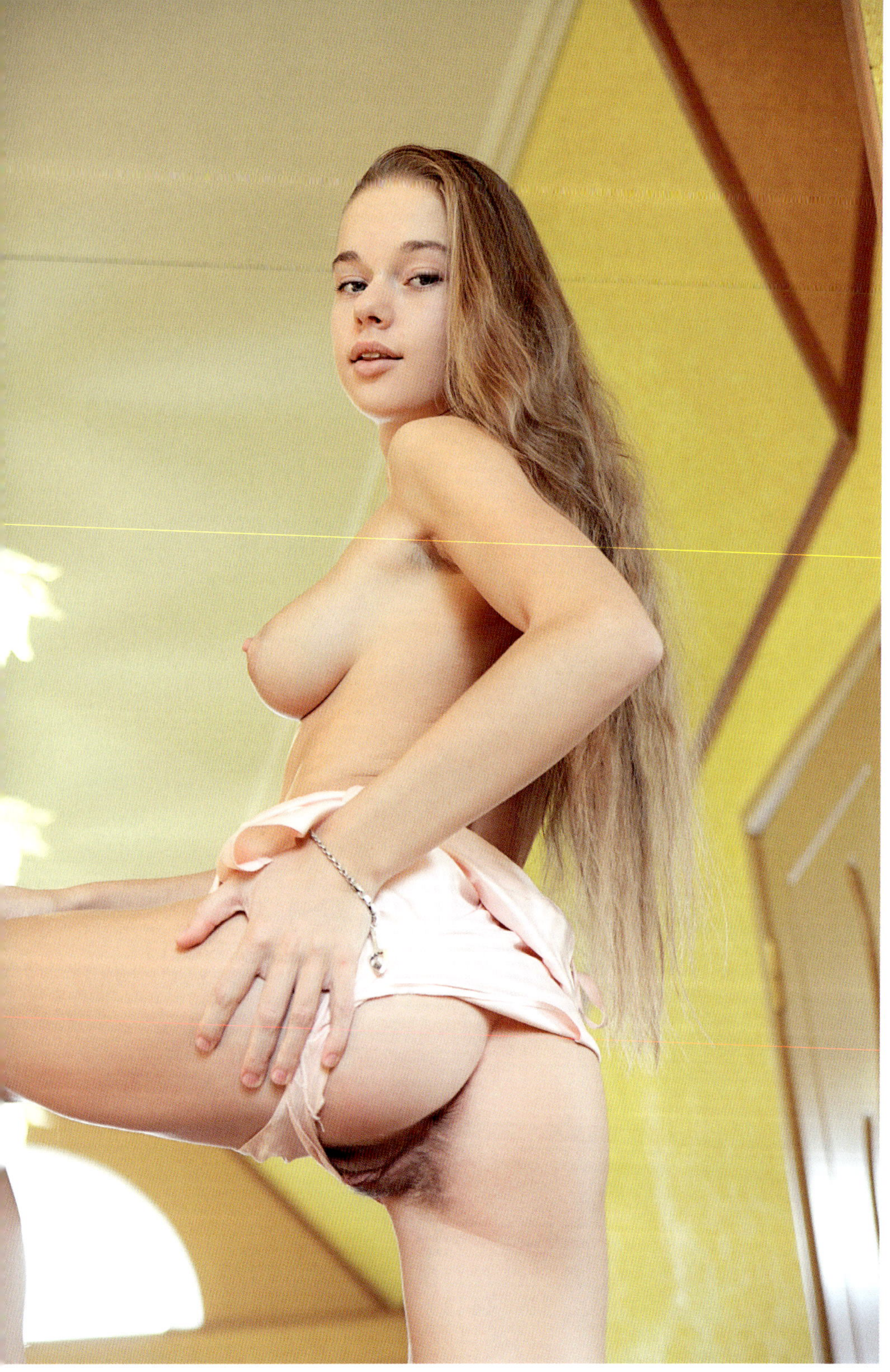

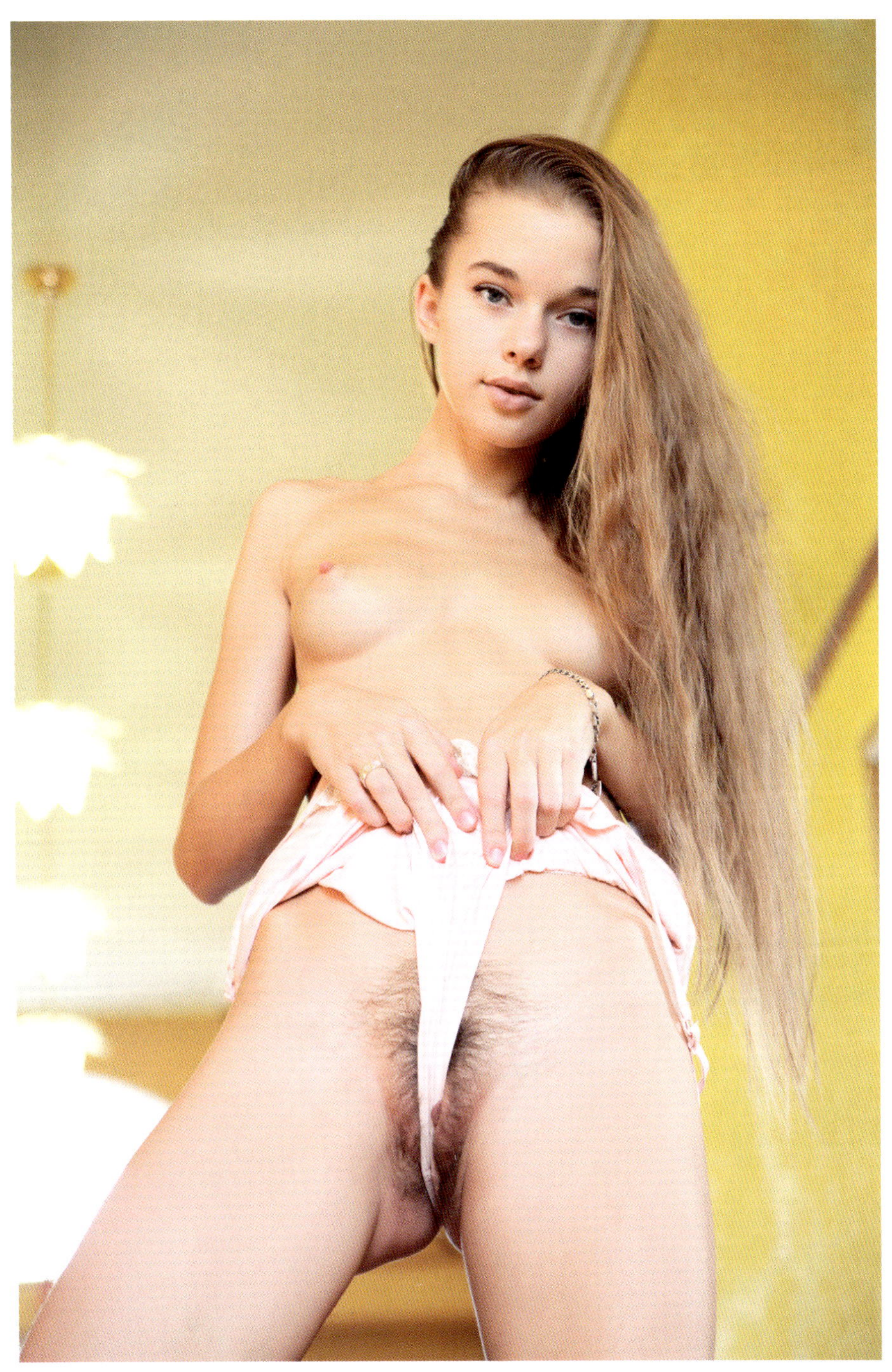

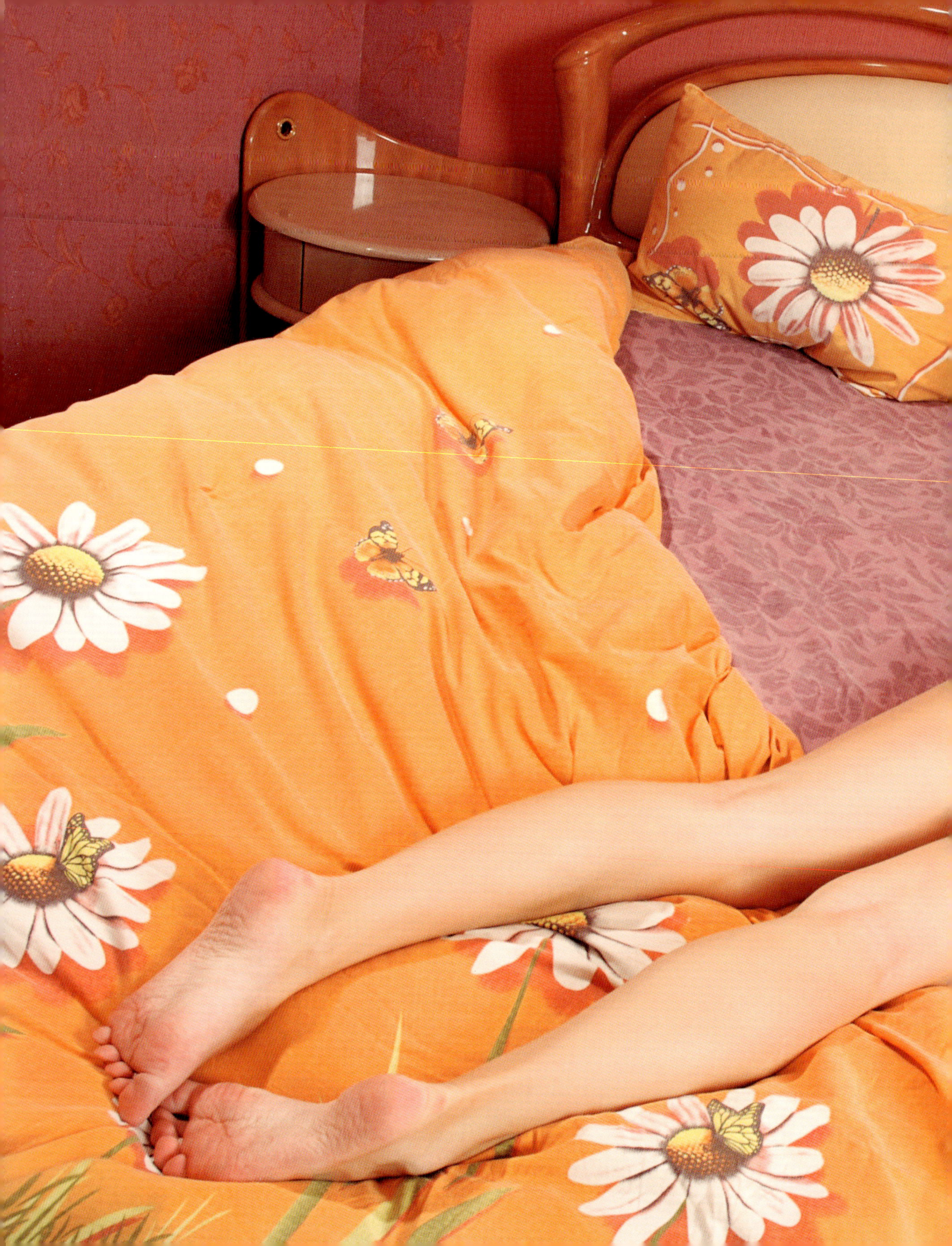

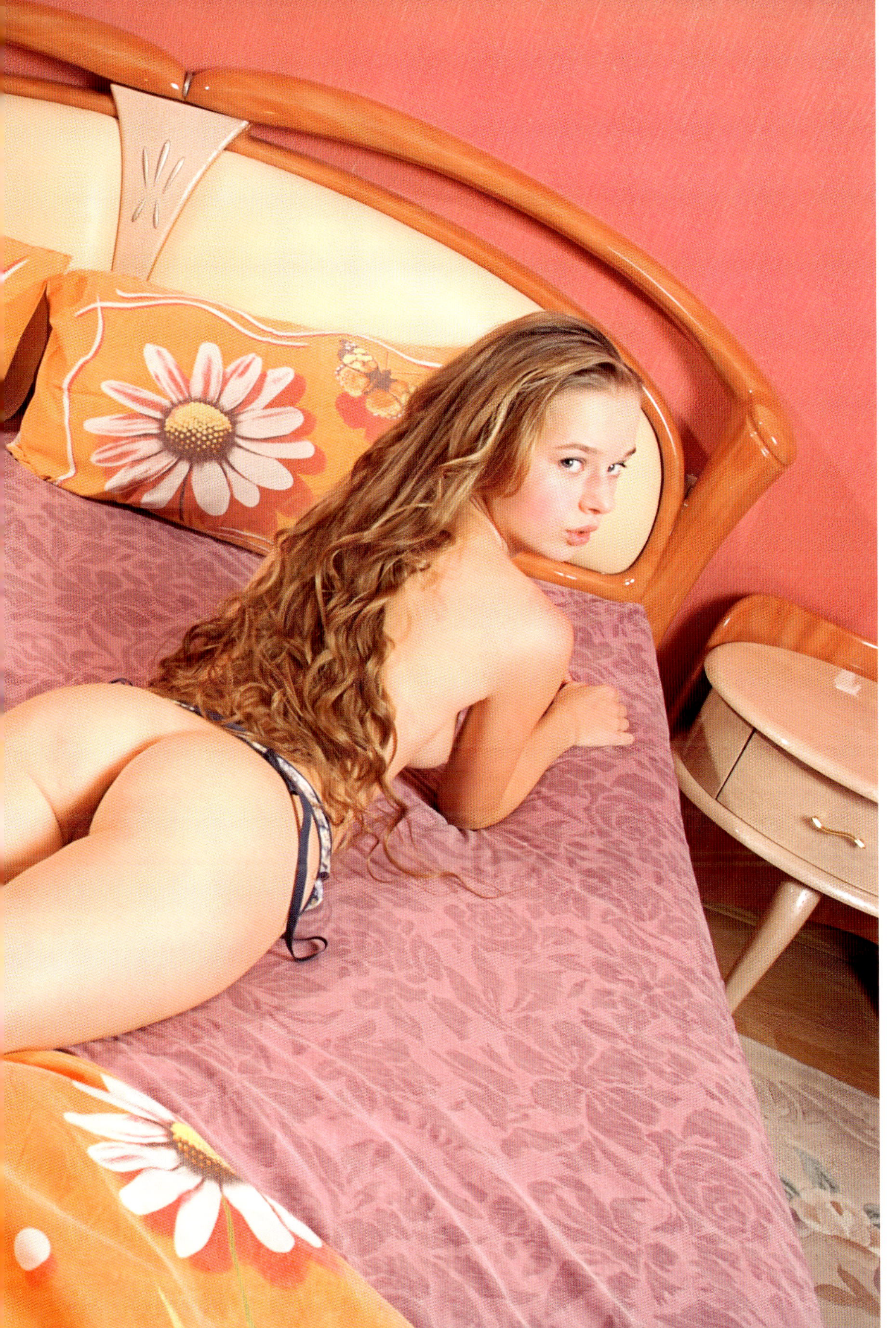

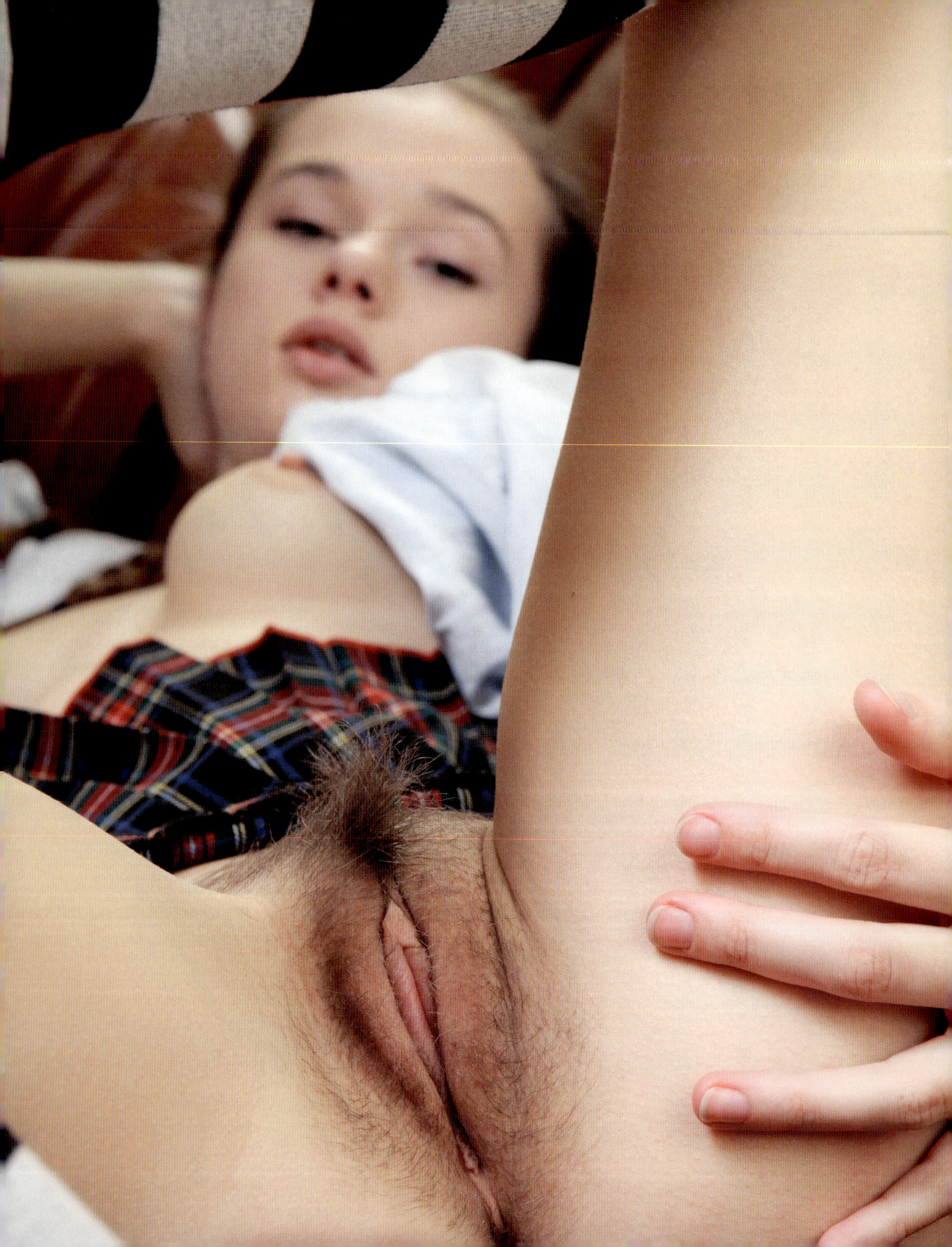

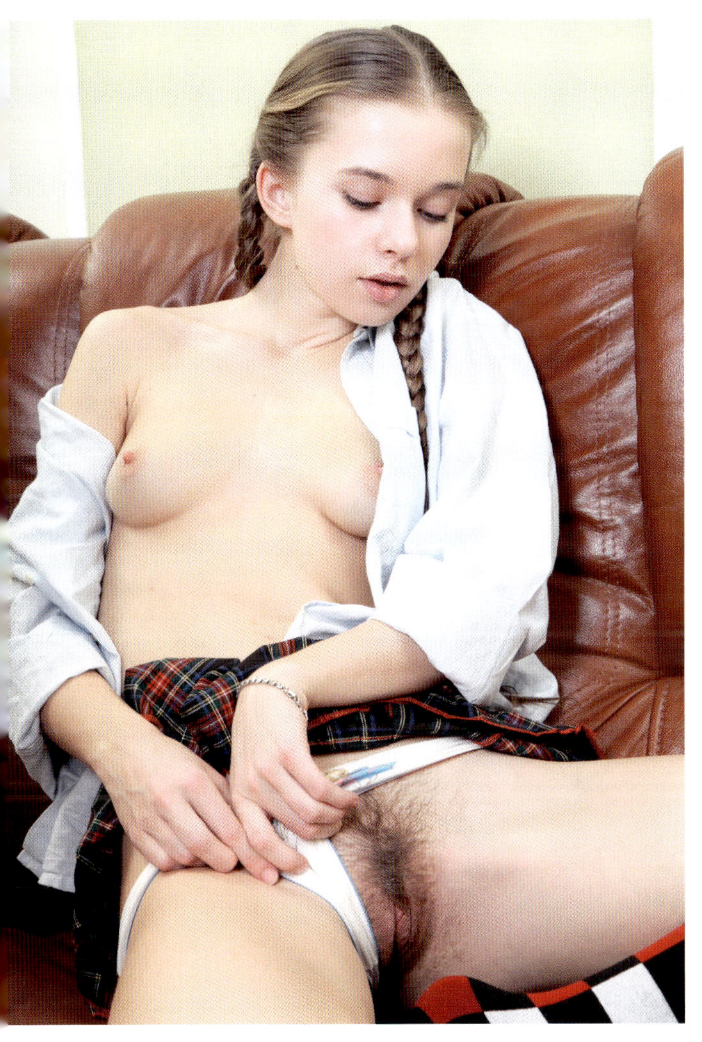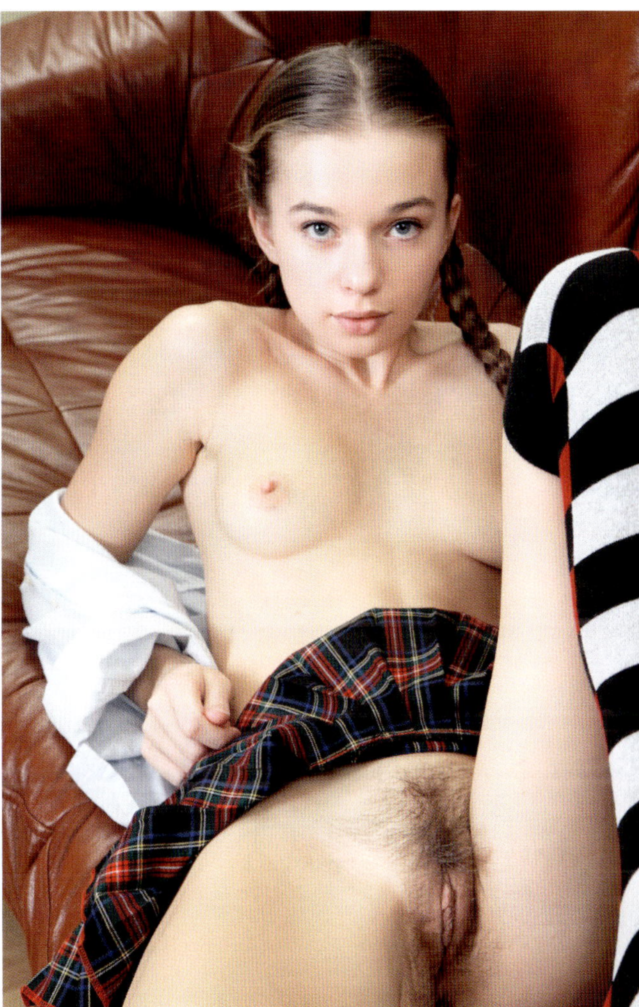

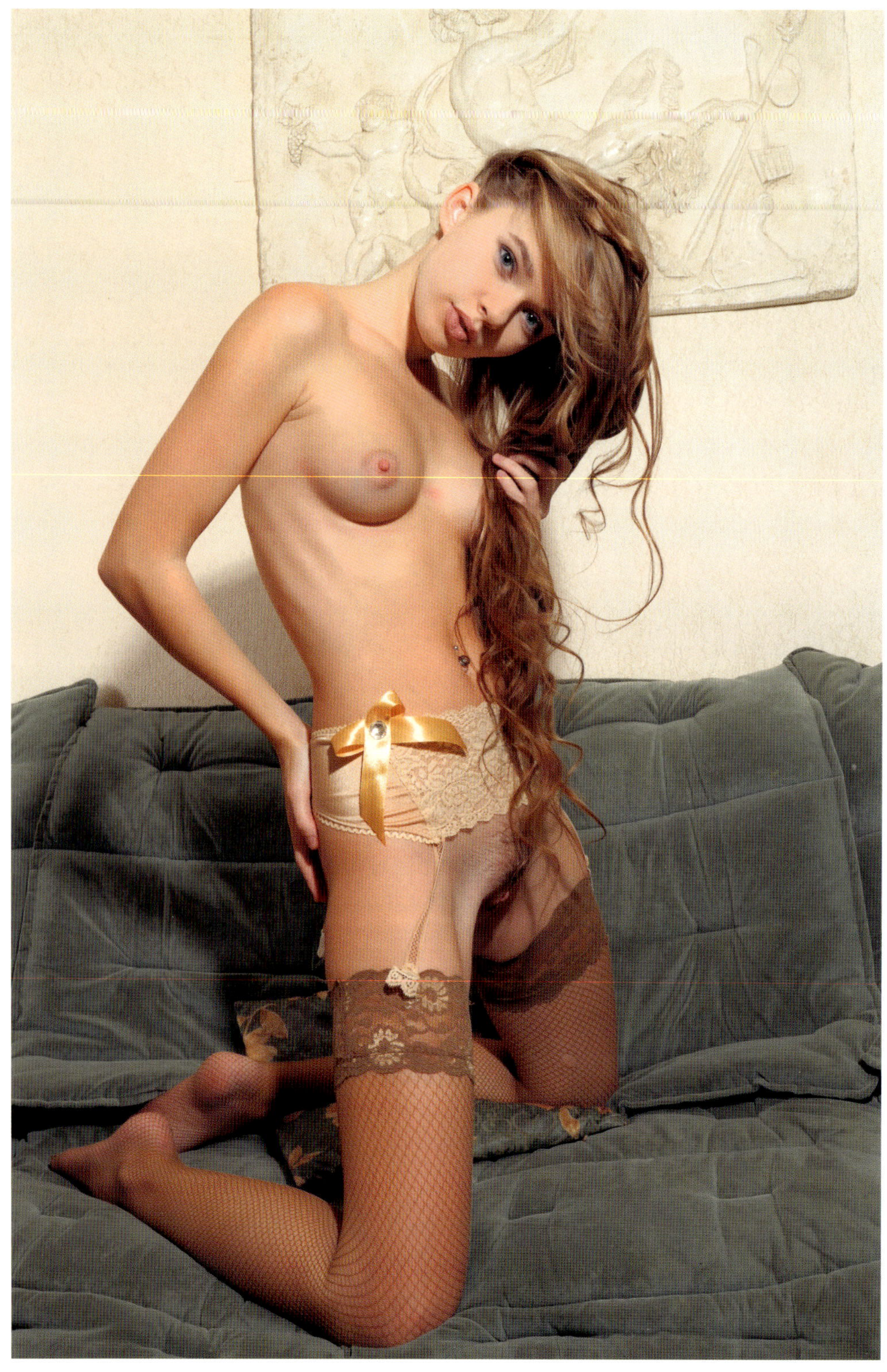

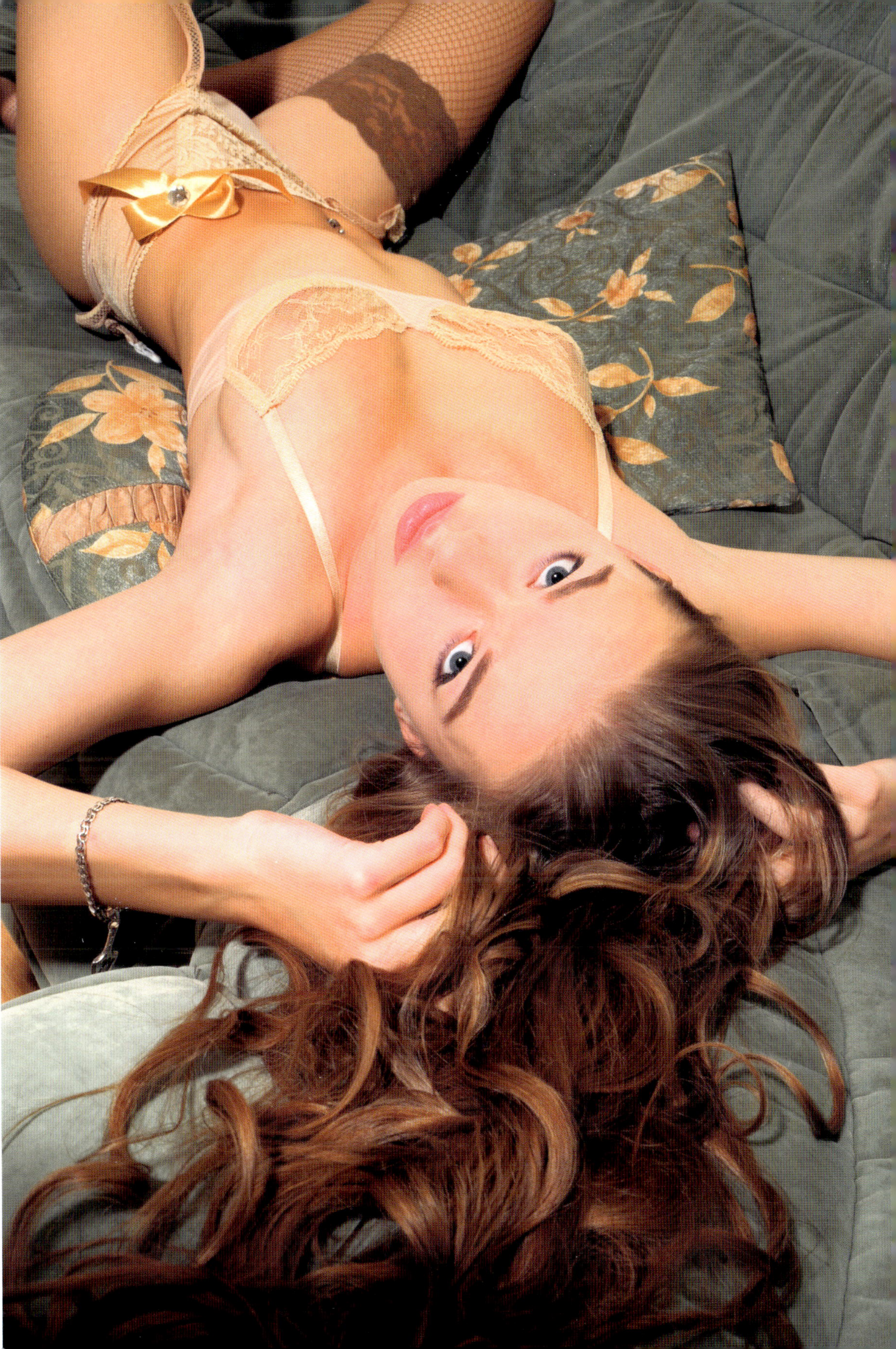

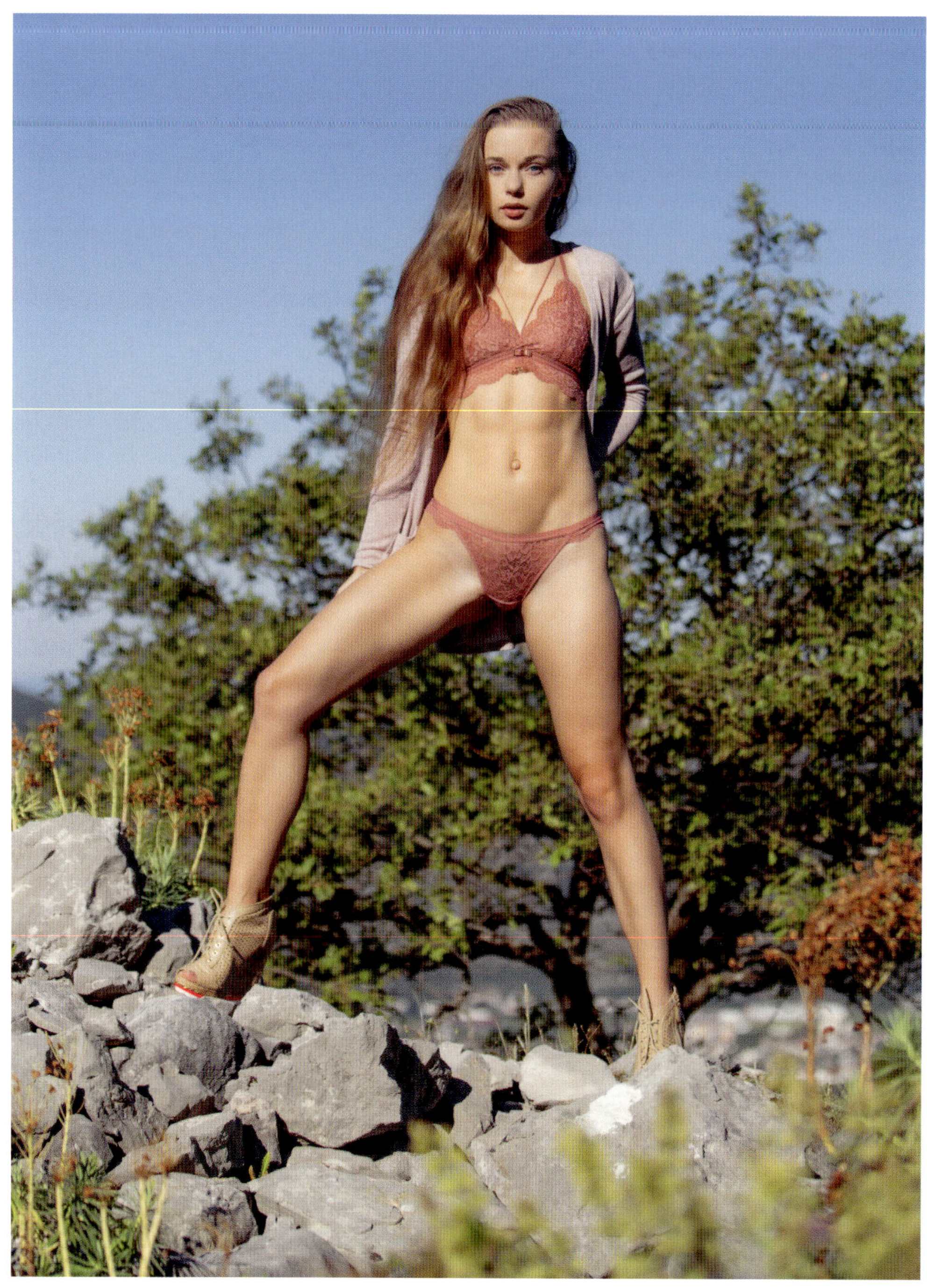

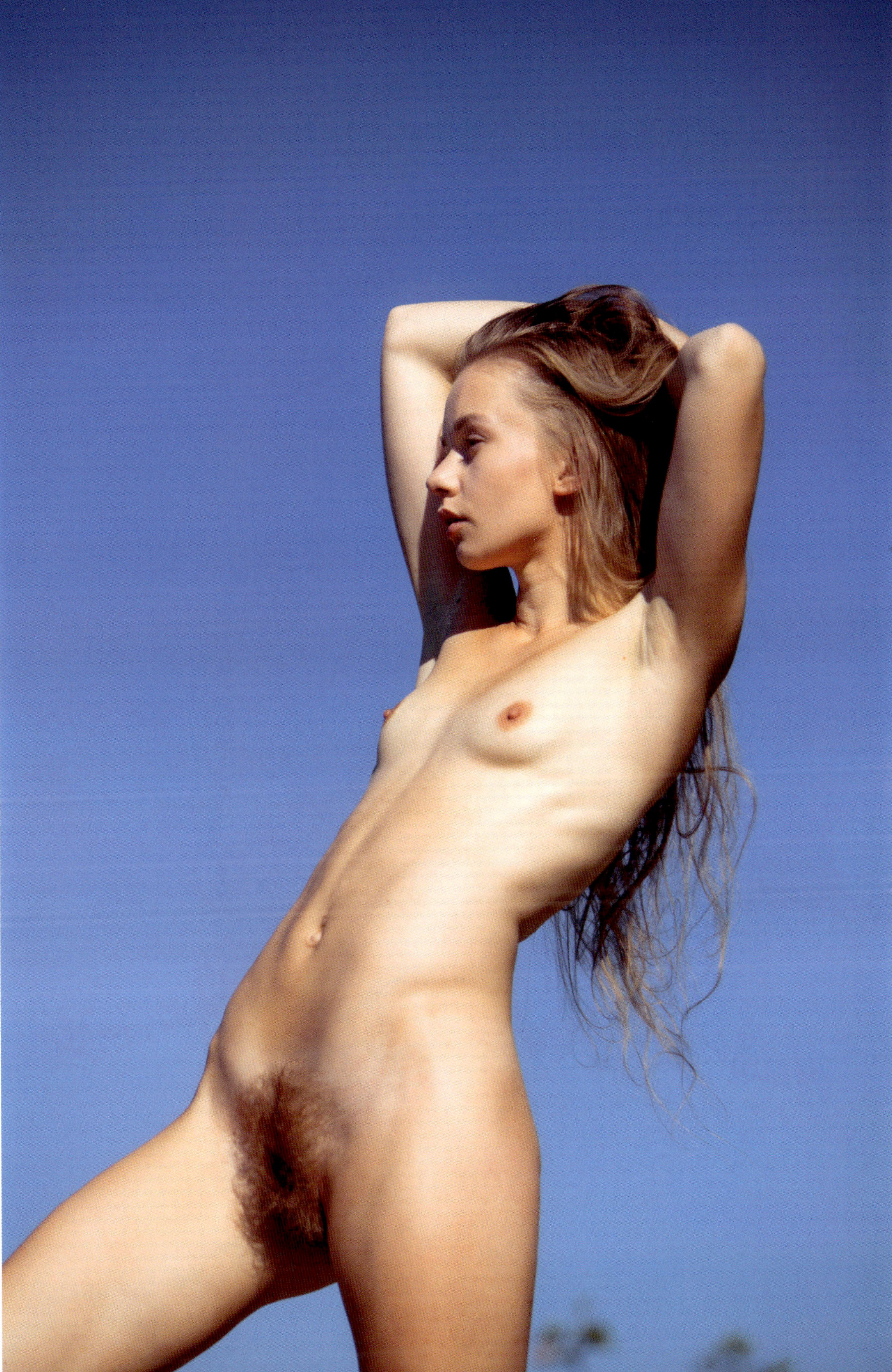

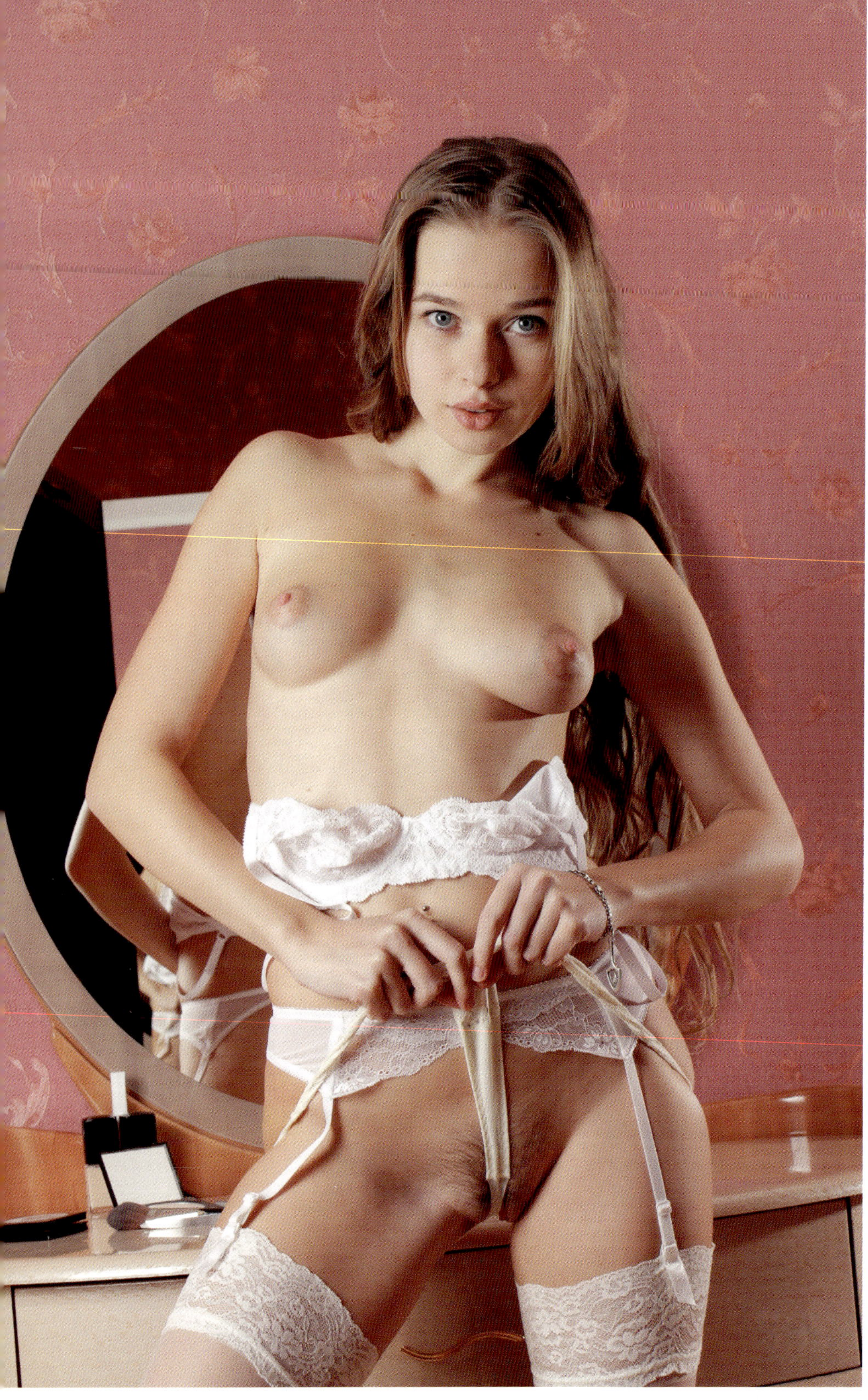

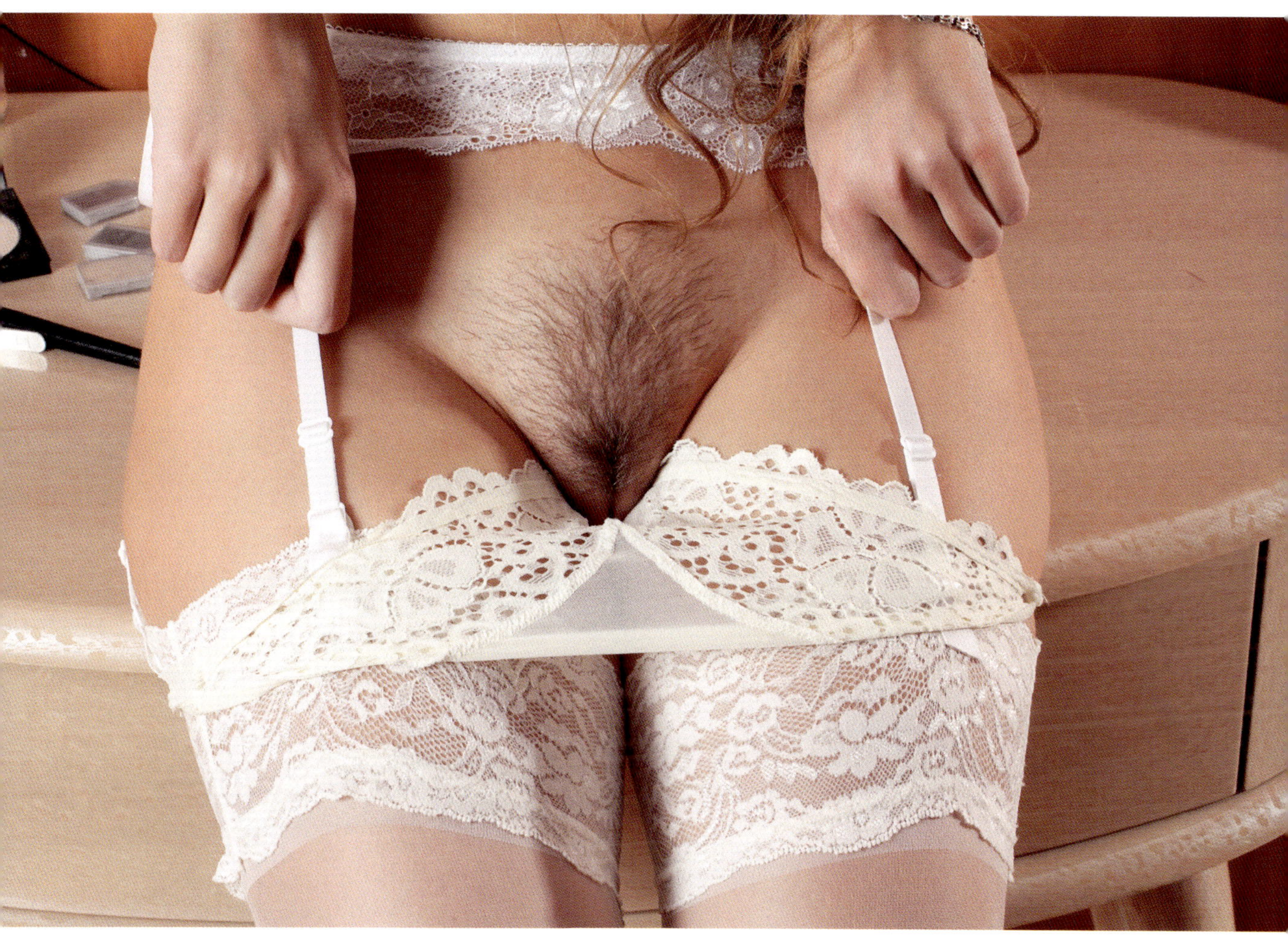

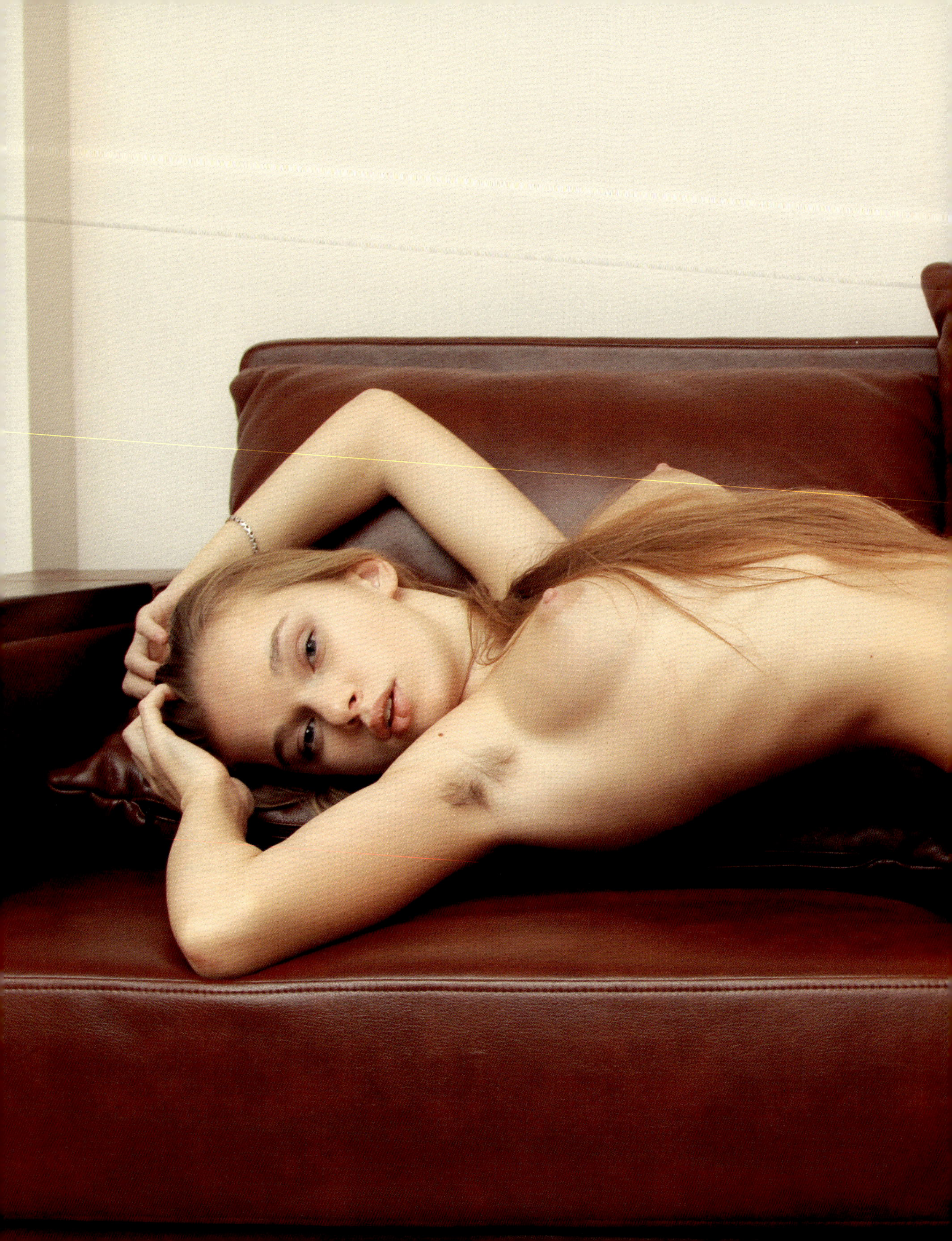

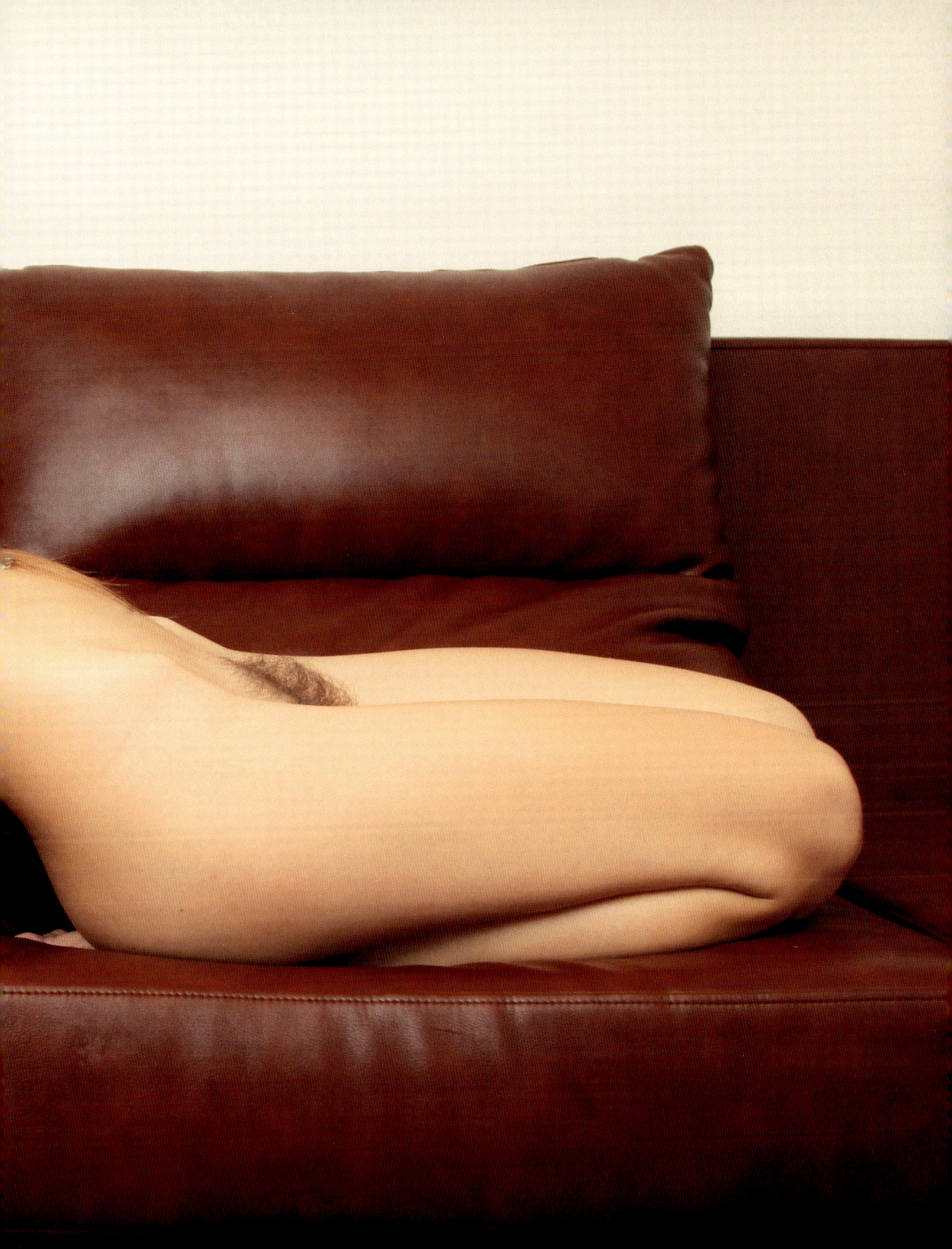

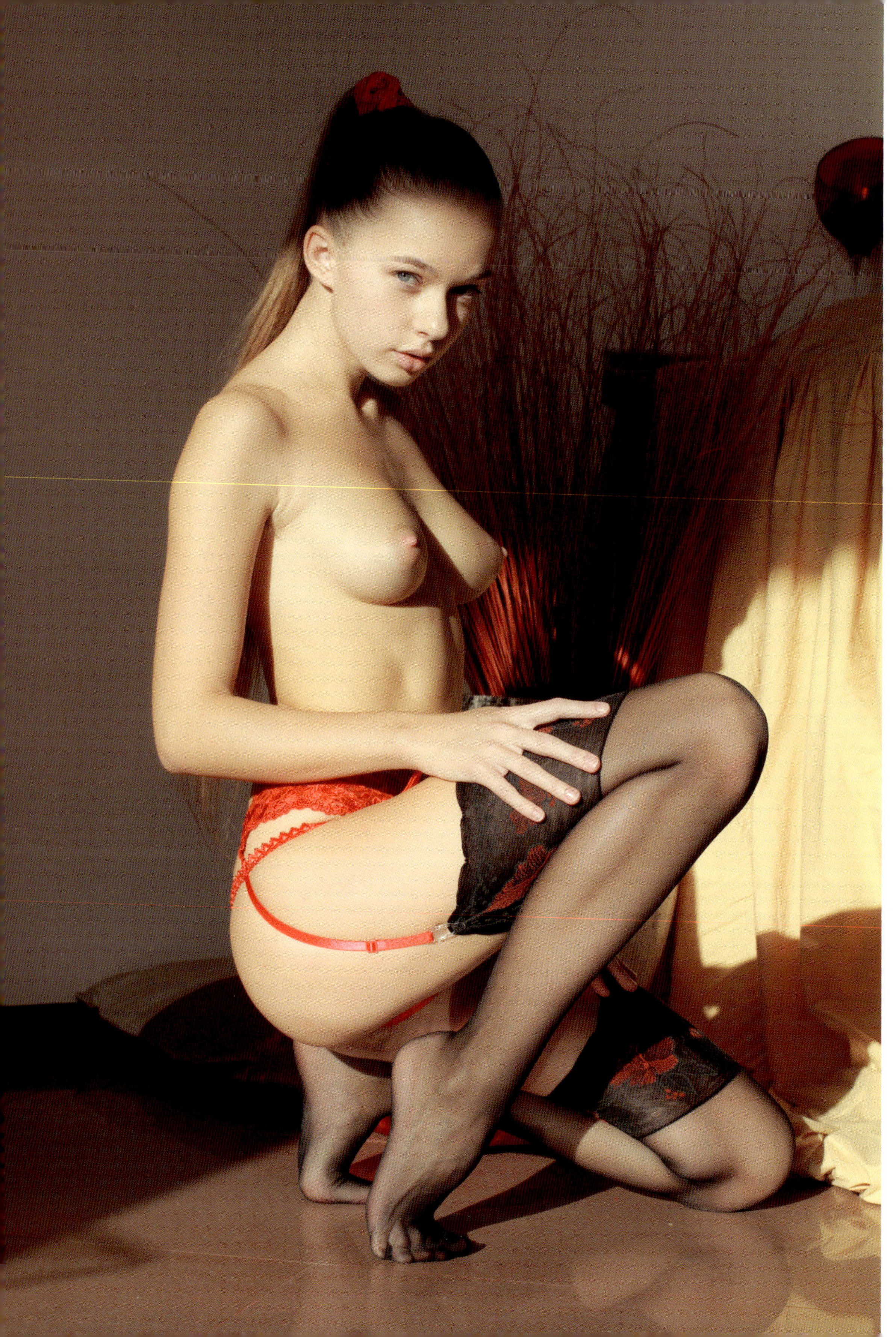

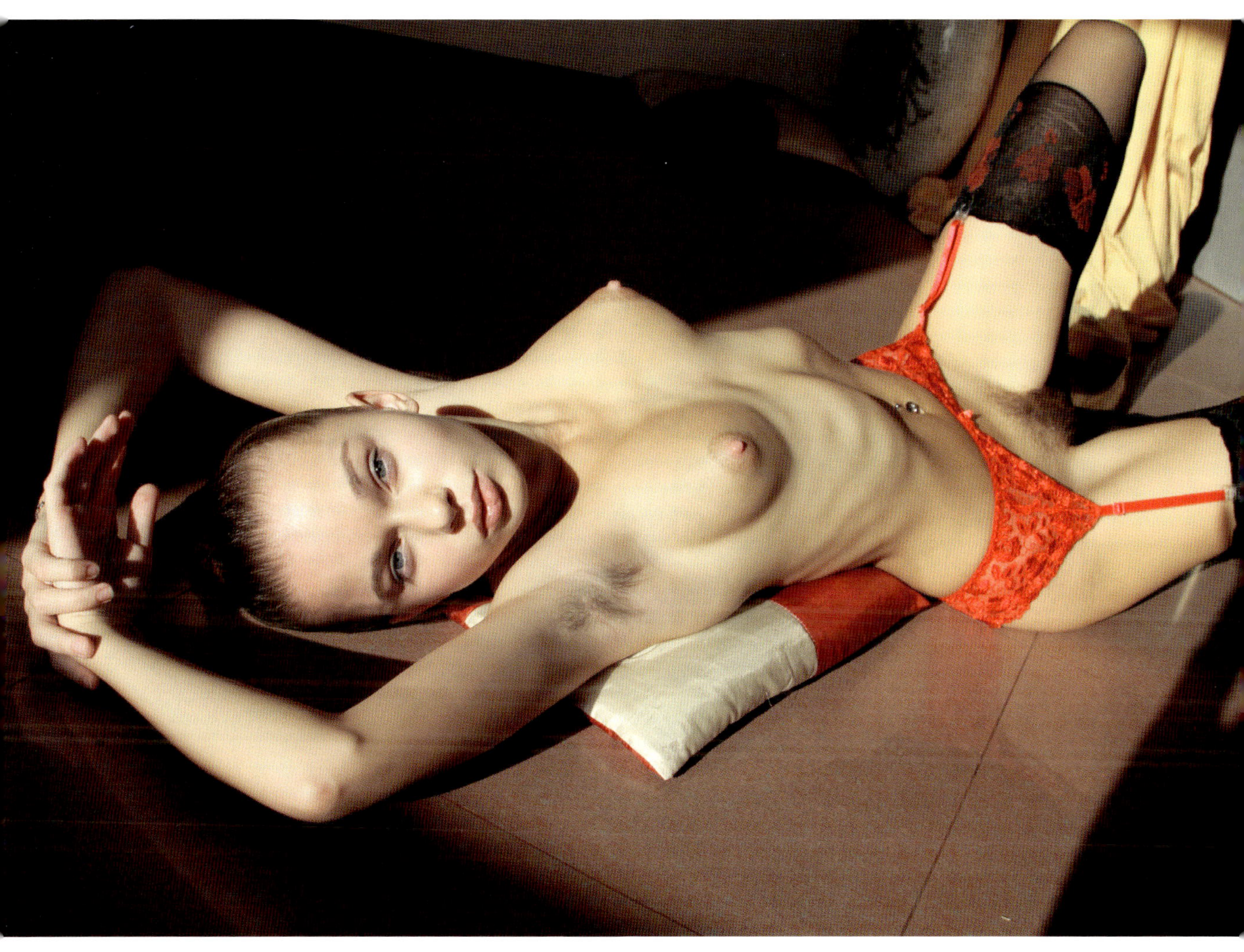

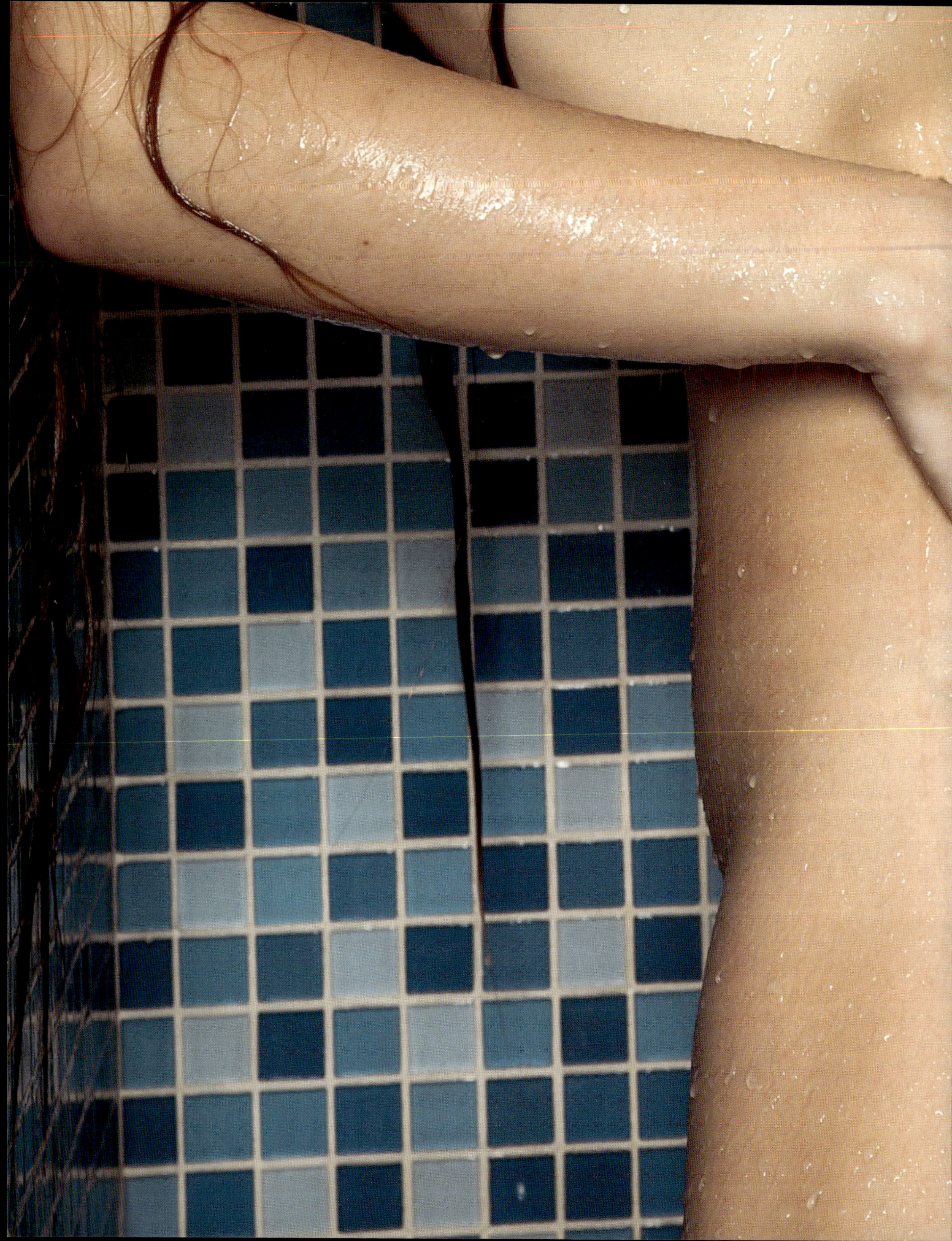

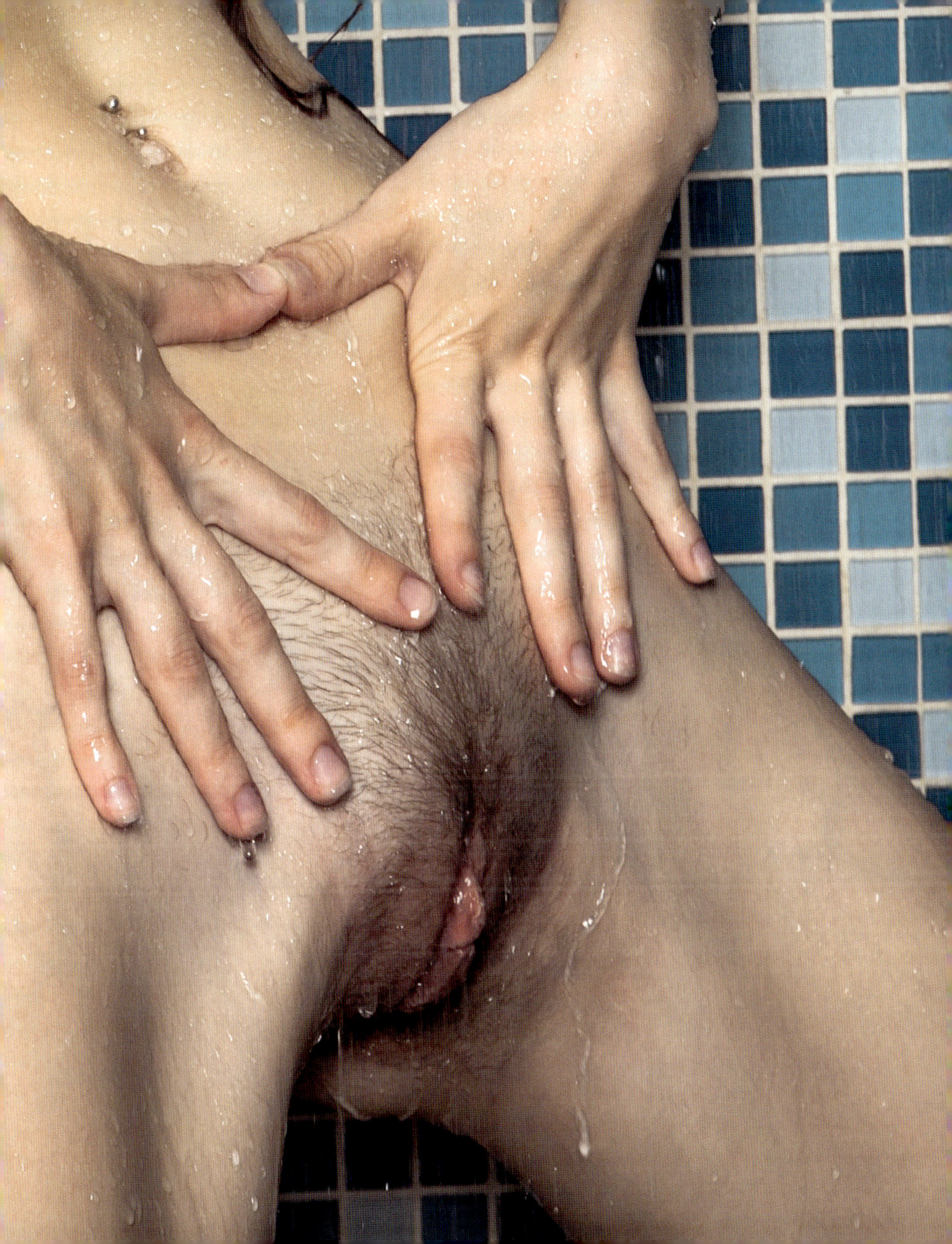

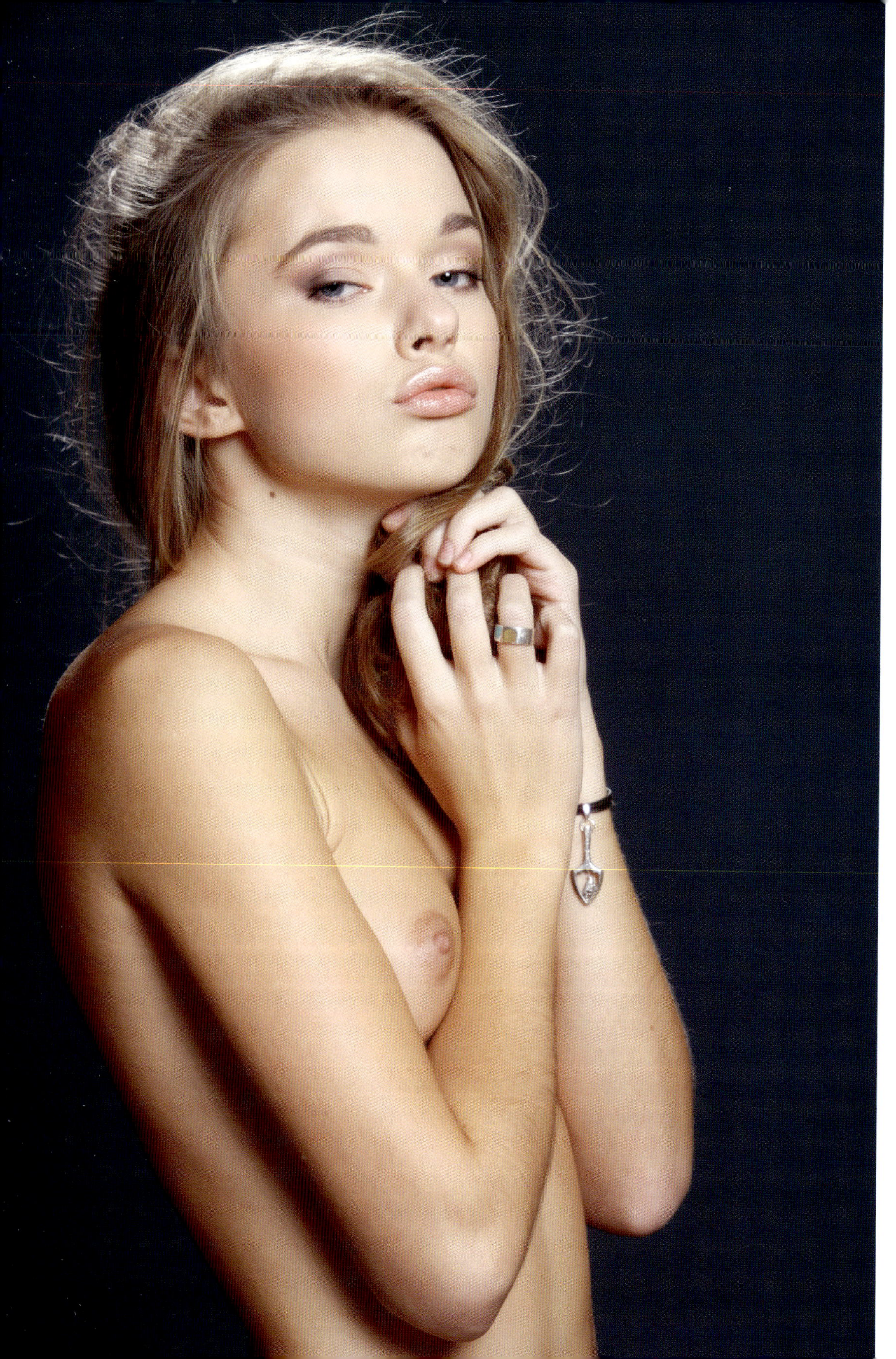

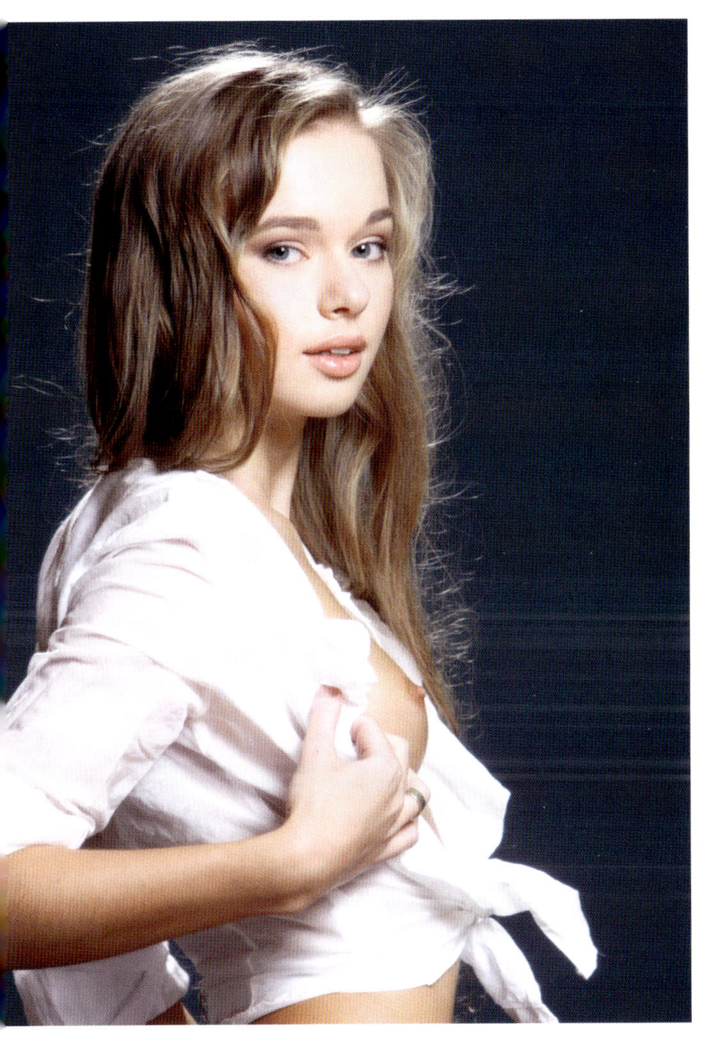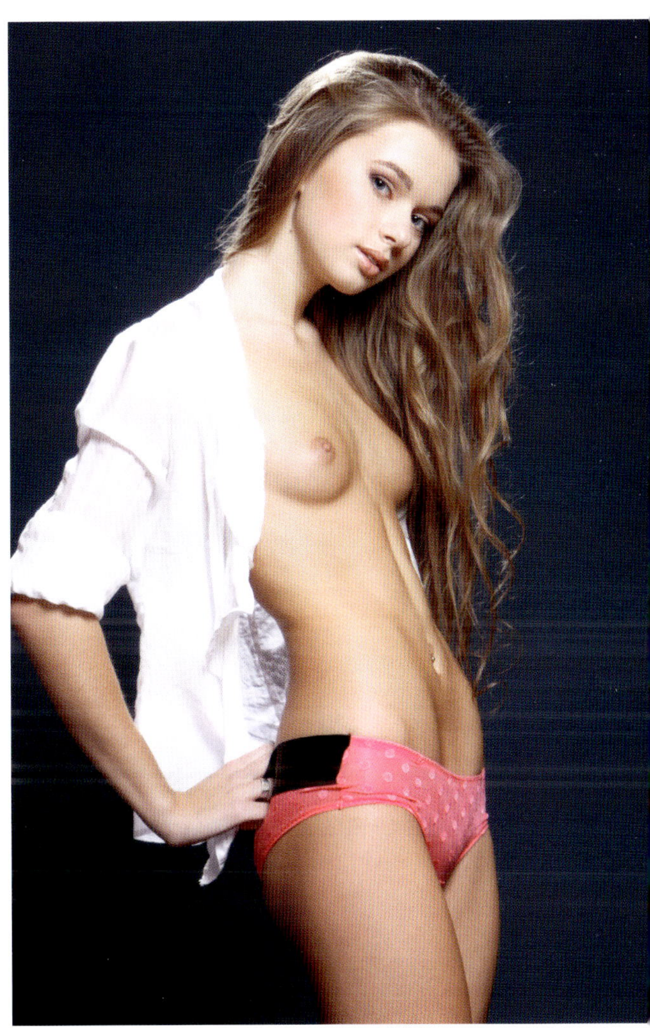

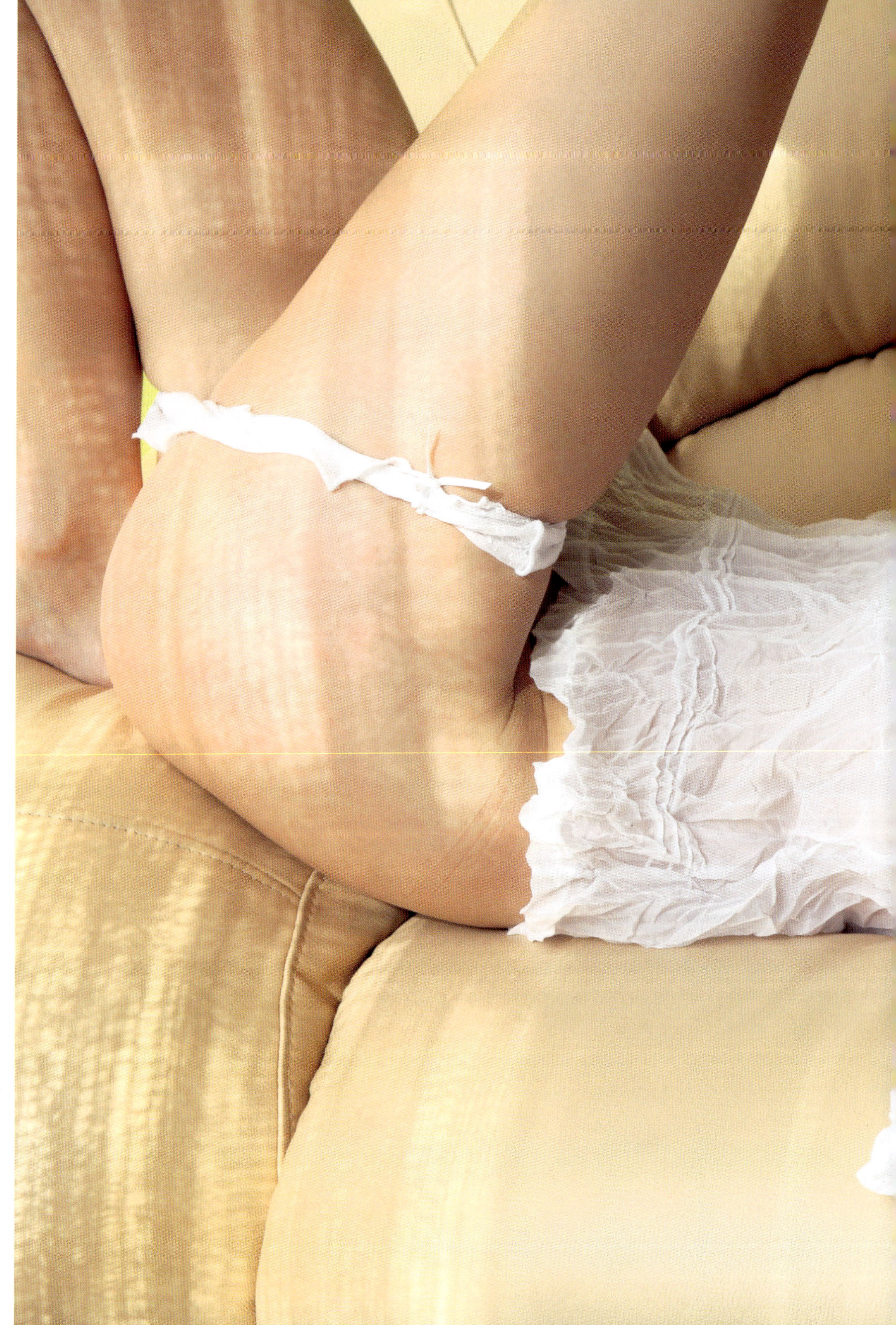

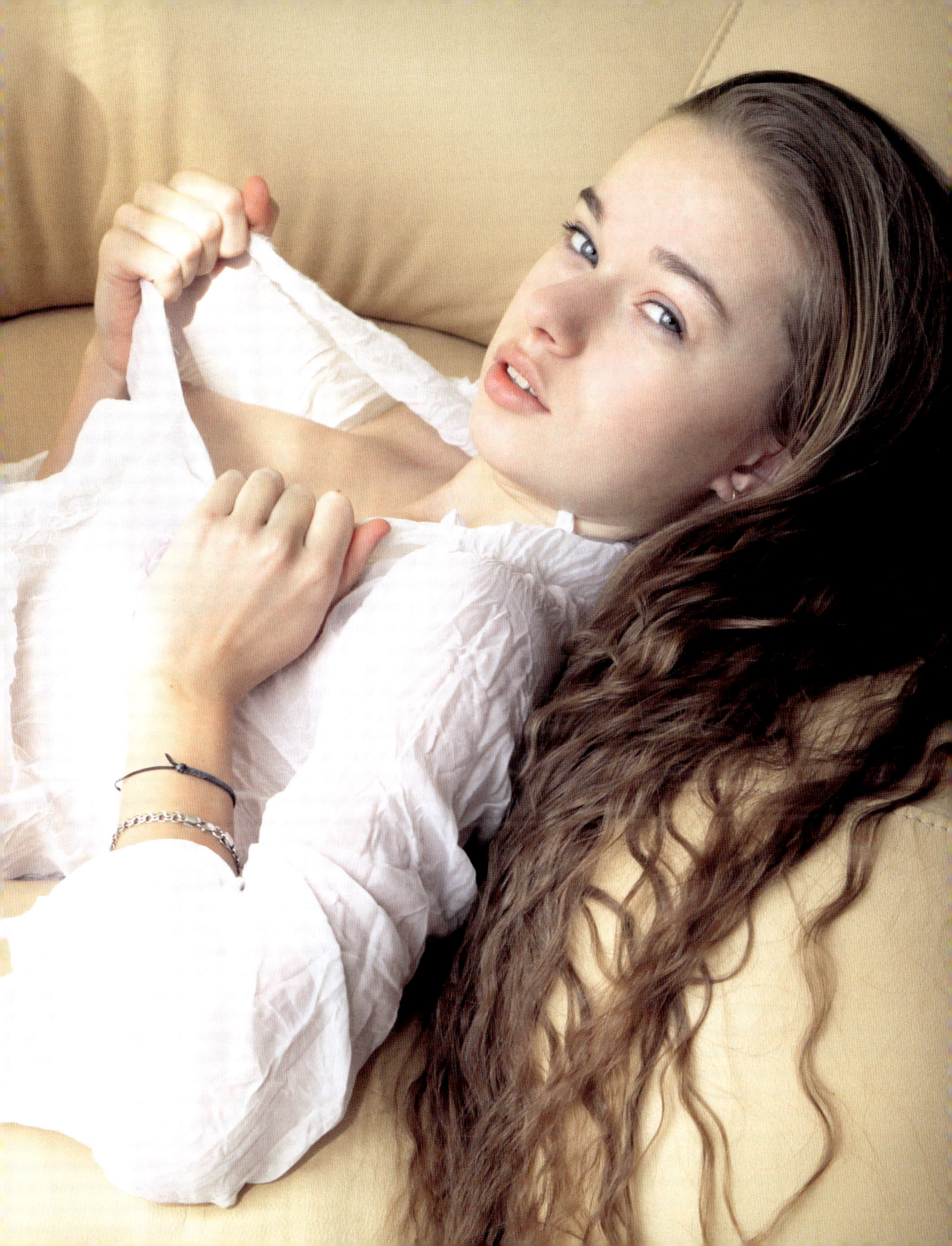

COLLECT THEM ALL: OUR MOST BEAUTIFUL

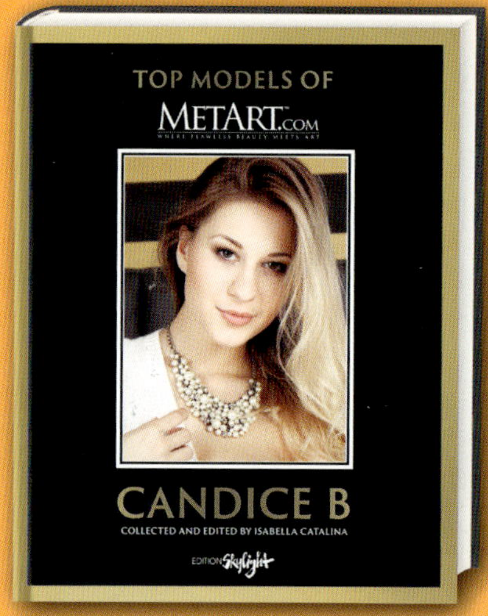

ISBN 978-3-03766-660-9

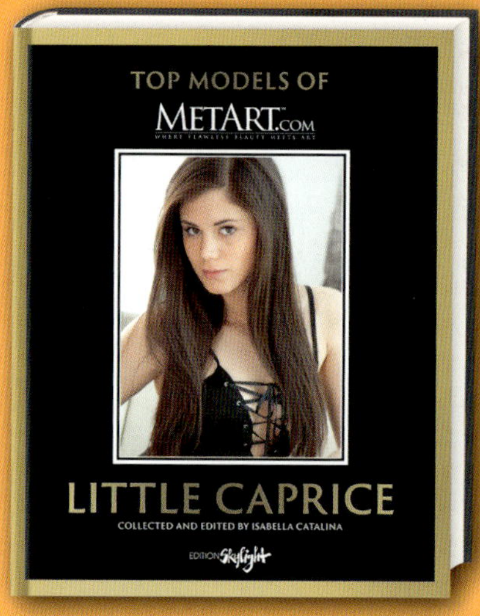

ISBN 978-3-03766-659-3

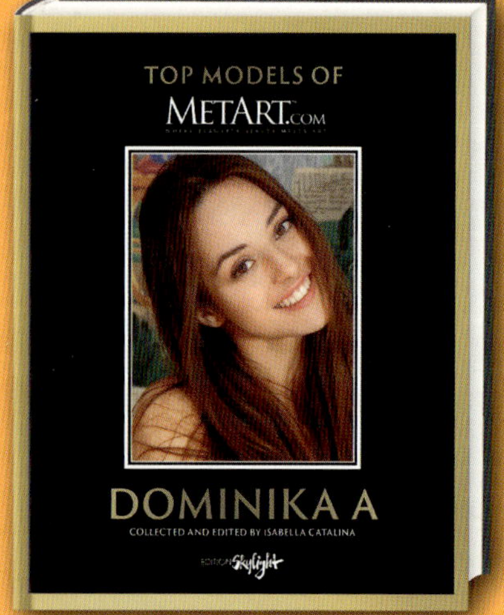

ISBN 978-3-03766-679-1

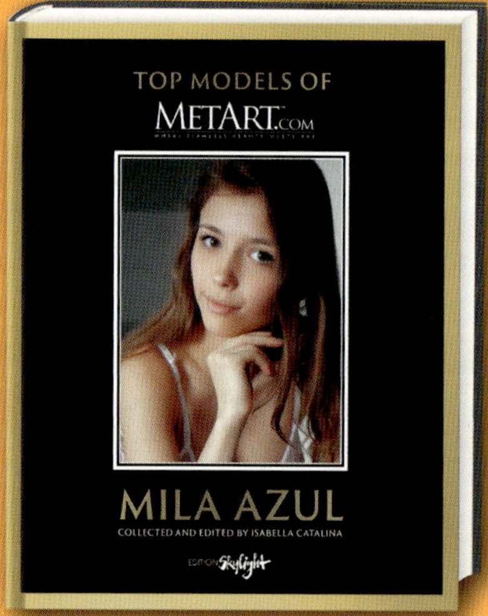

ISBN 978-3-03766-680-7

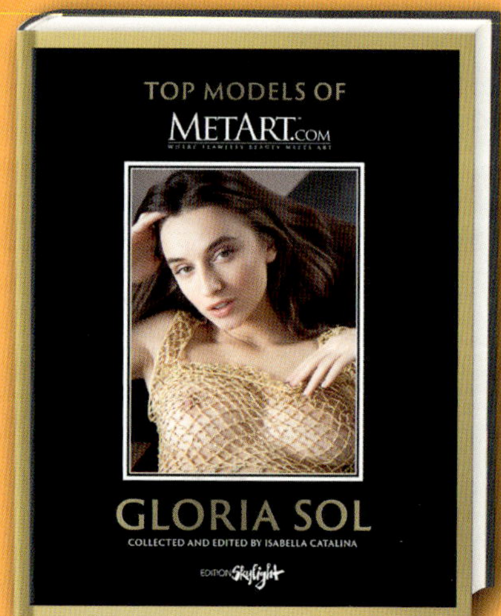

ISBN 978-3-03766-688-3

WWW.EDITION-SKYLIGHT.COM